MOUNT ARARAT

CASPIAN SEA

Ancient Land
of **MEDIA**

•NINEVEH
•HALAH
•ASSHUR

~POTAMIA
or the LAND OF SHINAR
"between the rivers"

TIGRIS RIVER

~ATES RIVER

BABYLON

~ginally

UR
(Abraham's early home)

Ancient Land
of **PERSIA**

F THE
~CHS
FLOOD

PERSIAN
GULF

D.M. & D.J.

THE FIRST
2000 YEARS

The
FIRST
2000
YEARS

By

W. CLEON SKOUSEN

BOOKCRAFT
SALT LAKE CITY, UTAH

23rd Printing, 1972

LITHOGRAPHED IN U.S.A.
BY

PUBLISHERS PRESS

SALT LAKE CITY, UTAH

PREFACE

This book brings to a conclusion fifteen years of research. In 1938 my wife and I decided to try and bring together in one volume everything which the Church has received thus far concerning the first 2000 years of human history—from Adam to Abraham. For both of us this has been a thrilling and faith-promoting adventure in exploratory research.

It will be observed that this study has not attempted to include apocryphal material from scriptural texts of doubtful authenticity. The principal sources for this study have been the standard works of the Church, the teachings of the Prophet Joseph Smith and certain corroborative historians who have made special studies of the period under consideration. The King James version was used for all Biblical references except in those instances where specific passages were clarified by Joseph Smith in the inspired version.

In quoting secular sources a special effort has been made to cite books which are readily available to the average student rather than quote obscure texts which the student would have neither the time nor inclination to search out.

Among the many who have offered encouragement and assistance in the preparation of this work I wish particularly to express appreciation for the suggestions of Dr. Sidney B. Sperry, head of the Department of Religion at Brigham Young University. And because much of the research for this work was done under circumstances which were crowded by the highly competitive pressure of professional life, I am deeply indebted to the persuasive persistence of interested friends who have provided continuous motivation for the ultimate completion of this study.

I also wish to acknowledge the splendid work of Mrs. Samuel Chandler, Barbara Pullan and Velora Gough who typed the manuscript and index.

Since this book deals with a relatively new field insofar as general Church literature is concerned, it does not pretend to be the final word on any portion of the period covered. Future revelation and future research will illuminate many areas which this work has merely opened for study. The author takes full responsibility for conclusions reached on the basis of available facts, and if improper evaluations or deductions have been made because of meager data, he will heartily welcome the results of additional research which will further clarify our knowledge of human history during the first 2000 years.

—W. Cleon Skousen

Brigham Young University
Provo, Utah
November 1, 1953

CONTENTS

CONTENTS

CHRONOLOGICAL TIME TABLE COVERING THE PERIOD OF THE EARLY PATRIARCHS

(According to Scriptural Sources*)

Years from Adam	Patriarchs	Years B.C.
0	Beginning of mortality for Adam	4,000 B.C.
130	Adam was 130 and begat Seth	3,870 B.C.
235	Seth was 105 and begat Enos	3,765 B.C.
325	Enos was 90 and begat Cainan	3,675 B.C.
395	Cainan was 70 and begat Mahalaleel	3,605 B.C.
460	Mahalaleel was 65 and begat Jared	3,540 B.C.
622	Jared was 162 and begat Enoch	3,378 B.C.
687	Enoch was 65 and begat Methuselah	3,313 B.C.
874	Methuselah was 187 and begat Lamech	3,126 B.C.
1,056	Lamech was 182 and begat Noah	2,944 B.C.
1,548	Noah was 492 and begat Shem	2,452 B.C.
1,656	(Noah 600) *The Flood* (Shem 108)	2,344 B.C.
1,658	Shem was 110 and begat Arphaxad	2,342 B.C.
1,693	Arphaxad was 35 and begat Salah	2,307 B.C.
1,723	Salah was 30 and begat Eber	2,277 B.C.
1,757	Eber was 34 and begat Peleg	2,243 B.C.
1,787	Peleg was 30 and begat Reu	2,213 B.C.
1,819	Reu was 32 and begat Serug	2,181 B.C.
1,849	Serug was 30 and begat Nahor	2,151 B.C.
1,878	Nahor was 29 and begat Terah	2,122 B.C.
1,978	Terah was 100 and begat Abraham	2,022 B.C.

*See article in the appendix. "The Chronological Time Table Covering the Period of the Patriarchs." Also see special chart at the back of the book.

CHAPTER ONE

Getting Acquainted with the Author of Genesis

When was Moses born?

Who gave Moses his name? What does his name mean?

Where did Moses receive his education and training?

How old was Moses when he left Egypt? Why did he leave?

What kind of people did Moses find in Midian?

Who was Jethro? Whom did Moses marry?

Who ordained Moses to the Melchizedek Priesthood?

How long did Moses remain with Jethro as the manager of his flocks?

Why did Moses resist his divine calling?

Did Moses see God "face to face" before he went into Egypt or did he just hear His voice?

How old was Moses when he received his special calling?

What great prophet saw a vision of the entire world and all the "children of men which are and which were created"?

While speaking with God Moses felt he missed a great opportunity. What was it?

After the conversation between the Lord and Moses what famous personality was permitted to cross the veil and appear before Moses?

Why was he frightened?

Who Was Moses?

Certain scholars have criticized Moses for daring to record as historical facts those things which admittedly happened more than 2,000 years before he was born.

Are such criticisms justified?

It is impossible to appreciate the reliability of the world's most ancient history—Genesis—unless we examine the remarkable life of this famous man who wrote it.

Moses was born in Egypt around 1,570 B.C. His parents were slaves—white slaves—who labored under the threatening lashes of Egyptian taskmasters. In fact, his parents belonged to that nation of Israelites who, as guarded prisoners in slave-labor centers, had been accumulating wealth for the lords of the Nile during more than three hundred years.

> "And the Egyptians made the children of Israel to serve with rigour; And they made their lives bitter with hard bondage, in morter, and in brick, and in all manner of service in the field." (Exodus 1:13-14)

Three hundred years earlier the Israelites had been few in number but now they had multiplied into several hundred thousand[1] and threatened Egyptian security by surpassing the total population of the native Nile-men.[2]

To prevent this the Egyptian Pharaoh issued a royal mandate of execution against all male children born in the future to Israelite mothers. Boy babies were to be slain upon birth by being drowned in the crocodile infested Nile.[3]

Such was the law when Moses was born.

An Infant Marked for Assassination

It is perhaps difficult to comprehend the terror of a mother who must await the birth of her child knowing

---

[1]Numbers ch. 2
[2]Exodus 1:9
[3]*Ibid.*, 1:22. (*Ibid.* indicates the same source as the last one cited).

that if he is a boy he will be assassinated on sight by the agents of the government.

Such was the state of fear in the mind of the mother of Moses which led her to devise a plan to preserve her son from the knowledge of tattling midwives or the spies of the heathen monarch. It required shrewd ingenuity for a slave woman to have the child in secret and then hide him away without detection.

However, the scripture says she was pleased when the child was born, and she found that God had blessed her with a "goodly" child, a son.⁴ But goodly, or not, at this moment he was a capital fugitive carrying a death warrant.

The mother of Moses was only able to hide him in her home for about three months.⁵ In such crowded quarters as the slaves occupied she knew that the cries of the child would eventually attract the attention of the night watchmen or paid informers. In desperation she took the chance of hiding him in a tiny waterproof casket made of bulrushes and coated with tar.* This was placed among the reeds of the very river which was supposed to snuff out his life.

Moses Becomes an Egyptian Prince

What happened after that is well-known history. The discovery of the infant Moses by an Egyptian princess who came to the river to bathe saved his life. It saved him because the Egyptian woman felt attracted to the handsome child and wanted him for her own. Thus he was adopted into the royal Egyptian household. But the quick thinking of Miriam, his sister, resulted in the employment of the real mother of Moses as his "nurse."

"And Pharaoh's daughter said unto her (the real mother of Moses), take this child away, and

---

⁴*Ibid.*, 2:2
⁵*Ibid.*
*The word *slime* in the Old Testament is translated from a word which means asphalt or tar; sometimes called "bitumen." (See Clarke's *Bible Commentary*, Vol. 1, p. 87, note on Genesis 11:3)

nurse it for me, and I will give thee wages. And the woman (the mother of Moses) took the child, and nursed it. And the child grew, and she brought him unto the Pharaoh's daughter, and he became her son." (Exodus 2:9-10)

Who will count the anguish of the mother of Moses as she gave her son back to the waiting arms of the Egyptian woman. She had saved her son, but for what?

It was the Egyptian princess who gave the child his name. "She called his name Moses . . . Because I drew him out of the water."[6]

During the next forty years[7] Moses received his education and training as an adopted prince of Egypt. The scriptural biography of Moses has nothing to say of these years, but we know they must have been crowded with exciting events, for this brilliant young Israelite was surrounded by the sophistry and treachery of a royal court which was famous for its cunning and intrigue.

And Moses knew he was not a true Egyptian. He was of a different racial pattern—with an entirely different code of human values. No doubt his real mother saw to it that he was taught the dignity and destiny of Israel.

Furthermore, the social gulf between Moses and his own people did not prevent him from observing with open eyes the cruel treatment they received. Through the years, no doubt, a spirit of indignation and rebellion arose within him as he watched the violent passion of the dark-skinned taskmasters welt the backs of their helpless wards. This resentment overflowed one day when Moses saw a belabored Israelite cringing under the lash of an Egyptian. Moses intervened and a violent struggle resulted. When the struggle was over the Egyptian was dead.

Moses hurriedly buried the body of the Egyptian in the sand. He knew that if this incident came to the ears of the Pharaoh there would be prompt vengeance.

---

[6]*Ibid.,* 2:10
[7]Acts 7:22-23

But even so the matter was not kept a secret for long. Moses learned the Pharaoh had issued orders that he should be captured and slain.

In fear of his life Moses fled from the land of Egypt.

Moses Finds Fellow Hebrews in Midian

With the desperate haste of a fugitive in flight, Moses made his way across the valley of the Nile, passed the Red Sea, and finally stopped in the land of the Midianites. He found this part of the country inhabited by a people who were also the descendants of Abraham. Because of his dress Moses was at first mistaken for an Egyptian[8] but after befriending the seven daughters of Jethro against a band of belligerent shepherds, these young women gratefully invited him to the home of their father. Jethro turned out to be the High Priest of the people.[9]

Moses soon gained the confidence of Jethro and became the manager of his flocks. Later he married Zipporah, one of Jethro's daughters,[10] and in due time he was ordained to the Melchizedek priesthood by Jethro. Jethro had received this priesthood by direct descent from the fathers back to the days of Abraham.[11]

Thus Moses began a new life. It was the peaceful, contented life of a pastoral society. Moses enjoyed it for forty years.

Moses Receives His Call at Eighty

As Moses neared the age of eighty[12] events began to occur which changed him from a manager of Jethro's flocks to one of the great prophets of all times. Moses had taken the herds of Jethro to the vicinity of Mount Horeb—about halfway between Midian and Egypt. As Moses walked in the cool of the afternoon he beheld a bush which appeared to be burning but was not con-

[8]Exodus 2:19
[9]*Ibid.*, 2:1-6
[10]*Ibid.*, 2:21
[11]D. & C. 84:6-16
[12]Acts 7:30

sumed. He approached it curiously, but suddenly he heard a voice coming from the midst of the fire which said: "Moses . . . draw not . . . hither: put off thy shoes from off thy feet, for the place whereon thou standest is holy ground . . . I am the God of thy father, the God of Abraham, the God of Isaac, and the God of Jacob."[13]

In the divine communication which followed, Moses learned that he had been chosen by God to rescue the children of Israel from their bondage in Egypt! This came as a tremendous shock to Moses, and as he weighed the meaning of the words which struck his ears, he began to offer numerous excuses. He feared to return to Egypt from which he had fled as a fugitive. It was necessary for the Lord to show forth His marvelous power in several miraculous incidents before Moses fully comprehended the fact that with God's power to sustain him, he could not fail. With this assurance he accepted the calling.

But Moses was not yet ready to go down to Egypt. Up to this time all he knew about God and His dealings with mankind were the scanty crumbs of knowledge he had picked up from his enslaved people in Egypt and the basic principles taught him by his father-in-law, Jethro. Before he could become the newly appointed teacher and prophet of the Israelites he had to be tutored himself. Moses had the distinction of receiving his religious education directly from the Lord in person.

To study the next events in the life of Moses we turn to a valuable scripture which came into our possession over a century ago. This scripture is called "The Book of Moses." The portion we shall now study was given to Joseph Smith by direct revelation in the year 1830. Here is disclosed for the first time how Moses was prepared for his great calling and how Moses happened to write Genesis.

How Moses Was Prepared for Leadership

To receive his spiritual education Moses was brought to "an exceedingly high mountain . . . the name of which

---
[13]Exodus 3:5-6

shall not be known among the children of men."[14] Then the record continues:

"And he saw God face to face and he talked with him, and the glory of God was upon Moses; therefore Moses could endure his presence. And God spake unto Moses, saying: . . . behold, thou art my son, wherefore look, and I will show thee the workmanship of mine hands; but not all, for . . . no man can behold all of my glory, and afterwards remain in the flesh." (Moses 1:2-5)

Here was a heavenly vision of the most extraordinary kind! In his "quickened" condition Moses was permitted to gaze upon the personage of God. He talked with the earth's Creator "face to face" and perceived the literal truthfulness of the scriptural principle that God created man in His own image.

It was apparently the purpose of the Lord to indoctrinate the mind of Moses with a quick but impressive vision of His power and government in the universe; to eliminate as rapidly as possible any foibles of error which Moses may have absorbed during his early life in Egypt. God warned Moses that what he was about to see was only a token of His glory and dominion, but at least it would give Moses some comprehension of the infinite power of the divine Personality who now stood before him.

"Behold," He said, "this one thing I show unto thee, Moses, my son . . . And it came to pass that Moses looked, and beheld the world upon which he was created; and Moses beheld the world and the ends thereof, and all the children of men which are and which *were* created." (Moses 1:7-8)

This would appear to have been a panoramic history of the race. If so, it must have taken a considerable period of time to present to Moses and when it was finished "he greatly marveled and wondered."[15] But even before he could regain his composure the vision suddenly vanished.

---

[14] Moses 1:1, 42
[15] *Ibid.*

Moses Misses a Great Opportunity

"The presence of God withdrew from Moses
. . . and as he was left unto himself, he fell unto the
earth. And it came to pass that it was for the space
of many hours before Moses did again receive his
natural strength like unto man; and he said unto
himself: Now, for this cause I know that man is
nothing, which thing I never had supposed." (Moses
1:9-10)

These words of Moses manifest the humbling effect
which the vision had upon him. As his strength began
to return Moses reflected upon the marvelous privilege
which had been granted him. In all probability this was
the first time since the days of Joseph—nearly four hundred years—that an Israelite had gazed upon a heavenly
vision. Then it suddenly occurred to Moses that he
had just missed a great opportunity.

All his life he had puzzled over the mysteries of the
universe. Over the years a thousand questions had come
tumbling into his mind. Why hadn't he taken advantage
of this wonderful opportunity to ventilate these problems while he stood in the presence of God? The very
fact that he had been granted such an interview, however, made him bold in hoping for another one. Said
he, "I will not cease to call upon God; *I have other things
to inquire of Him!*"[16]

But before Moses could receive another revelation
from the Lord he was to be subjected to a severe trial.
He was to be exposed to a satanical exhibition of power
administered by the prince of darkness in person. Apparently God wished to impress upon His newly commissioned servant that there are two great forces in the
universe—one constructive, the other destructive. He
wanted Moses to be able to distinguish between them.
Lucifer was, therefore, permitted to appear before Moses
and bring his whole influence to bear upon him. First he
tempted Moses just as he later tempted the Savior, and
when this failed to ensnare him Satan struck out in a

[16]Moses 1:18

violent rage and tried to intimidate him with a terrorizing demonstration which caused Moses to "fear exceedingly; and as he began to fear, he saw the bitterness of hell. Nevertheless, calling upon God, he received strength, and he commanded, saying: Depart from me, Satan, for this one God will I worship, which is the God of glory."[17]

The vital lesson which the Lord had wanted Moses to gain had been learned. When Satan saw that he had failed to deceive Moses he cried out against him in a wild denunciation. The record states that in the bitterness of his frustrated ambition he "cried with a loud voice, with weeping, and wailing, and gnashing of teeth."[18] Finally, he departed.

Moses was now prepared to receive one of the greatest revelations ever given to man.

[17]*Ibid.*, 1:18-22
[18]*Ibid.*, 1:22

CHAPTER TWO

The Revelation which Resulted in the Writing of Genesis

At the beginning of this revelation what special request did Moses make of the Lord?

Are there other inhabited planets in the universe?

The Lord told Moses He was going to place a definite restriction on the revelation concerning Genesis. What was that restriction?

Has God promised to reveal the rest of the story at some future date?

What did God tell Moses concerning the importance of the human race?

Is the book of Genesis a collection of the oral traditions of the Hebrews?

What did Peter say about the higher critics of the Bible who would appear in the latter days?

Did Moses know his writings in Genesis would be changed?

How did we acquire the opening chapters of the original Genesis for study in modern times?

Approximately how much scripture is missing from the first six chapters of Genesis as they appear in the modern Bible?

Where do we find a detailed description of the manner in which Moses obtained the information set forth in Genesis?

Moses Has A New Opportunity to Inquire
of the Lord

"And it came to pass that when Satan had departed from the presence of Moses, that Moses lifted up his eyes unto heaven, being filled with the Holy Ghost . . . and calling upon the name of God, he beheld his glory again, for it was upon him; and he heard a voice, saying: Blessed art thou, Moses, for I, the Almighty, have chosen thee, and thou shalt be made stronger than many waters; for they shall obey thy command as if thou wert God."[1]

With this, the vision of eternity suddenly opened again before Moses. He saw exactly what he had seen in the first vision—the earth and all of its inhabitants. Moses gazed intently at the scene. He "beheld the earth, yea, even all of it; and there was not a particle of it which he did not behold, discerning it by the spirit of God. And he beheld also the inhabitants thereof, and there was not a soul which he beheld not . . . and their numbers were great, even numberless as the sand upon the sea shore."[2]

This was the opportunity Moses had hoped for. This was his chance to ask directly concerning the questions which had been troubling him. Just as any modern scholar would have done, Moses longed to know the origin and purpose of all the things he had beheld. "Tell me, I pray thee, why these things are so, and by what thou madest them?"[3]

This was a decisive moment in the spiritual education of the man whose writings would later become part of the most widely read book in the world. In order that men of all races might afterwards appreciate the authoritative source of this revelation, Moses was endowed with additional glory so that once again he stood in the presence of God. "And the Lord God said unto Moses: For mine own purpose have I made these things."

---

[1]Moses 1:24-25
[2]Ibid., 1:27-28 (*Ibid* indicates the same source as the last one cited).
[3]Ibid., 1:30

Moses Learns That There Are Many
Inhabited Planets

Then the Lord gave Moses cause for more wonderment. Since he had been so impressed by the vision of this planet the Lord shared with him another secret of the heavens. He told Moses that there are millions of other inhabited planets in the universe. "Worlds without number have I created," said the Lord. "For behold, there are many that now stand, and innumerable are they unto man; but all things are numbered unto me, for they are mine and I know them."[4]

Moses had been a shepherd for forty years and on moonless nights he had gazed into the blue-black heights of the vaulted sky and watched the pinpoints of twinkling light coming through from the vast regions of outer space where great star-giants wheel their way through the orbits of our galaxy. Now he was told by this omnipotent and holy Personage—this divine Personality who stood before him—that many of these great solar dynamos are no different from our own sun; that they are circumscribed by whirling planets which —like our own earth—sustain life upon them.

Here was cause for real wonderment as Moses contemplated the vastness of the Lord's creations!

God Places Limitations on the Revelation
to Moses

But the Lord quickly added that He did not intend to emphasize distant things in this particular revelation. "Only an account of *this* earth and the inhabitants thereof give I unto you," said the Lord.

This was a most significant restriction placed upon the revelation which Moses was about to receive. It meant that nothing would be revealed at this time concerning possible relationships existing between this earth and other earths. It meant that if other, older planets were used as the source of plant and animal life for this

[4]*Ibid.,* 1:33, 35

earth, such facts would not be revealed because it would involve a discussion of planets other than our own. It meant that Moses would be required to accept some things without explanation for the time being.

History confirms the wisdom of God in refusing to excite the human imagination concerning matters which have no immediate bearing on life here, and would only distract the human race from the business of making life more profitable on our own planet. It is only a temporary restriction, however, for the Lord has promised that when the time is ripe all this information concerning faraway things and places will be fully revealed.[5]

It is understandable, nevertheless, why Moses was disappointed when he first learned of this restriction. The human mind is inherently desirous of knowing all truth—past, present and future; to learn not only existing facts but also the great "first causes" which lie behind them. But in spite of this Moses exhibited to the Lord the genuine faith of an obedient son. If he could not receive the whole answer, at least he was appreciative of the fragments. Said he, "Be merciful unto thy servant, O God, and tell me concerning *this* earth, and the inhabitants thereof . . . then thy servant will be content."[6]

MOSES LEARNS THE IMPORTANCE OF THE HUMAN RACE

But the Lord had one more seed to plant in the mind of Moses before He began the revelation on the "history of the race." The words which came next from the Lord constitute one of the most precious diadems of truth ever vouchsafed to man by heaven.

"Behold," said the Lord, *"this is my work and my glory—to bring to pass the immortality and eternal life of man!"* (Moses 1:39)

Here is the answer to the inquiry of King David when he said: "What is man that thou takest knowledge of him?"[7]

---

[5]D. & C. 121:28-32
[6]Moses 1:36
[7]Psalm 144:3

Man is the pride and pleasure of God and the object of His infinite devotion. He is no whimsical fantasy of God's creative power. He is no mere creature of chance cast upon the horizon of existing things by fickle circumstances. In fact, God was soon to reveal to Moses the thrilling fact that the spirit which is embodied in each and every human being is a *literal offspring of God* —a fact which Paul would later confirm, as does modern revelation.[8]

Man is so important in the "work and glory" of God that earths are created for the express purpose of being inhabited by him.[9] The plant and animal kingdoms which are placed upon these planets are for man to cultivate, subdue and make a part of his pleasant dominion.[10]

Here indeed is the God-given key to the identity and dignity of man!

Moses Is Finally Prepared to Receive Genesis

"And now, Moses, my son," said the Lord, "I will speak unto thee concerning the earth upon which thou standest; and thou shalt *write* the things which *I shall speak*. And in a day when the children of men shall esteem my words as naught and take many of them from the book which thou shalt write, behold, I will raise up another like unto thee; and they shall be had again among the children of men—among as many as shall believe."[11]

Original Text Refutes Modern Theories Concerning Genesis

The above passage reveals a glaring error on the part of many modern Bible scholars who have been teaching for many years that Genesis is not of divine origin but merely a compilation of the *oral traditions* of the Jews which Moses collected and wrote down for the first time. The teachings of these scholars has had

---

[8]Acts 17:29; Hebrews 12:9; D. & C. 76:24
[9]Isaiah 45:18
[10]Moses 2:26
[11]Moses 1:40-41

the effect of reducing the major portion of Genesis to the level of superstitious hearsay. Almost cheerfully, they have gone about the business of discrediting and destroying confidence in the historicity and authenticity of Genesis.

A typical example of this point of view is represented in the writings of Professor Frederick Carl Eislen of the Garrett Biblical Institute who recently wrote the following for present-day consumption: "If anyone is in search of accurate information regarding the age of the earth, or its relation to the sun, moon or stars, or the exact order in which plants and animals first appeared, or the rise of civilization, or the origin of languages and races, and similar questions, he should go to the books embodying the results of scientific and historical investigation and *not to the book of Genesis.* So far as the scientific or historical knowledge in the latter is concerned, it is of little more value than that contained in similar stories among the other nations."[12]

In other words, it is the opinion of this gentleman that Genesis is about on a par with the superstitions, traditions and legends of the Babylonians, Egyptians, Chinese, Greeks and so forth.

Continuing, the professor writes, "In any consideration of the historical value of the patriarchal narratives it must be kept in mind that, whatever the origin of the book of Genesis . . . *these stories were handed down for several centuries by word of mouth;* which means that they were exposed to all the dangers which ordinarily threaten narratives thus transmitted. . . . As a result it becomes impossible to regard the patriarchal stories as historical authorities in the proper sense of that term."[13]

In all of this a prophecy is literally fulfilled. As previously stated, the Lord told Moses that the day would come when his words would be esteemed as nothing. And speaking in the same spirit of prophecy, Peter, chief of the Apostles, declared: "There shall come in the

[12]*Encyc. Americana* (1946 Ed.), Vol. 12, p. 386 under Genesis
[13]*Ibid.,* p. 387

last days scoffers, walking after their own lusts." He said that these higher critics of the last days would be unmindful of the words which were spoken by holy prophets in ancient times but would say: "All things continue as they were from the beginning of the creation." Among other things, he said they would deny the Great Flood, being deliberately and "willingly" ignorant of that great cataclysmic event to which all of the ancient prophets and historians plainly refer.[14] ♦

In his introductory chapter Moses originally made it plainly clear that Genesis is *not* based on the oral traditions of the Hebrews, nor on their legends. Regardless of what men may think of the matter, Moses states that he was commanded of God to write the words of God. Jehovah was the source of this information. In its original text, Genesis was reliable, historical and true!

How the Original Genesis Was Restored In Modern Times

As we have previously mentioned, it was in the year 1830 that Joseph Smith received the "restored" text of Genesis. This text gives us the opening chapters of Genesis the way Moses originally recorded them. In this restored text we find answers to many of the questions which have puzzled scholars of the scriptures down through the centuries.

Joseph Smith received the complete text of the original Genesis up to chapter 6, verse 13 of our modern Bible. In the Bible this amounts to only 151 verses of scripture but in the restored version as given to Joseph Smith it comprises a total of 314 verses — more than *twice* as much!

In fact this indicates that 52% of the original Genesis up to verse 13 of chapter 6 had been lost. We do not know whether the chapter which tells how Moses received Genesis[15] was a part of this book in ancient times.

---

[14]2 Peter 3:3-6
[15]Moses, Ch. 1

If it was, then 65% of the original text is missing from the opening chapters of our modern Bible.

Now that the restored text of Genesis is available we find a wealth of new material to assist us in our study.

CHAPTER THREE

Beginning
The Story of Creation

What is the meaning of the original Hebrew word which was translated into English as "created"?

What then is meant by God's "power of creation"?

Why do you think the Lord felt that humanity could not comprehend a detailed account of the creative processes?

Scientists tell us we cannot understand many commonplace things with which we are familiar. What do you think they mean when they say, "We don't know what electricity is; we don't know what gravitation is; we don't know what life is"?

When was "the beginning" referred to in Genesis 1:1?

What kind of creation is the first chapter of Genesis talking about?

Has modern revelation taught us that "life" is much more complicated in structure than students had formerly supposed?

What happened the "first day"? What happened the "second day"? The "third day"?

On the "fourth day" something happened which demonstrates the similarity between physical and spiritual things. What was it?

What is the significance of the statement "be fruitful and multiply" during the spiritual phase of existence?

Do we have any hint as to how the various forms of "spirit life" were begotten or produced during the pre-existence?

How has the "restored" text of Genesis helped us better to understand the two creation stories?

BEGINNING THE STORY OF CREATION

Let us now examine the history of the creation as given to Moses. We should emphasize that the word "created" which some men have interpreted as "being made from nothing" really comes from a Hebrew word which means "to organize."[1] In other words, the Lord's power of creation is really his organizing power. Even with God there is no such thing as making something from nothing.

Apparently it was not easy for the Lord to present the creation story. It is obvious from His statements to Moses that He was conscious of the fact that the children of men do not have the present capacity to comprehend many of the eternal principles used during the creation process. To describe the creation in detail would have raised more questions than it would have answered.

In many respects we are like little children who might ask a scientist to explain how atomic bombs are made. Only simple generalities could be given because the complex procedures and scientific principles involved would not be understood. The Lord has a similar problem as He attempts to unfold to us the colorful panorama of the creation.

At the beginning of the millennium, however, the details of the creation story are to be revealed to us in all their magnificence.[2] The Lord says it will be knowledge which "no man knew." Meanwhile we must be content with the basic generalities which the Lord gave to Moses as a foundation for the greater revelation which is to come. We begin our study with the basic outline which Moses received.

"IN THE BEGINNING—" WHEN WAS IT?

The Lord declared: *"In the beginning* I created the the heaven and the earth upon which thou standest."

It is here that students of the Bible have often stumbled. They have assumed that this "beginning" of

---

[1] *Teachings of Joseph Smith,* pp. 350-351 and note
[2] D. & C. 101:33

the Lord's creative processes refers to the beginning of the temporal creation of this present earth. But the "beginning" of the earth's creation goes farther back. Thirty-five verses later in Moses 3:5 the Lord explains it. "I, the Lord God, created all things of which I have spoken *spiritually* before they were (created) naturally. . . ." Or, as the Lord explains in another place, all things were created "first spiritual, secondly temporal."[3]

In other words, the whole first chapter of Genesis which describes the organizing of a planet, the bringing forth of plants, animals and human beings, has nothing to do with the physical or temporal creation of our present earth. It is dealing with the *spiritual creation* of the earth and the placing of spiritual plants and creatures upon it.

The fact that all things had to be organized spiritually before they were "added upon" and brought into this present temporal sphere indicates that the earth and all things in it are much more complicated in structure than men have imagined. These things have a history reaching far back beyond the horizon of material things as we know them now.

THE SPIRITUAL CREATION

The spiritual creation was divided into six phases or days. On the first day the First Presidency of heaven undertook to organize the waters or the materials which were to form the spirit earth.[4] Although this was a "spiritual" creation the elements were real, substantive materials, but they were more refined than the elements with which we are presently acquainted. These spiritual materials were brought together on the first day.

"And again, I, God, said: Let there be a firmament in the midst of the water, and it was so, even as I spake; and I said: Let it divide the waters from the waters; and it was done;

---

[3] D. & C. 29:32
[4] Moses 2:2-5

"And I, God, made the firmament and divided the waters, yea, the great waters under the firmament from the waters which were above the firmament, and it was so even as I spake.

"And I, God, called the firmament Heaven; and the evening and the morning were the second day." (Moses 2:6-8)

On the second day the Lord divided the materials which had been collected. The waters or materials were divided into two parts and the space between them was called the firmament or heaven. The great waters or materials below the firmament eventually became the spirit earth. Nothing more is said of the water or materials which were left above the firmament.

"And I, God, said: Let the waters under the heaven be gathered together unto one place, and it was so; and I, God, said: Let there be dry land, and it was so.

"And I, God, called the dry land Earth; and the gathering together of the waters called I the Sea; and I, God, saw that all things which I had made were good.

"And I, God, said: Let the earth bring forth grass, the herb yielding seed, the fruit tree yielding fruit, after his kind, and the tree yielding fruit, whose seed should be in itself upon the earth, and it was so even as I spake.

"And the earth brought forth grass, every herb yielding seed after his kind, and the tree yielding fruit, whose seed should be in itself, after his kind; and I, God, saw that all things which I had made were good; and the evening and the morning were the third day." (*Ibid.*, 2:9-13)

So on the third day we see that the materials of the planet were concentrated and the dry earth became distinguishable. The Lord then undertook to organize and bring forth the spirit plant life—grass, herbs and trees are specifically mentioned.

"And I, God, said: Let there be lights in the firmament of the heaven, to divide the day from the night, and let them be for signs, and for seasons, and for days, and for years.

"And let them be for lights in the firmament of the heaven to give light upon the earth; and it was so.

"And I, God, made two great lights; the greater light to rule the day, and the lesser light to rule the night, and the greater light was the sun, and the lesser light was the moon; and the stars also were made even according to my word.

"And I, God, set them in the firmament of the heaven to give light upon the earth.

"And the sun to rule over the day, and the moon to rule over the night, to divide the light from darkness; and I, God, saw that all things which I had made were good;

"And the evening and the morning were the fourth day." (*Ibid.*, 2:14-19)

On the fourth day the new planet was given its fixed place in a solar system which confirms a modern declaration of the Lord that things which are spiritual are very much like the material things with which we are familiar.[5]

"And I, God, said: Let the waters bring forth abundantly the moving creature that hath life, and fowl which may fly above the earth in the open firmament of heaven.

"And I, God, created great whales, and every living creature that moveth, which the waters brought forth abundantly, after their kind, and every winged fowl after his kind; and I, God, saw that all things which I had created were good.

"And I, God, blessed them, saying: Be fruitful, and multiply and fill the waters in the sea; and let fowl multiply in the earth.

------

[5] See D. & C. 77:2

"And the evening and the morning were the fifth day." (Moses 2:20-22)

On this fifth day the Lord brought onto the spirit earth those forms of life which pertain to the realm of the sea. He also brought forth the various members of the bird family. As with the plant life previously mentioned, all these creatures were composed of spirit element. The command to "multiply" is similar to a command given a little later to the spirits of mankind,[6] but the scripture is clear that this command simply anticipated the time when they would be given physical bodies and be endowed with the power of procreation in mortality. As Mother Eve later declared: "Were it not for our transgression we never should have had seed."[7]

Where did these various forms of spirit life (plants and animals) come from? Since we know that the spirits of mankind were the offspring of resurrected beings[8] it is perhaps safe to assume that the other forms of spirit life were reproduced by parent stock in resurrected status.

"And I, God, said: Let the earth bring forth the living creature after his kind, cattle, and creeping things, and beasts of the earth after their kind, and it was so;

"And I, God, made the beasts of the earth after their kind, and cattle after their kind, and everything which creepeth upon the earth after his kind; and I, God, saw that all these things were good." (Moses 2:24-25)

This was the remainder of the animal kingdom. The Lord assures us that these creatures were also "spirit" at this stage of their existence.[9]

Then, last of all, the Father brought forth upon this spirit planet a large family of his own spiritual offspring

---

[6] Moses 2:27-28
[7] Ibid., 5:11 (Ibid. indicates the same source as the last one cited.)
[8] Brigham Young, Journal of Discourses 6:275
[9] Moses 3:5

"made in mine own image," and He gave them propri-
etory dominion over this magnificent new planetary home.[10]

Now the spirit creation was finished—not only the
planet but also "all the things" which were to inhabit it.
Then the Creator rested.

GOD'S GREAT SECRET CONCERNING THE CREATION

At this point in the narration the Lord inserted an
explanation to Moses so that he would not confuse
what had gone before with a description of the temporal
creation which was to follow. He declared: "Now,
behold, I say unto you that *these* (things which He
had been discussing) are the generations of the heaven
and the earth . . . in the day that I the Lord God made
the heaven and the earth and every plant of the field
before it was in the (temporal) earth, and every herb
of the field *before* it grew (on the temporal earth). For
I, the Lord God, created *all* things of which I have
spoken spiritually before they were naturally upon the
face of the earth."[11]

This is a marvelous contribution to the religious
understanding of modern man. Commenting on this
valuable addition to modern Christian knowledge, B. H.
Roberts had this to say: "To learn that the first account of the creation in the Bible is of a spiritual creation
and the second of an actual or natural one, gives some
comfort from the fact that it removes all appearances
of inconsistency or contradiction between the two accounts. For since they are descriptions of two different things instead of one thing, there is nothing in the
law of consistency requiring the accounts of different
events to be alike."[12]

It will be helpful to the student who is examining the
available texts on the creation to keep in mind that the
Lord does not give a distinct name to the spiritual or
pre-existent earth so as to distinguish it from the present temporal earth. He refers to it simply as "the earth"

---

[10]Moses 2:27-28
[11]*Ibid.*, 3:4-5
[12]Roberts, B. H., *The Gospel and Man's Relationship to Deity*, p. 277

regardless of whether He is speaking of the pre-existent abode of our spirits or its subsequent embellishment as our temporal abode. On certain occasions He has distinguished pre-existent things from temporal things by using a different name—such as calling the pre-existent Adam by the name of Michael, and we know that Noah was known by the name of Gabriel. With the earth, however, no such distinction is made, and the student must therefore keep this in mind to avoid confusion.

Now let us turn to a study of the temporal creation.

CHAPTER FOUR

The Temporal Creation

There is an unexpected surprise in the narration of the temporal creation as given to Moses. What is it?

How many things can you list which the earth would have to provide before it could sustain human life?

How many things can you list which the earth would have to provide before we could build a modern type of civilization?

What was Abraham told about the temporal creation?

During its period of preparation the earth was in a different environment. Where do the prophets say it was?

What was the time schedule on the earth before the Fall?

Should it be of some assistance to the student of science to learn about the interplanetary transplantation of life?

We have now been told what it means to be made from "the dust of the earth." What is the significance of this phrase?

Do we know where the Garden of Eden was?

Since the restoration of the gospel what have we learned about Adam that we didn't know before?

Which part of the earth is really the "old" world?

Was there any death in the Garden of Eden era prior to the Fall?

Adam and Eve and all the earth were brought to this state of existence for but one purpose. What was it?

Modern Scripture Illuminates Account of Temporal Creation

Just as the spiritual creation of the earth was a carefully engineered program so the temporal creation was the result of much thoughtful preparation. However, the Lord's revelation to Moses doesn't tell us a word about it!

To our amazement we observe that the revelation stops at the completion of the spiritual creation and then picks up the account at a much later period when the preparation of the physical earth is *presumed to have been completed.* Notice how the account of the temporal creation begins: "I, the Lord God, had not caused it to rain upon the face of the (temporal) earth . . . and there was not yet flesh upon the earth, neither in the water, neither in the air, but I, the Lord God, spake and there came up a mist from the earth and watered the face of the ground."[1]

From this it is apparent that the Lord is not going to tell us anything about the preparation of the physical earth. He is commencing the narration of the temporal creation at that period when the earth was completed and the various forms of life were about to be placed upon it.

We are certain, however, that the temporal earth had an extensive preparation before human beings were brought here.[2] Certainly Adam and Eve did not come to a globe of lava rock and salt water. They undoubtedly came to a prepared earth abounding in natural resources—coal, lime, oil, minerals and a layer of topsoil which would support advanced types of plant life. How was the earth prepared with these deposits of nature's wealth? Moses did not record a word concerning it.

Fortunately, however, we do have access to a revelation which was received by Abraham in which the Lord told him that prior to the arrival of Adam and Eve the temporal earth was carefully prepared so that

[1]Moses 3:5-6
[2]Isaiah 45:18

it would sustain the forms of life which the Lord desired to bring here. (See Abraham, Chapters 4 and 5)

Even with Abraham, however, the Lord did not disclose any details concerning the methods or procedures followed in preparing the earth. As we have already pointed out, this vitally interesting knowledge is being held in reserve, but it will not be kept a secret forever. As the scripture says: "In that day when the Lord shall come, he shall reveal all things—things which have passed, and hidden things which no man knew, *things of the earth, by which it was made* and the purpose and end thereof. Things most precious, things that are above, and things that are beneath, things that are *in the earth and upon the earth* and in heaven." (D. & C. 101:32-34)

This will be a great day of illumination for students of science and students of the scriptures. As indicated in the above passage, it will occur at the beginning of the millennium "when the Lord shall come." Meanwhile we will continue to study the crust of the earth to discover whatever we can find recorded there concerning the earth's illustrious past. In such a study, however, we must be humble students, for there have been many things occur to this remarkable sphere which no amount of "rock research" would reveal.

Knowledge by Revelation

As an example, the Lord disclosed to Abraham the fact that before the Fall this planet was on a different time schedule than at present. Before the Fall Adam's time on this earth was "after the Lord's time which was after the time of Kolob."[3] In another place we learn the significance of this statement. The time of Kolob is one thousand years for a single revolution or day![4]

Modern prophets have also received additional understanding concerning the status of the earth prior to the Fall. In his writings President John Taylor refers to "this earth which had fled and fallen from where it

[3]Abraham 5:13
[4]*Ibid.,* 3:4

was *organized near the planet Kolob*."[5] Brigham Young taught precisely the same doctrine.[6]

New knowledge of this kind should speak caution to the student of the earth's past. Undoubtedly a multitude of other dramatic historical events have occurred to this planet which nothing short of a revelation would disclose to us.

In connection with the bringing of life to the earth we now know that the interplanetary transplantation of life is a common procedure with the Lord. As President Brigham Young pointed out, when we learn the whole truth of the matter we shall see that all plant and animal life was brought "from other planets to this world."[7] In other words, older planets are used to provide parent stock for new planets.

How can this be done? At this very moment science is grappling with the problem of space travel. How can human beings—or any life for that matter—be safely transported through space? Scientists say it will be necessary to preserve earth conditions throughout the flight. Problems of providing correct pressure, adequate oxygen, supplies of water and sufficient food will all have to be solved. But the Lord approaches the problem differently because of His superior knowledge. He *changes the creature* so that it can endure space travel without reference to the prerequisites of earth life. The creature is temporarily "quickened" or "translated" and the transfer is made safely and without apparent discomfort of any kind.

We are not given the slightest hint as to the scientific principle underlying this procedure but the scriptures refer to a number of occasions when life has been transferred from this planet to other planets by this method. It happened to the entire city of Enoch,[8] to the people of Melchizedek,[9] to John the Beloved,[10] to the Three

[5]Lundwall, N. B., *The Vision*, p. 146
[6]Lundwall, N. B., *Assorted Gems*, p. 346
[7]Sermon of Brigham Young in Salt Lake City, April 20, 1856
[8]Moses 7:21; *Doc. Hist. of the Church*, Vol. 4, pp. 209-210
[9]Inspired Version, Gen. 14:32-34
[10]D. & C., Sec. 7

Nephites[11] and perhaps to many others about whom we have not yet been told.

Knowing the reality of the procedure it becomes possible to better appreciate the teaching of Brigham Young to the effect that when God is ready to populate a new planet he follows the economical and apparently simple device of transplanting parent stock from some older planet to the new one. By temporarily "quickening" the various forms of life this transfer can be accomplished quickly and safely.

Obviously, the methods of God are often beyond the imagination of man. It emphasizes the necessity of remaining open-minded and teachable as we approach the study of the earth's past history. Many students—sincere and hard working—have propounded theories concerning the history of the earth which conflict with the insight we have already received through the disclosures of the earth's Creator. Of such we should beware. And most certainly we should not allow ourselves to fall in among the "scoffers" of the last day referred to by Peter. He said the great mistake of our day and generation would be the false assumption that "all things continue as they were from the beginning of the creation."[12]

He said that men of our day, "walking after their own lusts" would deny such things as the great Flood and other manifestations of the intervening power of God in the history of the earth. This prophecy has been fulfilled and we live in a day when professional scholarship has denied many of the things which God has asserted to be true. In the pursuit of knowledge each man must judge for himself the reliability of his source material. It would seem that where God has revealed to His prophets events and circumstances which He has declared to be facts, the speculations of theorists to the contrary should carry little weight.

[11]3 Nephi, Ch. 28
[12]2 Peter 3:3-6

ORIGIN OF HUMAN LIFE ON THE EARTH

When the Lord was describing to Moses the manner in which human life first came to this planet, He summarily dismissed the subject with the simple statement that Adam's temporal body was made from "the dust of the ground" and that his spirit entered that body to sustain it with the "breath of life." *How* the Lord provided Adam with a body from the dust of the ground is not mentioned at this point and as a result a great many scriptural scholars made the same mistake certain scientists did. They concluded that by some mysterious means life was created spontaneously. They misled themselves into thinking that the Lord performed some kind of miracle by making a physical form out of earthly clay and then transforming it into a living human body.

Such a concept partakes of the dark ages and is nowhere justified in scripture.

In fact, the Lord originally told Moses precisely what it meant to be made from the dust of the earth. This is a technical phrase. It meant to be *"born . . . by water, and blood, and the spirit which I have made, and so became of dust a living soul."*[13] This is simply a description of the physical birth. That is also how Adam's physical body was made. It was born of a mother just as the body of every other human being has been made from the dust of the earth.

As President Brigham Young stated: "He (Adam) was made *as you and I were made* and no person was ever made on any other principle."[14]

Where was he born? Who were his parents? To have answered these questions in detail would have required the Lord to discuss events on other planets and He had already told Moses He did not wish to cover such matters at that time. (Moses 1:35)

*There are many exciting events behind the creation story which the Lord has deliberately left obscure. It is not difficult to discover the reason why. The history of eternity extends behind us like an endless thread. Some

---
[13]Moses 6:59
[14]*Journal of Discourses*, Vol. 3:319
*The next four paragraphs were added in the third edition.

place along that thread the Lord decided to select a point which would be called the beginning of our history. He decided to tie a knot so to speak, in the thread of eternity at the point where Adam became a resident of the earth. It is difficult for the human mind to accept this "terminal point" designated by the Lord and many scholars have therefore tried to penetrate the obscure past and build up theories and suppositions which would satisfy the human thirst for knowledge.

In this connection, however, it is interesting to observe that while the Lord has temporarily declined to tell us the details of Adam's origin, he at least assures us that:

1—Adam did not evolve from lower animals.

2—There were no pre-Adamic men.

Here is what the Lord says: "And man (Adam) became a living soul, the *first flesh* upon the earth, the *first man* also."[15]   Obviously, if he were the *first* flesh upon the earth he could not have evolved from earlier flesh and if Adam was the *first* man then there were no pre-Adamic men.

Such statements are a great challenge to the student but the Lord counsels us not to worry too much about it because when we get the whole story we will find these statements to be literally true.   The Lord has said that when he reveals the full account it will be knowledge "which no man knew."[16]   It is most profitable, therefore, to leave these obscure matters for future revelation and get on with the known facts of history which begin at the Garden of Eden.

THE GARDEN OF EDEN

The meaning of "Eden" is described as connoting "Paradise" or "Pleasure."

Concerning the introduction of plant life onto the earth at this time the Lord states: "And I, the Lord God, planted a garden eastward in Eden, and there I put the man whom I had formed.   And out of the ground made I, the Lord God, to grow every tree, naturally, that

---

[15]Moses 3:7
[16]D. & C. 101:33

is pleasant to the sight of man; and man could behold it. *And it became also a living soul.* For it was spiritual in the day that I created it."[17]

Here again the Lord is emphasizing the dual nature of all things. Even the plants had a spirit creation before they were brought forth and made to grow "naturally" upon the face of the earth. Thus they, too, each became "a living soul"[18] which means the combining of spirit and temporal matter.

Finally all types of animal life belonging to the orders which were considered profitable for mankind during his sojourn upon the earth were brought to the earth. The Lord states that "they were also living souls; for I, God, breathed into them the breath of life, and commanded that whatsoever Adam called every living creature, that should be the name thereof."[19]

During this period of embellishment when parent stock of the plant and animal kingdoms was being transplanted to this earth, Adam took an active part in supervising this work under the Lord's direction as he also must have done during the earth's preparation. This is referred to by President Young, "Though we have it in history that our Father Adam . . . knew nothing about his God previous to being made here, yet it is not so, and when we learn the truth we shall see and understand that he helped to make this world and was the manager of that operation. *He was the person who brought the animals and the seeds from other planets to this world.*"[20]

Who was Adam? During Adam's own lifetime the Lord revealed the true identity of this great patriarch to Adam's children. He was none other than Michael in the pre-existence.[21] He was the mighty Archangel spoken of by John the Revelator who led the offensive against Lucifer and his hosts[22] during the First Estate in the spirit world when Satan undertook to destroy the plan of sal-

[17]Moses 3:8-9
[18]D. & C. 88:15
[19]Moses 3:19
[20]Jour. of Disc. 3:319
[21]D. & C. 27:26; 128:21
[22]Rev. 12:7-9

vation which the Lord had offered us. In the pre-
existence Adam or Michael was a prince of God. He
was one of the "noble and great ones" seen by Abraham
in vision.[23] His name, "Michael," is said to have meant
"Who is as God."[24] It was no mere matter of accident
that this personality was selected to be the first great
leader and patriarchal ancestor among the children of
men.

Undoubtedly Eve held a corresponding position of
eminence. When Adam and Eve assumed the management of the Garden of Eden the earth became honored
with the presence of two of the Father's most noble
servants.

Where Was The Garden Of Eden?

The whereabouts of the Garden of Eden has
prompted men to engage in continuous debate down
through the centuries. The position of modern scholars
is represented in the following: "The account given in
Genesis of the situation of Eden *is not such as to enable
us to identify it with any existing locality.* It is said to
have had a garden in the eastern part of it, and we are
told that a river went out of Eden to water this garden,
and from then it was parted into four heads which were
called respectively, Pison, Bihon, Hiddekel and Euphrates."[25]

This last named river has led scholars of Biblical history to assume that the location of Eden was in Mesopotamia somewhere along the Euphrates. However, all
other descriptive data which appear in the Bible concerning Eden seem to dispute the possibility of its having
been in that location.

The true location of the Garden of Eden was made
known to Joseph Smith in this dispensation as well as
the location of the residence of Adam and Eve after they
fled from Eden. Brigham Young stated, "Joseph, the

[23]Abraham 3:22-23
[24]*D. & C. Commentary,* p. 183
[25]*Encyc. Americana,* Vol. 9, p. 580, 1946 Edition, under "Eden"

prophet, told me that the Garden of Eden was in Jackson County, Missouri. When Adam was driven out he went to the place we now call Adam-ondi-Ahman, Daviess County, Missouri. There he built an altar and offered sacrifices."[26]

To know the exact location of the Garden of Eden leads one to appreciate more fully the personal reality of the life and labors of Father Adam and Mother Eve. It also teaches us that America or the Western Hemisphere is the cradle of the race. It is the *old* world— the most anciently inhabited part of the earth. Of course, in ancient times America was not separated from the mainland of Eurasia but was joined together in "one land."[27] The division of the land into continents and islands did not occur until the days of Peleg around 2,240 B.C.[28]

During the Garden of Eden era prior to the Fall there was no death.[29] Everything that existed in the Garden of Eden was endowed with the capacity to live forever. It was as though all things were in a state of suspended animation. There was no degeneration, no breakdown of cellular structure, no disease, no predatory influence of any kind to rob mankind or his companions in the animal kingdom of their power to go on existing forever.

And as there was no death, neither was there any reproduction. Although the commandment to multiply and replenish the earth was given long before,[30] we shall see later that the power to fulfil it did not come until after the Fall.

The sublime condition which existed in the Garden of Eden was not intended to last. It was a temporary taste of paradisiacal glory which anticipated an event of great historical importance that was about to take place. Adam and Eve and all the earth had been brought to this state of existence for but one purpose—to Fall!

---

[26]Cowley, M. F., *Wilford Woodruff*, p. 431
[27]D. & C. 133:23-24
[28]Genesis 10:25
[29]2 Nephi 2:22
[30]Moses 2:28

CHAPTER FIVE

The Purpose of Earth Life

Was it an important contribution to modern religious knowledge to learn that "fallen" earth life had a divine purpose instead of being merely a man-made blunder? Why?

Can you think of any reasons why it would have been impossible to obtain physical bodies in the spirit or pre-existent estate?

What are some of the distinctive characteristics of this life which would not be found in the pre-existent estate?

Is there a difference between "pleasure" and "joy"?

Why do you think a resurrected person is the only type of individual capable of registering a "fulness of joy"?

What special significance does the Lord attach to the power of procreation? Is this new knowledge?

Have human beings been "tested" before this life?

Why is the testing period in this life so important?

Was it possible to learn the difference between good and evil "in heaven" as effectively as we are able to learn it here? Why?

Why is it particularly important to the Father to have us schooled against rebellion at this stage of our existence?

Is it a blessing to live in an environment where judgment is "temporarily suspended"? Is that one of the exclusive conditions of earth life?

Why would repentance be of little value without the Atonement of Jesus Christ? What does the Atonement do?

Is there repentance in heaven?

THE FIRST PURPOSE OF EARTH LIFE

For many centuries unenlightened professors of religion have taught that man's greatest calamity was the disobedience of Adam and Eve in the Garden of Eden which precipitated the Fall. Modern scripture clarifies the problem, however, and teaches that the Fall was a carefully planned project of the Father which he not only anticipated but *intended* should occur. In fact, a careful perusal of the ancient and modern scriptures reveals that the Lord attaches the greatest significance to the temporal, fallen, mortal estate through which we are now passing.

At least five profoundly important purposes are fulfilled in this fallen or mortal estate which could not be achieved in any other way.

First, it was the only way several billion spirit children of the Father comprising our own particular family group could be provided with temporal bodies.

In the pre-existence or spirit world we secured all that could be obtained there. We enjoyed the privilege of being provided with spirit tabernacles in which our individual personalities or intelligences could dwell.[1] But these bodies had definite limitations. Further progress was closed to us unless we were "added upon" by acquiring bodies of temporal material.[2] These could not be obtained in the spirit world. To secure bodies of temporal matter we had to leave the spirit world and subject ourselves to a lower plane of existence where bodies of temporal matter were available. And when we obtained these bodies we had to learn the laws by which the materials of these bodies could be controlled.

THE SECOND PURPOSE

Secondly, this was the course the Lord said we had to follow in order to attain "a fulness of joy," like unto our Heavenly Father.

---

[1]Abraham 3:22-23
[2]*Ibid.,* 3:26

The warm, excitable, and thrilling emotion which the body registers in response to conditions which are for its stimulation or welfare is called "joy." This is something we apparently did not have abundantly while in the spirit world. The Prophet Lehi indicates that unless we had come into this world after the Fall and received physical bodies we could not have known the abundance of this rich emotional experience called "joy."[3]

$\rightarrow$ Joy is the emotional marriage of the mind and the body. For centuries men have misunderstood the prerequisites of true joy and have considered it merely a physical expression of subtle and fleeting duration. They have therefore attempted to manufacture the sensation of joy by artificial means. Some resort to alcohol, some to narcotics, some to physical dissipation. But all of these return dissolute and disappointed.

The true components of joy are found not only in the physical responses but in a spiritual and intellectual reaction as well. In this life we may learn to a limited degree the sweetness of true joy.

However, a "fulness of joy" can only be attained when our bodies have been resurrected and are inseparably connected with our spirits forever. As the Lord has said: "Spirit and element, inseparably connected, receive a fulness of joy."[4] Then He adds this significant postscript: "And when *separated,* men cannot receive a fulness of joy."[5] Our spirits, when alone, are for some reason incapable of enjoying this experience in its fulness.

In the fusion of our physical and spiritual tabernacles we achieve an exalted and glorified medium of expression which alone is capable of reflecting the same thrilling and transcendent exhilaration of continuous physical pleasure such as our Heavenly Father enjoys.

Mortality is the gateway through which mankind had to pass before they could possess a fulness of joy like unto God. Concerning those who achieve this great

[3] 2 Nephi 2:25; see also D. & C. 93:34
[4] D. & C. 93:33
[5] *Ibid.,* 93:34

blessing the Lord had this to say: "They are they into whose hands the Father has given all things—they are they who are priests and kings, who have *received of his fulness*, and of his glory . . . wherefore, as it is written, they are gods, even the sons of God—wherefore, all things are theirs, whether life or death, or things present, or things to come, all are theirs and they are Christ's, and Christ is God's.[6]

THE THIRD PURPOSE

Third, mortality made it possible for us to be endowed with the powers of procreation for the first time.

Procreation was another blessing reserved for the Second Estate or mortal existence here on the earth. This functional endowment was given as an exclusive and divine dispensation to those who were found worthy and willing to enter this Second Estate. Parenthood is a portion of the power of Godhood and therefore this privilege of participating in the organizing or creative processes of God was barred from us until we had scaled the heights of aeons of loyal obedience in our antemortal existence—first as intelligences and then as spirits. Only at this late stage of our development when we have become potential candidates for a place in the councils of the gods are we permitted to partake of these powers.

Of course, many—in fact, the vast majority—of those who enter mortality and enjoy the temporary power of procreation will not attain the ultimate status of Godhood, and all those who fall short of the goal—which is the highest degree of the celestial kingdom—will lose this divine capacity to perpetuate themselves through their posterity.[7]

One of the most profound and significant disclosures to come forth in the Dispensation of the Fulness of Times is the fact that parenthood upon this earth is but a training period for parenthood in eternity. The divine power of procreation is described by the Lord as being a funda-

[6]*Ibid.*, 76:55-59; see also 2 Nephi 9:18
[7]*Ibid.*, 131:1-4

mental quality of Godhood. In fact, eternal parenthood *is* Godhood.[8]

It is interesting to note that when Adam and Eve were first placed in the Garden of Eden, they were still incapable of having mortal children.[9] According to the scripture if they had not subjected themselves to the metamorphosis of the Fall they *never* could have had children.[10] Not only they, but we ourselves, had to pass through the gateway of mortality to receive these blessings.

THE FOURTH PURPOSE

Fourth, mortality was designed to subject the human race to its *final* period of probationary testing.

After aeons of progression and testing we, who have been fortunate enough to make the Second Estate, now face our last screening test for evaluation purposes. We were undoubtedly tested as intelligences and we know we were tested in the spirit world because the Lord spoke of the spirits in the pre-existent estate and said: "We will prove them herewith, to see if they will do all things whatsoever the Lord their God shall command them; and they who keep their first estate shall be added upon, and they who keep not their first estate shall not have glory in the same kingdom with those who keep their first estate."[11]

It must be kept in mind that down through the corridors of eternity there has been a highly competitive program of eternal progression which has been a constant challenge to us. It has resulted in a wide variance among us as to individual integrity, initiative, intelligence and quality of character.[12]

The scriptures hint that all along the path there were many casualties. From time to time myriads of our brother and sister intelligences would voluntarily choose a course of conduct which permanently dammed them off from the stream of progression which we were following.

[8]*Ibid.,* 132:19-20
[9]2 Nephi 2:23
[10]Moses 5:11
[11]Abraham 3:25-26
[12]*Ibid.,* 3:19

In fact, as late as our recent pre-existent estate, one third of the hosts of the Father's spirit children chose to forsake the struggle and thereby cut themselves off forever from the possibility of attaining the fulness of joy for which we are now striving.[18]

For the rest of us, however, this life is in the final probation. This is our last test. That is why the Lord constantly attaches so much importance to our perseverance in this life. We are so near the end of the race; but the risk is correspondingly great. As Alma declared: "Behold, this life is the time to prepare to meet God; yea, behold the day of this life is the day for men to perform their labors. And now, as I said unto you before, as ye have had so many witnesses, therefore, I beseech of you that ye do not procrastinate the day of your repentance until the end; for after this day of life, which is given us to prepare for eternity, behold, if we do not improve our time while in this life, then cometh the night of darkness wherein there can be no labor performed. Ye cannot say, when ye are brought to that awful crisis, that I will repent, ... For behold, if ye have procrastinated the day of your repentance even until death, behold, ye have become subjected to the spirit of the devil, and he doth seal you his; therefore, the Spirit of the Lord hath withdrawn from you, and hath no place in you, and the devil hath all power over you; and this is the final state of the wicked."[14]

Although comparatively speaking, the human family is now close to the ultimate goal of eternal lives and exaltation, nevertheless there will be very few who will satisfy the stringent prerequisites of this final test. As the Lord himself declared: "Strait is the gate, and narrow is the way, which leadeth unto life, and few there be that find it."[15]

THE FIFTH PURPOSE

Fifth, mortality is designed to condition us forever against rebellion.

---

[18]D. & C. 29:36; 76:33-34
[14]Alma 34:32-35; see also 1 Nephi 10:20-21
[15]Matt. 7:14; D. & C. 132:22

Because the Father has lost so many of His choice intelligences through misguided rebellion down through the ages, He desired to immunize us effectively against rebellion in the future. He wanted us to come in direct contact with sin and rebellion but under circumstances where we would not become permanently scarred by the experience. He wanted us to discover for ourselves that sin never will bring happiness—that there are no short-cuts to exaltation—which is what Lucifer rebelled over. The Lord wanted us to convince ourselves for all time that God's way is the safe, proven, reliable way, so that never, in all the eternities of the future, would we allow ourselves to be lured into rebelling against Him as were a third of our brothers and sisters in the pre-existence. Earth life, therefore, was set up and designed to give us this opportunity of distinguishing through actual experience the difference between the bitterness of sin and rebellion and the sweetness of righteous obedience.[16]

This was not possible "in heaven." There celestial law prevails which means that perfection is maintained and any sin or rebellion is not tolerated with even the "least degree of allowance."[17] Of course, like our brothers and sisters of the pre-existence we *could* have rebelled, but not without suffering the immediate consequences. In heaven there is no opportunity to "learn" about rebellion, for those who indulge in it feel the immediate impact of judgment.

In order to learn what sin and rebellion are like we had to be removed from the celestial kingdom of the Father into an environment where good and evil exist side by side. It had to be a place where we could "taste" and then have time to decide which we would choose.[18] It had to be a place where judgment was *temporarily suspended* so that in case we became enmeshed in grievous error during our learning process we would still have time to turn back before a judgment was pronounced or a final penalty imposed. In other words, provision had to be made so that there was "*a space* granted unto man

[16]D. & C. 29:39
[17]*Ibid.*, 1:31
[18]*Ibid.*, 29:39

in which he might repent,"[19] a time in which to turn back and, insofar as possible, regain the lost ground.

Finally, the Father said that as rapidly as we turned away from evil and overcame it He would blot out the offense through the atonement of Jesus Christ so that it would not be held against us. It is important to realize that even though we learned the difference between good and evil and decided to govern our lives by the good, we nevertheless could *not* return to the perfection of the celestial kingdom if it were not for the Atonement of the Savior which "blots out" the offenses which are tabulated against us during the learning process. How this is accomplished will be discussed elsewhere.* It is sufficient at this point simply to restate the divine assurance that every sin which we overcome sufficiently to bring under the cloak of the atonement will be so completely erased from our record that when we receive our final judgment it will be as though that particular mistake *had never happened!* This is the principle of repentance.[20]

From this it will be seen that the principle of repentance is a very great blessing that can only operate in a very carefully prepared laboratory which is isolated from the Father's immediate presence. To be efficacious it must operate in an environment: 1—where good and evil exist side by side, 2—where there is a "time" of suspended judgment in which men can choose and, if they desire, "turn back" through repentance, and 3—where there is an infinite atonement provided through which all sins that are overcome by repentance can be blotted out forever.

The Lord states that when this earth is celestialized and rolled back into His presence, "repentance shall be hid from mine eyes."[21] In other words, *there is no*

---

[19]Alma 12:24; see also 42:4
*See article in the appendix "Why Was the Atonement Necessary?"
[20]Isaiah 1:18; 43:25; 44:22; D. & C. 58:42; Ezekiel 33:14-16; Alma 7:13
[21]Hosea 13:14

repentance or suspended judgment in heaven! As Alma
says: "*This* life is the time to prepare to meet God; yea,
behold the day of *this* life is the day for men to perform
their labors!"[22]

---

[22]Alma 34:32

CHAPTER SIX

Why the Fall of Adam and Eve Was Difficult to Achieve

Since the Lord wanted Adam and Eve to obtain a "knowledge of good and evil" why was the fruit in the Garden of Eden declared to be forbidden?

From the Lord's point of view what was the nature of the problem involved in the Fall?

Does this Second Estate involve a high degree of risk for mankind?

How did Lucifer try to capitalize on this fact during the pre-existence?

Could the Lord have been assured that Adam and Eve were acting "independent" of the Lord unless they had acted in opposition to His expressed will?

Did Adam and Eve know how the Fall was going to be brought about?

Does it appear that they knew there was going to be a Fall?

Was there anything significant about the "place" where God located the tree of "knowledge of good and evil"?

What do you think motivated Lucifer when it says "he sought to destroy the world"?

Does Lucifer know the mind of God so that he can anticipate all of the Lord's plans for the welfare of the human race?

Did the serpent lie to Eve when he tempted her?

What argument seems to have had the greatest influence in persuading Eve to partake of the fruit?

Why did Adam partake of the forbidden fruit?

Did he knowingly act in opposition to the Lord's expressed will?

What does Paul mean when he says "Adam was not deceived"? (1 Timothy 2:14)

NATURE OF "THE PROBLEM" INVOLVED IN THE FALL.

The casual student of the scriptures may miss the rather dramatic fact that the engineering of the Fall of Adam and Eve represented a tremendous challenge to the First Presidency of heaven. Not that the problem was new—nor was the solution new. Undoubtedly the Fall was achieved by following the same blueprint as that which had proved most successful in engineering the Fall on other planets. Nevertheless, it was a delicate operation requiring the utmost skill in maneuvering our first parents into a position where they would deliberately and voluntarily take the step which would precipitate them down into a temporal sphere of mortality.

Why did the Lord place the fruit in the Garden of Eden which He knew would bring about the Fall and then tell Adam and Eve it was forbidden?

Superficially it would almost appear as though the Father did not want them to fall, but, as we have previously observed, the scripture plainly teaches that the Fall was expected, predicted and that provisions for it were carefully planned in advance. In fact, the Father indicated that it was the next step in the plan of eternal progression for the human race.

Why then, did He prohibit Adam and Eve from doing the very thing which He knew would precipitate the Fall and put the plan into effect?

The answer requires that we project our thinking back to conditions as they then existed and examine them from the Lord's point of view.

First of all, it must be appreciated that the Father was extremely anxious that the Fall be accomplished without *His* direct participation. Obviously, He did not want this to be brought about through *His* will, but by the voluntary and independent will of Adam and Eve. The reason the Father did not want to be a party to the actual mechanics of the Fall appears to be based on the fact that He knew the Fall would entail a tremendously high rate of risk for the vast majority of his spirit children. For a few it would mean the realization of Godhood and exaltation, but for the vast majority it would mean something else—it would mean an assignment to one of the lesser degrees of glory where they would have every blessing to which they were entitled but be forever excluded from the privilege of enjoying the presence of the Father.

Concerning these teeming multitudes who would fail to make their Second Estate completely profitable the scripture declares: "But where God and Christ dwell they cannot come, worlds without end."[1]

CAN THE RISK BE ELIMINATED FROM THE PLAN OF SALVATION?

Knowing, therefore, the tremendous risk involved and the fact that there would be many casualties, the Father took every precaution to make certain that all those who entered the Second Estate of mortal probation did so voluntarily and on their own initiative. That was why the entire matter was presented to us for discussion and our sustaining vote in the pre-existence; and reflect for a moment upon the fact that even though we were told that it was the next step in the plan of eternal progression, nevertheless, one third of the hosts in the spirit world were afraid to go forward. The risk was too great.

Lucifer rallied these around him and gained their support for a plan which *would not entail any risk*. He proposed to prevent any spirits from falling short of salvation by simply forcing them to live throughout the Second Estate or mortal estate in strict compliance with celestial law.[2] He would have to admit that his plan involved a violation of personal free agency—a principle on which God had evolved the entire cosmic universe,[3] but undoubtedly he justified himself on the ground that it was for a good end. When the Father said He would not accept the plan, Lucifer whipped his followers into an open rebellion against God, and so violent did the dispute become that it finally resulted in the complete ejection of Lucifer and his hosts from the presence of the Father.[4]

[1] D. & C. 76:109-112; see also verse 77
[2] Moses 4:3
[3] D. & C. 93:30
[4] Moses 4:3; Revelations 12:7-9

The rest of us voted to accept the risk of going forward and shouted for joy at the prospect of this new and
exciting experience,[5] but the Father knew that before we
had finished the travail of mortality many of us would
change our shouts of joy into wails of lamentation.

It was for this reason, therefore, that He desired that
Adam and Eve—as our representatives—should actually
bring about the cataclysm of the Fall on their own initiative and not permit us afterwards to say that the Fall was
the fault of the Father, rather than of our own making.

It seems clear from subsequent events that Adam and
Eve had no idea *how* the Father was going to effect the
Fall. They apparently knew it was about to occur but
undoubtedly presumed that the Father would bring it
about in His own way whenever the time was ripe. It
is very clear that Adam and Eve did not know *they*
were going to precipitate the Fall.

The Father's problem was further complicated by the
fact that He not only intended that Adam and Eve should
initiate the Fall but they should do it *independent* of the
Father's expressed will. The only way to insure such
independence would be to have Adam and Eve launch
the Fall through some act which was in *opposition* to the
Father's expressed will.

Here then is the reason for the "forbidden" fruit. It
was the key to the Fall. By placing a ban upon it the
Father was assured that if they partook of it they would
be acting entirely on their own initiative.

The next problem was getting Adam and Eve to
partake of the fruit through the exercise of their wills
in opposition to the expressed will of the Father. This
was not as easy as it may appear. It must be kept in
mind that Adam and Eve had no desire to exercise
their wills in opposition to that of the Father. They had
no guile, no secret ambitions. In fact, at this stage of
their existence they were "innocent."[6] Their relationship with the Father was one of implicit faith. They
were like children who trusted their every need to the

Job 38:4-7
D. & C. 93.38

counsel, direction and will of the Godhead. It will be appreciated, therefore, that here indeed was a delicate and challenging maneuver wherein the First Presidency of heaven undertook to arrange surrounding circumstances in such a way that this noble man and woman who were honored in the pre-existence for their fidelity and faithfulness would express their will in opposition to that of the Father.

How The Fall Was Achieved

Now let us consider the ingenuity and care with which the Lord set up the circumstances designed to lead to the Fall. It appears that there were four different ingredients necessary to start the chain reaction of events that ultimately permitted Adam and Eve to make their decisions under conditions acceptable to the plan and purposes of the Father.

First, as we have previously mentioned, Adam and Eve seem to have been placed in the Garden of Eden with a knowledge that they were soon to fall and thereby enjoy the blessings of mortality. Note that they were united in marriage and are consistently referred to as husband and wife.[7] Such a union was void of meaning except as it anticipated the time when they would enter the realm of mortality where their marriage would be consummated and they would enjoy the God-given powers of procreation. From this and subsequent events it would appear that the Fall was expected by them. *How* the Fall would be effected was not made known to them, but they were confident that God, in his wisdom, would bring it about when the circumstances were propitious.

Second, the Lord placed in the Garden of Eden the degenerate fruit containing the seeds of death which would introduce into the bodies of Adam and Eve those ingredients necessary to scientifically precipitate the Fall. This was called the fruit of "the knowledge of good and evil." God placed the tree which bore the fruit in the heart of the garden where it had a place of prominence and was easily accessible.[8]

[7]Moses 4:12, 14, 22, 23, 27
[8]*Ibid.,* 4:9

Third, the Lord placed a ban on this fruit. Note the strange way in which this prohibition was couched: "But of the tree of the knowledge of good and evil thou shalt not eat of it, nevertheless, thou mayest choose for thyself, for it is given unto thee; but remember that I forbid it, for in the day thou eatest thereof thou shalt surely die."[9] Looking back over that period it is now possible to appreciate that the Father was saying: "You can eat of this fruit if you want to, even though I forbid it, and I want you to decide for yourselves whether or not you will eat of it."

However, neither Adam nor Eve caught the subtle hint. As far as they were concerned it was categorically prohibited and that was the end of the matter.

They knew they were supposed somehow to obtain a knowledge of good and evil incidental to the Fall (which was used as an argument by Lucifer when he tempted Eve) but at this particular time it did not occur to either Adam or Eve that they would get the desired knowledge by partaking of this forbidden fruit in violation of a specific commandment of the Lord.

Lucifer Furnishes The Initiative For The Fall

It was for this reason that the Lord introduced the fourth element into the scene. This was Lucifer's initiative. Without Lucifer's seductive persuasion it is doubtful whether Adam or Eve would ever have partaken of the forbidden fruit. It was no mere accident that the permanent exile of Lucifer had been temporarily delayed and that he and his fallen hosts were consigned temporarily to the earth. The Lord intended to use the proud ambitions of Lucifer to accomplish something which the latter never dreamed of.

Lucifer seems to have misunderstood the reason why he was placed upon the earth and assumed that it was just another opportunity to prove his superiority over Jehovah whose plan was accepted in preference to his own.

---

[9]*Ibid.*, 3:17

For this reason, the scripture says, "he sought to destroy the world."[10]   He resolved to do everything possible to thwart, dismantle, demobilize and otherwise frustrate all the constructive work which Jehovah attempted to do. But the scripture also says, "he knew not the mind of God"[11] and therefore he didn't realize that his forces of destruction would provide the initiative necessary to accomplish many of the things which Jehovah had in mind for the consummation of His plan of salvation.

One of these purposes was accomplished at this time. Lucifer's cunning and unholy ambition led him to try and make Adam and Eve violate the first negative commandment they had received. He resolved to lure them into eating the "forbidden fruit."

LUCIFER APPROACHES EVE INDIRECTLY

The first step in Lucifer's plan to beguile Adam and Eve was to cultivate the confidence of certain animals in the Garden of Eden who were of subtle intellects. For this purpose he concentrated on many of the serpents. The scripture specifically states that "he had drawn away many after him."[12]

Why Lucifer wished to approach Adam and Eve indirectly through one of these creatures is not entirely clear but he must have felt that his deceitful arguments, if delivered in person, would have been completely unacceptable to these two beings who had both participated in his expulsion from the mansions of the Father. In any event, we know that he either did not dare or did not desire to approach Adam and Eve directly. Instead, he used one of these serpents as his medium or spokesman.

The fact that the scripture speaks of the serpent as being articulate is worthy of brief comment. Josephus, in summarizing the ancient Jewish tradition on this subject states that before the Fall, "all the living creatures had one language."[13] William Whiston of Cambridge University comments on this statement in a footnote

[10]*Ibid.*, 4:6
[11]*Ibid.*
[12]*Ibid.*, 4:6
[13]*Antiquities of the Jews*, Book I, Chapter 1, paragraph 4

saying, "Many inducements there are to a notion that the present state that they (the animals) are in is not their original state; and that their capacities have been once much greater than we now see them, and are capable of being restored to their former conditions."[14]

In line with this thought is the most unusual but apparently possible phenomenon of animals being quickened and being permitted to express themselves intelligibly.[15] It is given further credence from the fact that animals will apparently enjoy some power of articulation after their resurrection as seen by John in an open revelation.[16] He describes them as "praising God." Joseph Smith was told that John saw the actual condition of these animals as they shall exist in the full felicity of their glory following their redemption or resurrection.[17]

Returning to our text, the scripture expressly states that one of the serpents in the Garden of Eden did speak to Eve in her own language and did reason with her after the manner of the deceitful eloquence which had been "put into the heart of the serpent" by Lucifer.[18]

Note the subtle insinuation of the serpent's opening remark, "Yea, hath God said—Ye shall not eat of *every* tree of the garden?" This placed Eve on the defensive. It was as though she were being accused of not enjoying the garden which God had provided for them. It called for a defensive answer—an explanation of why she and Father Adam were not partaking of *every* tree in the garden. She said: "We may eat of the fruit of the trees of the garden, but of the fruit of the tree which thou beholdest in the midst of the garden, God hath said—Ye shall not eat of it, neither shall ye touch it, lest ye die."[19]

Now the serpent came back with a challenging declaration which was pure lethal vitriol from the tainted vial of Satan's dark intellect. With the utmost self-assurance the serpent said: "Ye shall *not* surely die!" Then he

[14]*Ibid.*
[15]Numbers 22:28; 2 Peter 2:16
[16]Revelations 4:6
[17]D. & C. 77:3-4
[18]Moses 4:6
[19]*Ibid.*, 4:8-9

reasoned with Eve along the same line of argument which Lucifer had previously used to convince the serpent: "God doth know that in the day ye eat thereof, then your eyes shall be opened, and ye shall be as gods, knowing good and evil."[20]

As previously indicated, Eve knew that she was on the earth to enter mortality and gain a knowledge of good and evil but she had been waiting for God to bring this about. Now the serpent tells her that this "forbidden fruit" which is in fact called "the tree of knowledge of good and evil" is the very thing which will give her that for which she and Father Adam were placed upon the earth.

Note the insinuation of the serpent when he said the reason why God forbade them to eat the fruit was because it would make them "as gods," implying to Eve that God was selfishly trying to prevent them from obtaining their great blessing.

The next thing that happened, Eve found herself gazing admiringly upon the tree "in the midst of the garden." She deliberately tormented herself with the serpent's tempting challenge. As she gazed upon the fruit of the tree "it became pleasant to her eyes," and when she reflected on the words of the serpent that it would make her wise and that *she would not die*—God to the contrary notwithstanding—she felt herself swept along to the inevitable moment when she would decide to "taste it and see." Reaching forth her hand, she plucked some of the fruit from the tree and pressed it to her lips. Note that the scripture nowhere describes the species of the fruit. It does not say that it was an apple although artists and writers, without authority, have so indicated for centuries.

Adam Is Confronted with a Dilemma

When Eve had partaken of the fruit, and found that it was indeed pleasant, she hastened immediately to her companion and husband.

---

[20]*Ibid.,* 4:11

As she held forth the fruit temptingly to Adam he scarcely could believe his eyes. Here was his wife, given to him by God as a helpmate, tempting him to violate a specific commandment of the Lord.

Adam reasoned with her. She had been deceived. Eve reasoned right back. What if she had—were not the purposes of God being fulfilled by thus unlocking the doorway to mortality and gaining the longed for capacity to learn for themselves a knowledge of the difference between good and evil? Furthermore, what would happen if she fell and Adam did not? If they were separated they never could fulfil the commandment to multiply and replenish the earth.

It was obvious to Adam that this was true, nevertheless, he undoubtedly felt that a great mistake had been made. He, too, knew there was going to be a Fall, but no doubt he continued to feel that the Lord would have brought it about in his own due time and by his own infinite wisdom and power. That Adam carried a certain burden of remorse for Eve's conduct appears evident from statements subsequently made by Eve which we will discuss later.

But mistaken or not, the fact was plainly apparent to Adam that Eve had brought about the Fall and was at that very moment in a state of metamorphosis whereby she would soon be permanently separated from the level of existence which they had been enjoying together.

Confronted by the enigma of these circumstances, Adam resolved to take the step. When all the facts are known to us we may perhaps discover greater elements of heroism in this bold act than any of us can presently appreciate. Eve had partaken of the fruit in a deceived spirit of experimental curiosity but not so with Adam. He pressed the ripened pulp of death-charged fruit to his lips knowing as he did so the cataclysmic consequences which would follow.

These facts led Paul to exclaim, "Adam was not deceived, but the woman being deceived was in the transgression."[21]

---

[21] 1 Timothy 2:14

CHAPTER SEVEN

The Eviction of Adam and Eve from the Garden of Eden

Did God appear to Adam and Eve immediately after they had partaken of the forbidden fruit?

When Adam and Eve heard the voice of the Lord what did they do?

Did Adam take the blame for what had happened? What did he say?

Did Eve take the blame for what had happened? What did she say?

What did the Lord say would happen to Mother Eve?

Was this a "punishment" or was the Lord simply reciting the circumstances which would characterize their new mortal existence?

In your opinion why didn't the Lord take Adam and Eve into His confidence at this particular time and explain to them just what was happening?

The Lord said to Eve: "Thy desire shall be to thy husband and he shall rule over thee." What appears to have been the purpose of the Lord in setting up this procedure?

When this procedure is carried out according to the instructions of the Lord is it an equitable and efficient arrangement?

What did the Lord say would happen to Adam?

What did He mean when He said the ground would be cursed for "thy sake"?

What is meant by the "Gospel of Work"?

Did Adam and Eve have clothing prepared for them before leaving the Garden of Eden? Where did they get it?

Upon leaving the Garden of Eden how far away did they go to make their home? Do we know where it was?

The Lord Returns to the Garden of Eden

God did not seek out Adam and Eve immediately after they partook of the forbidden fruit. He waited until the new physical processes of their bodies had made them suddenly aware of their nakedness and had driven them to devise coverings of fig leaves which they "sewed together" and made into aprons.

It was in the "cool of the day" or probably late afternoon while Adam and Eve were walking among the trees of their garden home that they suddenly heard the voice of God. Notice the natural and unpretentious manner in which the Lord returned. He did not appear unexpectedly before them in a blinding blaze of thunderous indignation. Rather, He deliberately spoke aloud while He was yet hidden from their view so that they would hear Him and be forewarned.

The Lord knew what they would do. Filled with a newly discovered sense of guilty terror, they fled fearfully to the nearest grove of sheltering trees. There the Lord came upon them. Calling Adam by name, the Lord said: "Where goest thou?"

Adam replied with childlike honesty, "I heard thy voice in the garden, and I was afraid." He was conscience-stricken to be caught fleeing from the Lord whom he loved. Without even being asked why he was fleeing, Adam volunteered the information, "I beheld that I was naked and I hid myself."

"Who told thee thou wast naked?" inquired the Lord. God knew the answer fully as well as Adam, but He wanted Adam to confess what he had done. To bring the issue quickly to a head He challenged Adam directly, "Hast thou eaten of the tree whereof I commanded thee that thou shouldst not eat—if so, thou shouldst surely die?"

Adam's reply is clear proof that the Fall had taken full effect. Instead of answering the Lord's question with a simple "yes"—which was what the question called for— Adam proceeded to present an explanatory alibi. His newly acquired instinct of self-preservation drove him to pass the blame for what he had done to somebody else: "The woman thou gavest me, and commandest that she should remain with me, she gave me of the fruit of the tree and I did eat."

Immediately the Lord turned to Eve.

"What is this thing which thou has done?"

Eve had no defense. As the Lord gazed at her, all the persuasive arguments which Lucifer's reptile-medium had given her seemed to crumble away like dikes of sand before the flood. What had previously seemed so logical, desirable and justifiable now loomed up in her mind as a monumental blunder. She had violated a specific commandment of the Lord and she knew it.

A surging, instinctive passion to escape the guilt which she felt, swept over her. Like the many billions of mortal children who would descend from her, Mother Eve felt compelled to avoid responsibility for what she had done.

"The serpent beguiled me," she cried, "and I did eat!"

The Lord wasted no time as he turned upon the serpent. This creature was one of those subtle intellects of the animal kingdom who, with many of his kind, had deliberately fallen under Lucifer's influence. The Lord pronounced judgment upon him immediately.

"Because thou hast done this thou shalt be cursed above all cattle, and above every beast of the field; upon thy belly shalt thou go, and dust shalt thou eat all the days of thy life."[1]

That some change took place in the physical capacities of the serpent as a result of this rebuke seems apparent since otherwise the form of the rebuke would be meaningless. "Upon thy belly shalt thou go" came as a judgment. This would indicate that previously this branch of the animal kingdom had enjoyed some other means of locomotion.

It might also be worthy of mention here that the close allegiance which existed between Satan and the members

---

[1]Moses 4:15-20

of the serpent kingdom during the Garden of Eden era resulted in Lucifer also being designated thereafter as a "serpent."[2]

GOD'S JUDGMENT OF MOTHER EVE

The Lord then addressed Mother Eve with these words: "I will greatly multiply thy sorrow and thy conception. In sorrow thou shalt bring forth children."

Had the Lord desired, He could have taken the first parents into His confidence and said: "You have now projected yourselves into the Second Estate by eating of the fruit of the Tree of Knowledge. The great blessings which I planned for you from the beginning will now be available to you. You will have the powers of procreation. However, the fallen, mortal condition of your bodies makes them subject to pain and suffering and the power of begetting your kind will therefore involve passing through the valley of the shadow of death and bringing forth your children at the cost of sorrow and great travail. This is the only way this blessing can be obtained while your mortal bodies are so constituted."

In the wisdom of the Lord, however, He did not share this intimate confidence with Adam and Eve at this time. Knowing human psychology as He did, He merely recited the consequences of the Fall without entering into any detailed explanation. He wanted Mother Eve to be constantly reminded that the trials of mortal life, particularly the travail of childbirth, were brought about by her own choosing. It is one thing to invite opportunity for progress by voting to enter the Second Estate and quite another thing to count the cost. In moments of suffering the Lord did not want His children to wail against the heavens and say: "Look what the Lord has inflicted upon us!" The Lord wanted Mother Eve to remember that what was coming to her as a result of entering mortality was precipitated by her own volition and her own acts.

Then the Lord continued: "And thy desire shall be to thy husband, and he shall rule over thee."

[2]D. & C. 76:28; 88:110; Revelations 12:9

This was not intended as a punishment as some have claimed that it was. This was a statement of administrative procedure under the patriarchal order of the Priesthood. The fact that one person is placed under another in the Priesthood does not necessarily mean that the person in higher authority is any better or more highly exalted in the eyes of the Lord than the one in a lower position of authority. It is done for one purpose and one purpose only: *to establish order in the kingdom of God.*

Those placed in presiding offices may well be considered as simply "first among equals." As long as this attitude prevails among Priesthood holders a wholesome spirit prevails, but just as soon as a man looks upon his office in the Priesthood as a token of his superiority over his fellow men then priest*craft* replaces Priesthood.[3]

The same principle applies with relation to husband and wife. The husband is simply "first among equals." For the sake of order in the family, in the community and in the kingdom of God, the husband is considered the head. But he is head only for administrative purposes. He is simply first among two personalities both of whom are equal in the eyes of their Heavenly Father. The equality of the sexes as viewed by the Lord was cogently stated by Paul: "Nevertheless neither is the man without the woman, neither the woman without the man, in the Lord."[4] In other words, a husband and wife are joined in an eternal co-partnership and neither can progress to the highest degree of the celestial kingdom separately and alone.[5]

So long as a husband looks upon his wife as a symbol of equality he can exercise his office in the family as a righteous administrator. Just the second he undertakes to exercise any unrighteous dominion the Spirit of the Lord will leave him.[6]

Whenever the light of the gospel has prevailed among any people they have held womanhood in high esteem. Only during ages of apostasy, darkness and un-

---

[3] D. & C. 84:109-110
[4] 1 Cor. 11:11
[5] D. & C. 131:1-4
[6] *Ibid.,* 121:36-37

civilized degeneracy have women been made chattels and slaves by those whom God intended to be their companions and protectors.

Originally, it was intended in the divine economy of the Lord to set up an order wherein the mission of life for both men and women would be equal. Through motherhood women acquire a superior position of influence over each rising generation. This could completely eclipse the influence of their husbands. Having given so great a mission to the mothers of the race, our Heavenly Father placed them under the presidency of their husbands to preserve a proper balance of power, influence and division of labor. For this reason there is no power of presidency or Priesthood given to women. The blessings of Priesthood which they enjoy must come to them through their husbands. In this way a balance is maintained. There was great significance behind the solemn declaration to Mother Eve: "Thy desire shall be to thy husband and he shall rule over thee." It was not to make Mother Eve inferior to her husband—it was simply designed to keep them equal! Family unity is promoted in that home where the wife encourages and sustains her husband in taking the lead. That is his calling. It is his duty and responsibility to serve as an alert and righteous governor in the home.

God's Judgment of Adam

Finally the Lord turned to Adam. "Cursed shall be the ground for thy sake," He proclaimed; "in sorrow shalt thou eat of it all the days of thy life."

This appears to have imposed a great affliction upon the race. Note, however, that the Lord told Adam that the ground was being cursed for *"thy sake."* Many trials and difficulties are really blessings in disguise and they are imposed upon us by a wise and prudent Heavenly Parent for the specific purpose of helping us to learn as much as we can during our probationary estate. Who can doubt that the exigency of garnering a frugal harvest from the rebellious and reluctant elements of this temporal earth has not built character, patience and appreciation into the moral and spiritual fiber of Adam's toiling descendants?

Note also that Adam was not only subject to the necessity of conquering the stubborn and unyielding sod but also the competitive enemies of the crops he would raise: "Thorns also, and thistles shall it (the ground) bring forth to thee."

Then the Lord announced something which was probably new to our first parents: "Thou shalt eat the herb of the field."

In the Garden of Eden, Adam and Eve had apparently found a degree of satisfaction in eating the fruit of the tree and vine. Now the eating of food took on a new and significant importance as Adam and Eve came to rely upon it for the continuous restoration of their physical strength. For this purpose the Lord commanded that in addition to fruit they should "eat the herb of the field." To sustain life Adam and Eve were now going to need grains and vegetables. Later on they would also be allowed to eat meat moderately.

"By the sweat of thy face shalt thou eat bread." Thus God proclaimed the "Gospel of Work." He hallowed the sanctity of physical labor. Next to learning obedience, the greatest lesson of life accruing to Adam and Eve during mortality would be this eternal diadem of truth that no thing of worth can be gained but by labor.

In later years when Adam toiled beneath a scorching sun with blistered hands and weary body—when the swirling dust rolled up to choke off his breath and cake his perspiring countenance—in that day Adam would learn the literal significance of God's words when he said: "By the sweat of thy face shalt thou eat bread!"

In this brief conversation the Lord also condemned Adam for listening to the counsels of his wife when he knew that her counsels were directly opposed to the commandments of God. No woman has a right to ask her husband to break a commandment of God. No husband has a right to require evil of his wife. The Lord intended that a man and woman united in marriage should counsel together but He never intended that either of them should follow the other into paths of unrighteousness and disobedience. The Lord therefore took advantage of this occasion to emphasize this principle.

THE EVICTION OF ADAM AND EVE FROM THE GARDEN OF EDEN

Now the Lord prepared to send Adam and Eve away from their garden of paradise. In a short time they would leave the beautiful array of flowers, foliage and fruit which covered the trees of their garden home. They were commanded to depart from its comforting security and take up their residence in the dreary, cold and hostile world that lay just outside the borders of Eden.

Before doing so, however, the Lord desired to prepare them somewhat for the rigors of their new life. He brought them clothing made from the skins of animals.[7] It is doubtful that either of them had seen the phenomenon of death up to this time. They probably took the new clothing more or less for granted, never realizing that the comfort of this raiment had cost the lives of two or more creatures over which Adam and Eve had formerly exercised friendly dominion. Immediately after their exile from Eden they must have paused in horrified astonishment as they saw the members of the animal kingdom mercilessly destroying each other in the great battle for survival which the Fall had launched upon the earth.

Even after their exile Adam and Eve did not go far from the Garden of Eden. In fact, they made their home in the vicinity of Adam-ondi-Ahman which is only forty miles from the site of the Garden of Eden. As previously indicated, Brigham Young declared: "Joseph, the Prophet, told me that the Garden of Eden was in Jackson County, Missouri. When Adam was driven out he went to the place we now call Adam-ondi-Ahman, Daviess County, Missouri."[8]

[7]Moses 4:27
[8]Cowley, M. F., *Wilford Woodruff*, p. 481

There Adam and Eve began the task of working out their temporal salvation. The level plains near Adam-ondi-Ahman were named "Olaha Shinehah." Shinehah means "sun"[9] and Olaha is possibly a variant of the word "Olea" or "moon."[10] If this is correct, then the name "Olaha Shinehah" would be the plains of the Moon and the Sun—the place where Adam is specifically described in the scriptures as having made his habitation.[11]

It became the cradle of civilization, the geographical wellspring from which poured the hundreds of millions of human beings who later spread across the face of the earth.

[9]Abraham 3:13
[10]*Ibid.*
[11]D. & C. 117:8

CHAPTER EIGHT

Significance of the Tree of Life

What does the scripture say would have happened if Adam and Eve had partaken of the Tree of Life?

What is the key to the resurrection process which the Lord has revealed in modern times (D. & C. 88:28)?

How does this help us to appreciate why it would have been disastrous for Adam and Eve to have partaken of the Tree of Life?

What contribution did Alma make in adding to our understanding of the problem?

What is the difference between "immortality" and "eternal life"?

From the scripture it would appear that one is much easier to achieve than the other. Which is it?

The restoration of the gospel brought a much more comprehensive understanding of "eternal life." What were some of the concepts which added materially to modern Christian knowledge?

What is the purpose of life in the spirit world?

What does the scripture say about the "spirits of just men made perfect"?

Why can a few of the children of men be changed from mortality to immortality "in the twinkling of an eye"?

Can any human being attain resurrection status without passing through the change called death?

WHAT IS THE SIGNIFICANCE OF THE TREE OF LIFE

So frequently in the scriptures great eternal concepts are hidden behind casual and sometimes insignificant passages. Pre-existence, the three degrees of glory, the literal fatherhood of God and work for the dead are but a few examples of cosmic and eternal truths which are barely referred to in the Old or New Testaments. They were so completely taken for granted by the prophets and apostles of ancient times that they only referred to them summarily without feeling the necessity for any exposition or explanation.

In the story of the Fall there is one of these obscure passages which is usually glossed over by the casual reader. It contains, however, a dynamic and thought-provoking statement: "And the Lord God said: Behold the man is become as one of us, to know good and evil; and now, lest he put forth his hand and take also of the tree of life and eat and *live for ever* . . . He (God) placed at the east of the Garden of Eden Cherubims and a flaming sword which turned every way to keep the way of the tree of life."[1]

There is a great lesson to be learned from the story of the Tree of Life so briefly referred to in the above scripture.

It is designed to teach us that God had it within his power to make us immortal beings without requiring us to pass through the misery and physical travail called death. It means that just as Adam and Eve partook of the forbidden fruit and thereby caused a metamorphosis in their bodies by violating certain natural laws and injecting into their systems the seeds of death, so also they could have turned about—had God permitted it—and immunized themselves against these destructive elements by partaking of the Tree of Life. The above scripture specifically states that had they eaten of this fruit they would have *lived forever!* in their sens,

That this was a literal, scientific possibility is borne out by several scriptural authorities. Alma, for example, declared:

[1] Genesis 3:22-24; Moses 4:28-31

"And now behold I say unto you that if it had been possible for Adam to have partaken of the fruit of the tree of life at that time there would have been no death." (Alma 12:23)

"For behold, if Adam had put forth his hand immediately and partaken of the tree of life he would have lived forever." (*Ibid.,* 42:5)

And if the Lord could do this for Adam and Eve, He could have done it for all their children. In other words, human beings *could* be made to live forever without passing through death.

WHY MUST MEN DIE?

The question which immediately arises is, "Why did the Lord want Adam and Eve to die?" If He had it within His power to make them live forever without passing through death, why did He prevent it? Why did He want them to die?

There appears to be a very specific reason why it was necessary to have humanity pass through the portals of death so that their spirits could be separated temporarily from their bodies.

First of all, the Lord tells us that man cannot be exalted "in the flesh." "Neither can any natural man abide the presence of God," explained the Lord.[2] There is something inherently mundane about the mortal clay which prevents it from being elevated to a celestial glory *in and of itself*. It can only be elevated by combining it with glorified spirit matter. In other words, a temporal body can only be exalted by becoming "inseparably connected"[3] with spirit matter *after* the spirit matter has been glorified or celestialized. This is the secret to the mechanics of the resurrection as the Lord clearly described it in a modern revelation.

Speaking of the process wherein the temporal body is fused with the spirit body at the time of the resurrection, the Lord said: "They who are of a *celestial*

[2]D. & C. 67:12; Moses 1:5
[3]*Ibid.,* 93:33

spirit shall receive the same body which was a natural body . . . and *your* glory (which obviously would have to be the glory of one's spirit) shall be the *glory by which* your bodies are quickened."[4]

In other words, the Lord has to have the opportunity of redeeming and glorifying the spirit first—then the glorified spirit is used as the quickening medium to refine the physical body.

From this it becomes obvious why it would have been disastrous for Adam and Eve to have partaken of the fruit of the Tree of Life so that they *could not die!* Their spirits would have been imprisoned within their temporal bodies forever—incapable of redemption, incapable of exaltation. The entire plan of salvation would have been annihilated by this single act.

This enlightening contribution to our understanding of a most difficult scriptural problem is one of the valuable gems in the Book of Mormon. The prophet Alma enjoyed particularly keen insight into the problem. Said he:

"If Adam had put forth his hand immediately, and partaken of the tree of life, he would have lived forever . . . and also the word of God would have been void, and the great plan of salvation would have been frustrated."[5]

Then he tells why it would have been frustrated. Because "the soul could never die"[6]—which means the spirit could never be separated from the body.

Alma points out that "living forever" or conquering temporal death was not important at this time: "Now behold, it was not expedient that man should be redeemed from this temporal death, for that would destroy the great plan of happiness."[7] It was first "expedient that mankind should be reclaimed from this spiritual death,"[8] which means to return to the presence of God. And since the physical body cannot endure the presence of God in its mundane state it was necessary to permit

---

[4] *Ibid.*, 88:28
[5] Alma 42:5
[6] *Ibid.*, 42:9
[7] *Ibid.*, 42:8
[8] *Ibid.*, 42:9

the spirit to be released from the body. When the spirit
had been "reclaimed from the spiritual death" and, as
the Lord says made into a "celestial spirit,"[9] then it could
be used as the refining medium to exalt the elements of the
temporal body.

The Problem of Gaining Eternal Life

It must be realized that our Heavenly Father is not
only anxious to have us conquer death but also gain eternal life.[10] The existence of the Tree of Life in the Garden
of Eden was designed to teach us that conquering the
seeds of death which presently prey upon our temporal
bodies is a relatively simple thing. For the reasons just
stated, however, it was most important that the conquest
of physical death be postponed. Bringing us back into the
presence of God was the real problem. And partaking of
the Tree of Life would not have brought Adam and Eve
back into the presence of God. As Alma states:

"And now behold, if it were possible that our first
parents could have gone forth and partaken of the tree
of life they would have been *forever* miserable."[11]

It would *not* have returned them to their state of
paradisiacal innocence. It would have made them immortal *in their fallen state*! It would have left them in
their "misery"—their sorrow, ignorance and spiritual
darkness. It would have left them with their capacity to
distinguish between good and evil but without the power
to conquer evil. It might have even left them with their
power to beget children, but they would have been left
without the means of redeeming themselves or their
children.

It would have truly been a great disaster and a frustration to the entire plan of salvation. That was why Adam
and Eve were ejected from the Garden of Eden and
threatened with immediate destruction if they attempted
to partake of this fruit from the Tree of Life.

[9]D. & C. 88:28
[10]Moses 1:39
[11]Alma 12:26

Immortality and "Eternal Life" Mean Different Things

Perhaps this is an appropriate place to analyze the distinction between immortality and "eternal life." Immortality means to live forever but *"this* is life eternal, that they might know thee the only true God, and Jesus Christ whom thou has sent."[12] The only way to know our Heavenly Father is to return to His presence and there learn to become like Him. This is the only way a child ever learns really to know his father. Acquiring eternal life means to return to the presence of God in the celestial kingdom. And those who are particularly faithful receive "eternal lives."[13] This means to become exalted just as our Heavenly Father is and enjoy a fulness of celestial glory, "which glory shall be a fulness and a continuation of the seeds forever. . . . Then shall *they be gods,* because they have no end; therefore shall they be from everlasting to everlasting, because they continue; then shall they be above all, because all things are subject to them. . . . Verily, verily, I say unto you, except ye abide my law ye cannot attain to this glory. For strait is the gate, and narrow is the way that leadeth unto the exaltation and continuation of the lives and few there be that find it."[14]

This is what God is seeking to achieve for as many of His children as possible. He wants them to return to Him, to become like Him, to become kings, priests and joint sovereigns with Him in the cosmic universe over which He rules.[15] And for those who fall short of this great goal He has other, lesser kingdoms where they can enjoy all of those things to which they are entitled but where they will contribute a lesser part as servants of the Father.

Therefore, "eternal life" means to gain the celestial kingdom, and "eternal lives" means to gain the highest degree of glory in that kingdom.[16] All of this would have

[12]John 17:3
[13]D. & C. 132:24
[14]*Ibid.,* 132:19-22
[15]*Ibid.,* 88:107; 76:58-59
[16]*Ibid.,* 131:1-4

been impossible if Adam and Eve had suspended the seeds of death by partaking of the Tree of Life and thereby shackled their spirits within their bodies forever. Alma says they would have sacrificed their opportunity to go through the "preparation" which was carefully set up to take them back to the Father.[17]

THE PREPARATION OF THE SPIRIT FOR THE RESURRECTION

When the spirit leaves the body and passes into the spirit world it is entering a kingdom specifically organized to prepare each spirit for the resurrection. Alma had a revelation concerning it and said: "Now there must needs be a space betwixt the time of death and the time of the resurrection."[18] This "space" of time is used for the cleansing, redemption and education of the spirit. The spirit is prepared for as high a degree of glory as it is capable of receiving. How the individual conducted himself during mortality determines, to a very large extent, what that degree of glory shall be.

Only those who lived as righteously as they knew how and made the atonement effective in blotting out their former transgressions are redeemed as "celestial spirits." They are then prepared to be resurrected as soon as the Lord authorizes them to do so.

We know that some of these "celestial spirits" are not immeditaely resurrected but serve a temporary mission in the mansions of the Father. As Joseph Smith stated, these are "the spirits of just men made perfect, they who are not resurrected (for the time being) but *inherit the same glory.*"[19]

CONCERNING THOSE WHO ARE CHANGED IN THE TWINKLING OF AN EYE

As we have already noted, Alma was told that "there must needs be a space betwixt the time of death and the resurrection," but in the case of certain individuals who

---

[17] Alma 42:10
[18] *Ibid.,* 40:6
[19] D. & C. 129:1-3

have lived unusually righteous lives the space is of such short duration that it is described as "the twinkling of an eye." This almost instantaneous transition from mortality to immortality is to be a common procedure during the millennium.[20] The righteous will not require an extensive period of preparation for the resurrection. In fact, speaking of the righteous of that day, the Lord says: "when he dies he shall not sleep, that is to say in the earth, but shall be changed in the twinkling of an eye, and shall be caught up, and his rest shall be glorious."[21]

CONCLUSION

We have taken time to consider the problem of "death and the resurrection" in considerable detail at this point in our narrative so that the significance of the Tree of Life in the Garden of Eden might be better appreciated.

A study of the scriptures, a study of science and a careful scrutiny of the experiences of life teach us the plain and simple truth that in God's great plan everything is accomplished in the most direct and economical manner possible. No procedure or design is superfluous or whimsical. When we observe the Creator following a rather complex or circuitous pattern of procedure we may be certain that a program of a more simple design would have somehow defeated God's ultimate purposes. This principle applies to the problem of death. The temporary separation of the spirit from the body at the time of death was an inescapable necessity in the plan for human redemption. If the Father could have achieved our exaltation without death and without the "space betwixt death and the resurrection" for preparatory purposes, He would have done so. Wherever possible He has cut down the "space" of preparation, and in some instances he has been able to reduce its duration to "the twinkling of an eye."

But all mankind must pass that way in order to gain bodies which are not only immortal but are also exalted to some degree of glory. And not only must man follow

[20]*Ibid.,* 63:51
[21]*Ibid.,* 101:31

this procedure, but the animals as well, and the plants. Even the earth must die before it can be resurrected and exalted![22]

We see, therefore, that death is not a curse. It is a blessing. Knowing this we can better appreciate the wisdom of the Lord in preventing Adam and Eve from following the procedure which would have immunized them against death. Closing the narrative at this point, the Lord says:

"So I drove out the man, and I placed at the east of the Garden of Eden, cherubim and a flaming sword, which turned every way to keep the way of the tree of life." (Moses 4:31)

[22]*Ibid.,* 88:26

CHAPTER NINE

Human History Begins at Adam-Ondi-Ahman

Do you visualize Adam and Eve undergoing any hardships as the world's first pioneers?

Do you see a hint of struggle in the statement that Adam "began to till the earth and to have dominion over all the beasts of the field, and to eat his bread by the sweat of his brow"?

What is the significance of the statement that Eve "did labor with him"?

Is it possible that Adam and Eve may have received some instructions concerning earth life before they left the Garden of Eden?

After their eviction from the Garden of Eden how long does the scripture indicate that Adam and Eve had to wait before they received a divine communication?

Do you think this long period of spiritual excommunication and the early struggle of Father Adam to perform his life's labor will make him more understanding when he sits as "the Ancient of days" to judge the race?

Do we know the name of the first child born to Adam and Eve?

Did all of their early children grow to maturity without serious accident or mishap?

Why are close relatives prohibited from intermarrying today?

At the very beginning did Adam and Eve have any knowledge of the plan of salvation to teach to their children?

What was the first revelation received by Adam and Eve
in their "fallen" condition? What were they commanded to do?

How do you think the children of Adam and Eve reacted
to this revelation? At that time was there any rational
or logical explanation for the Lord's commandment?

Is there any indication that any of Adam's sons participated with him at this time in offering sacrifices?

The Beginning of a Great Human Adventure

Exploratory expeditions are always a source of great
personal satisfaction to the bold and curious spirit who
seeks to invade the unknown and satisfy the human thirst
for new knowledge and exciting experience. However,
when a venture into the unknown is forced upon a person
in the form of exile—with nothing in prospect but hardship, frustration and imprisonment—then the thrill of
adventure is smothered by the ominous presence of
threatening dangers which lurk at every turn. Nevertheless, even this fearful, unwanted type of adventure sometimes produces historic sagas of human victory over adversity. Such was the case with Adam and Eve.

When these two noble personages migrated from
the boundaries of Eden in keeping with the Lord's command they projected themselves into a strange, belligerent habitation where life and even the very elements
seemed arrayed against all else in a fury of perpetual,
offensive destruction. Adam and Eve found themselves
engulfed in a world of rebellious, defiant forces where the
heavens were split by barbs of forked lightning and dark,
forbidding skies roared with a thousand thunders; where
the forests hid a host of dangers and the night resounded
with the shrill cry of hunted beasts. Adam and Eve
passed from the sublime and peaceful Eden into an environment of chaos and competitive confusion.

Surely it was a terrifying adventure and a most
dramatic episode in this real-life drama of Paradise Lost.

As previously indicated, the place of residence chosen
by Adam and Eve was not far from Eden and was called

Adam-ondi-Ahman. Surrounding this first human settlement were the plains of Olaha Shinehah which were incorporated into the residential estate of Adam and Eve.[1]

On this estate Adam "began to till the earth and to
have dominion over all the beasts of the field, and to eat
his bread by the sweat of his brow."[2] Then the scripture
adds a poignant and significant postscript: "and Eve, his
wife, did labor with him."

In their struggle for existence this valiant man and
woman labored shoulder to shoulder to survive. Like all
the great pioneer women of every age, Eve did not con-
fine herself to "wifely duties" but labored *with* her
husband.

THE COLD AND DREARY WORLD

The early years at Adam-ondi-Ahman witnessed
scenes of drama not surpassed perhaps in any other period of history. Life, of necessity, was simple and frugal
—reduced temporarily to its lowest denominator. For
clothes they wore at first the skins of slain animals. The
Lord Himself taught Adam and Eve how to fashion
them.[3] For food they had only what they could produce
from the backward and reluctant ground. For a home
they had only what they could fashion with their bare
hands—using wood and stone in their crudest form.
Nothing came to them save through difficult and stren-
uous exertion. They were the first pioneers of the race.

Nevertheless, this was not the so-called age of "cave-
men" nor was it the so-called "stone-age." Adam was
no beetle-browed, primitive *Homo Sapiens*. Adam and
Eve came forth from the Garden of Eden and out
from the presence of God in the full bloom of physical
and intellectual maturity. Few, if any, save Jesus Christ
alone, of all the billions of human beings who have
descended from these first parents, excelled them either
in nobility of person or superiority of mind. Adam was
Michael, the leader and archangel of the First Estate,

[1] D. & C. 117:8
[2] *Ibid.*, 4:27
[3] Moses 5:1

"the father of all, the prince of all, the ancient of days."[4]
Eve was his worthy companion—a help *meet* for him.
The fact, therefore, that Adam and Eve began this early
pioneering stage of their earthly probation under primitive circumstances should not detract in the least from
the dignity of their true character.

Within Adam's own lifetime the ingenuity of himself
and his children was such that they were able to "build
a city,"[5] produce musical instruments such as "the harp
and the organ,"[6] mine and work the basic metals to make
brass and iron tools and artifacts,[7] speak the same "pure
and undefiled" language which they had used in the
Garden of Eden,[8] teach their children how to read and
also instruct them in the art of writing and the method
of recording histories and genealogies in a "book of
remembrance."[9]

It should also be kept in mind that perhaps much of
the remarkable knowledge evidenced by Adam and Eve
and their children may have come to them directly from
the Lord prior to their exile. Just as He taught them how
to fashion their clothes, He may have taught them how
to sow and cultivate seed, how to construct buildings,
mine and refine metals, build cities, write in the Adamic
tongue, produce instruments for the making of music and
even how to serve as their own physicians.

On all of these matters the scripture is silent, but it will
be recalled that in subsequent years the Lord concerned
Himself with just such details as the construction of the
buildings,[10] the layout of cities,[11] the seed time and harvest,[12] the recording of history,[13] the teaching of children,[14]
and the rules of good health.[15]

---

[4]D. & C. 27:11
[5]Moses 7:19
[6]*Ibid.*, 5:45
[7]*Ibid.*, 5:46
[8]*Ibid.*, 6:6
[9]*Ibid.*, 6:5
[10]Exodus Chapters 25-28; Ezekiel Chapters 40-43
[11]Ezekiel Ch. 48; D. & C. 94:1-3
[12]Exodus 23:10-11; Leviticus 25:3-4
[13]3 Nephi 23:11-13; D. & C. 47:1
[14]D. & C. 55:4; 68:25-28; 93:40
[15]Leviticus Ch. 11, 12, 13, 17

It would seem improbable that God would have launched the patriarchal ancestors of the race into the highly competitive conflicts of mortal life without some understanding of these basic truths upon which both they and their children were dependent for existence. The unusual rapidity with which the children of Adam soon surrounded themselves with a high degree of security, culture and comfort would indicate the probability that Adam received much of his first knowledge from the Lord at the same time he was instructed in the manner of making clothing.

Two Generations of Spiritual Excommunication

We know that Adam received the grand key-words of the Priesthood before leaving the Garden of Eden, and no doubt some of the Priesthood ordinances were described to him. (See Pearl of Great Price, p. 35, explanation to cut 3.)

But regardless of the knowledge and understanding which may have been given to Adam and Eve in the very beginning—just prior to their exile—the scripture is very plain that once they had established themselves beyond the pale of Eden they were completely cut off from the presence of the Lord.

It is also surprising to discover how long the Lord waited before He condescended to speak to them again. Ordinarily the student visualizes the Lord as responding to their every beck and call during this early period. Available scripture indicates, however, that such was not the case. In fact, it would appear from the opening verses of the fifth chapter of Moses that Adam and Eve were without revelation or direct divine guidance for a period which, in the normal course of events, must have been from fifty to sixty years. This scripture indicates that *they were grandparents* before the voice of the Lord was heard again.[16]

This would mean that they were left groping alone during two generations of spiritual excommunication.

---

[16]Moses 5:2-4

It was during this period of time that their first children were born to them. In the beginning no doubt the miraculous fruition of the propagative powers promised to them by the Lord must have provoked in them the utmost astonishment and concern. With feelings of uneasy anxiety they must have waited the arrival of their first child. It must have been a moment of both tragedy and triumph when Adam's helpmeet and companion finally fulfilled her days and slipped away into the valley of the shadow of death and underwent the predicted travail which made it possible for her to finally come forth bearing in her arms the first tiny infant of the human race!

Whether it was a boy or girl we do not know. Nor do we know its name. All that the scripture records is the fact that this first little personality was followed in later years by numerous brothers and sisters,[17] and that all of them grew to maturity without serious accident or mishap.[18]

Eventually, when the older ones had reached maturity, they gradually divided off into couples according to their mutual inclinations. No doubt they were encouraged in this by Adam and Eve who knew the sanctity of marriage and fully appreciated the Lord's plan for the uniting of husband and wife in covenants of matrimony for it had been taught to them in the Garden of Eden.[19]

Then the scripture continues: "And from that time forth, the sons and daughters of Adam began to divide two and two in the land, and to till the land, and to tend flocks, and they also begat sons and daughters."[20]

Today brothers and sisters or other close relatives are prohibited from marrying because the congenital weaknesses which have crept into many family strains may be compounded through such a union and their children would then come into the world handicapped both physically and mentally. In the beginning, however, when the race was new and uncontaminated, the mar-

[17]*Ibid.*
[18]D. & C. 29:42
[19]Moses 3:24
[20]*Ibid.,* 5:3

riage of relatives within the limits of consanguinity had no such ill effects.

Since the first two generations of descendants from Adam and Eve were raised during this period of spiritual exile, their rearing would have been made doubly difficult. At this time Adam and Eve could remember nothing further back than their life in the Garden of Eden. As subsequent events will show, they had completely forgotten their pre-existence or First Estate; they had forgotten the plan of salvation and had no way of knowing whether or not the Lord had any intention of rescuing them from the decadent environment into which they had fallen. All they knew for certain was the fact that eventually they would die and that while they lived they would have to exert every faculty to protect themselves from hostile elements and provide their bodies with physical sustenance.

From the later joyful expression of Mother Eve,[21] it would appear that during this dark period they bitterly condemned themselves for their error in partaking of the forbidden fruit and apparently entertained not even a suspicion that the Fall—though filled with a multitude of tribulations and dangers—was in reality a great blessing and an event deliberately and carefully consummated as part of God's plan for the exaltation of the human race.

Undoubtedly these first two generations of children pressed upon Adam and Eve a multitude of searching questions concerning the purpose of earth life and why they had to undergo so much hardship and live out their lives in sorrow. But to all such queries the first parents would have had no answers, for they themselves were mystified and perplexed by the enigma of life. Perhaps it is significant that none of these children later accepted the gospel when it was first given to Adam. They personify the classical lesson of the ages that children who grow up without faith seldom find it in maturity.

It is for this reason that none of the names of these first children are recorded in the genealogies of the race.

[21]*Ibid.*, 5:11

As we shall see later they lost their heritage through traitorous conduct against their parents. All of them, however, were born before Cain and Abel.

The Voice of the Lord Heard at Last

In the passing years the afflictions which Jehovah had predicted for them had been poured out upon their heads with unabated intensity, and no doubt Adam and Eve were led in their hearts to feel that perhaps they were cut off forever. In spite of this, however, they finally felt such an irresistible impulse to seek divine assistance that it gave them courage to try to communicate with God.

It was no doubt a crucial moment in the lives of these two human beings as they knelt together in fervent prayer to attempt to penetrate the stony silence of the heavens with their humble supplication for help.

As they unburdened their hearts they had no way of knowing that this was the moment heaven had been waiting for. They must have stopped in startled surprise as their prayer was suddenly interrupted. It was the soft but powerfully penetrating "voice of the Lord from the way toward the Garden of Eden."[22] They had been heard!

To have uttered their prayer in the first place was a great moral victory, but to gain the portals of heaven and hear the voice of the Lord responding to their fervent plea —here was a triumph indeed.

Although they peered earnestly in the direction from which the voice was coming they could see no personage but they definitely recognized the voice as being that of the Lord.[23] And they listened intently as the Lord instructed them.

By inference they were commended for approaching the Lord in prayer, for He told them that they should draw near unto the Lord and worship Him.[24] This was more of a comfort to Adam and Eve than the simple statement in the scripture may seem to convey. The fact that God

[22]*Ibid.*, 5:4
[23]*Ibid.*, 5:4
[24]*Ibid.*, 5:5

would command them to worship Him proved that they were not entirely cut off from His good will and beneficence. If He were still willing to receive their devotions and oblations then surely there was hope that someday, somehow, they might again be restored in His confidence.

But God required more at their hands than mere lip worship. He commanded that the first-born of every ewe or she-goat and the first-born of every heifer among the flocks of Adam should be slain and burned on an altar as a token of devotion to God. This was a strange commandment. It was incomprehensible. Why should the young lamb or kid or newborn calf be slain and burned as an offering unto the Lord? Where was the Lord's pleasure in it? What did it accomplish? There was no logical answer to such queries. The Lord gave no explanation, and between themselves, Adam and Eve could devise none.[25] Ordinarily the human mind revolts against that which is beyond understanding, but in this instance the scripture pays tribute to the faithfulness of Adam for it says: "And Adam was obedient unto the commandments of the Lord."[26]

Herein is reflected one of the greatest truths to be discovered during earth life—that the commandments of God should always be obeyed. The history of the human race is replete with examples of great men who paused in perplexed contemplation before strange, incomprehensible commandments of the Lord. And history is just as replete with examples which prove that those who obeyed the commandments of God were always in the right.[27]

Often the wisdom of God is foolishness to men, but the greatest single lesson to be learned in mortality is that when God commands and a man obeys, that man will always be right.

Ibid., 5:6
Ibid., 5:5
"For example, 1 Nephi 4:10-13

CHAPTER TEN

Adam and Eve Get Answers to some of their Questions

While Adam was alone an angel appeared before him. What did the angel ask Adam? What was Adam's reply?

When the Lord appeared before Adam how did He identify Himself?

What was the question which Adam asked the Lord after being commanded to repent and be baptized? What does this show?

The Lord did not answer Adam's question immediately but made a thrilling announcement to Adam. What was it? Was it a surprise?

What did Adam learn about the principle of repentance?

How do you account for the fact that humanity stubbornly refuses to believe God is an "exalted man" even though He has revealed it over and over again? What did He tell Adam?

Was Peter the first one to preach that except for Jesus Christ there is none other name under heaven given among men whereby we must be saved? (Acts 4:12)

What did Adam learn about "the new birth"?

After baptism what must the "Spirit" do before there is a remission of sins through the atonement?

How old is the gospel of Jesus Christ. How old is the Church of Jesus Christ?

Who was the first person in the world to be baptized and endowed with the gift of the Holy Ghost?

Who was the first person to receive the Priesthood?

Do we know whether or not there were temple ordinances
in the days of Adam and Eve?

Adam was given a rich outpouring of the gift of prophecy. Would he have been comforted by the things
which the scripture says he saw?

What are the three things which stand out in Adam's
psalm of praise to God?

ADAM IS VISITED BY A MINISTERING ANGEL

When the voice of the Lord broke through the tomb-
like silence of the spiritual void in which Adam and Eve
had been living for so many years and commanded them
to offer sacrifices, they went forth obediently to perform
this work. However, the scripture does not describe the
reaction of their children to these strange proceedings.
From subsequent events it would appear that they were
probably shocked and disdainful toward their parents'
actions. To them the sacrifices may have appeared
wasteful, cruel and, worst of all, meaningless.

Surely Adam and Eve could not have presented any
persuasive reasons why the Lord should have demanded
blood sacrifices for it was incomprehensible even to them.[1]
But the significant thing is that they obeyed the commandment.

Then the scripture states, "After many days an angel
of the Lord appeared unto Adam."[2] "Many days" is
always used in the scripture to signify the passing of a
considerable period of time,[3] frequently many years. It
is obvious from this assertion that the faithfulness of
Adam and Eve was tested for an extended period of time
by the Lord.

The heavenly messenger inquired of Adam, "Why
doest thou offer sacrifices unto the Lord?" Adam truthfully and humbly replied, "I know not, save the Lord
commanded me."[4]

[1]Moses 5:6
[2]*Ibid.*
[3]Isaiah 24:22; Ezekiel 38:8 Hosea 3:4
[4]Moses 5:6

This was probably the answer the angel expected. He hoped to hear Adam confess his lack of understanding so that he might be more receptive to the instructions which were about to be given him. Adam must have been greatly impressed as he looked upon the personage of this glorious messenger from across the veil. "These sacrifices," said the angel, "are a similitude of the sacrifice of the Only Begotten of the Father."[5] For the first time Adam heard the beginning of the gospel story.

The angel explained that the spilling of the blood of the first-begotten offspring of Adam's domestic flocks was intended as a tangible, heart-stirring reminder that in the Meridian of Time the Heavenly Father would be required to permit the sacrifice of His Only Begotten Son as an atonement for the human race. The Father wanted Adam and all his children after him to memorialize this great event. He wanted Adam to understand that the surge of emotion and aroused sympathy which welled up within his breast each time he took up the knife to slaughter the first and choicest of his flocks was simply a teaching device. It was initiated by a wise and prudent Heavenly Parent to impress upon His weak, mortal children the reality of the greatest sacrifice of all which would be consummated some four thousand years hence when the anguish, cruelty and sweat of blood at Gethsemane and Golgotha would mark the crowning climax to the life and mission of Jesus Christ.

But Adam must have wondered why such a supreme atoning sacrifice by the very Son of God was necessary. Who demanded that the life of the Son of God be sacrificed? What would it accomplish?* For the moment Adam had no answer. He had only the assurance of the angel that it was to be a most important event in the history and salvation of the human race.

Then the angel continued: "Wherefore, thou shalt do all that thou doest in the name of the Son, and thou shalt repent and call upon God in the name of the Son forevermore."[6]

---

[5]*Ibid.*, 5:7
*See Appendix: "Why Was the Atonement Necessary?"
[6]Moses 5:8

Here were two strange commandments! What did it mean to repent? And why must the Father be approached indirectly hereafter through the name of the Only Begotten Son?

But apparently Adam never had the opportunity of propounding these questions to the angel because the glorifying influence of the Holy Ghost suddenly overshadowed him, and an instant later he heard the voice of God speaking directly to him.

This thrilling conversation between Adam and his Creator is summarized by Moses in a single verse of scripture.[7] However, in a later part of the book of Moses we have a quotation from Enoch where this conversation between Adam and the Lord is given in remarkable detail.[8]

ADAM IS INSTRUCTED BY THE LORD

At the very beginning of this significant interview this glorious Personage identified Himself to Adam by saying: "I am God; I made the world, and *men before they were in the flesh*."[9] From this and subsequent passages it is obvious that Adam no longer remembered anything about his pre-existence and had to have the Lord explain anew this thrilling epic of mankind "before they were in the flesh," because Adam and Eve had forgotten it as a result of the Fall.

The Lord then elaborated upon the commandments announced by the angel just a few moments before: "If thou wilt turn unto me, and hearken unto my voice, and believe, and repent of all thy transgressions, and be baptized, even in water, in the name of mine Only Begotten Son . . . ye shall receive the gift of the Holy Ghost."[10]

All this meant nothing to Adam. He could not comprehend these new concepts. He grew bold, therefore, and inquired directly of the Lord: "Why is it that man must repent and be baptized in water?"

[7] *Ibid.*, 5:9
[8] *Ibid.*, 6:51-68
[9] *Ibid.*, 6:51
[10] *Ibid.*, 6:52

The answer which the Lord gave him must have come as a tremendous surprise. Instead of explaining the reasons for the first ordinances and principles of the gospel, the Lord held up to Adam the shining diadem of hope which the ordinances were designed to achieve. Said the Lord: "Behold, I have *forgiven thee thy transgressions in the Garden of Eden!*"

What an impact this must have had on the mind of Adam. It was almost too much to believe. How was it possible—after all the vicissitudes and tribulations they had endured—that God could finally forgive them for their disobedience in the Garden of Eden? In reply, the Lord began to unfold the "good news" or the gospel of salvation for the redemption and exaltation of the human race.

The first thing the Lord wanted Adam to understand was the fact that the Fall was *intentional*. It was designed as a blessing, not a curse. The Lord pointed out that in their fallen condition Adam and Eve now had the power to beget children and that these children would learn the difference between good and evil as a result of their experiences in mortality. "They taste the bitter," said the Lord, "that they may know to prize the good. And it is given unto them to know good from evil; wherefore they are agents unto themselves."[11]

In other words, when Adam and Eve precipitated the Fall by partaking of the forbidden fruit they had actually fulfilled the intended purposes of their Heavenly Father.

Here Adam and Eve had been living in sorrow—bitterly condemning themselves for their irreparable mistake—when, as a matter of fact, they had done the very thing which was necessary to provide for the advancement and exaltation of themselves and their children! Adam must have been stunned by the overwhelming implications of this thrilling revelation. As the literal reality of the Lord's words gradually received rational acceptance in his mind Adam must have felt the guilt complex, which he had been carrying about his neck like a lodestone, vanish away. For the first time in this

---

[11]Moses 6:55-56

mortal life, Adam saw himself in the reflected vision of his own true light. He was not an outcast. He was not a disobedient renegade cut off forever from the presence of God. He was a valiant and faithful son of God who would eventually return to the mansions of his Heavenly Father.

ADAM LEARNS THE MEANING OF REPENTANCE

Now the Lord was ready to answer Adam's question concerning repentance. What did it mean? Why was it necessary? The Lord's explanation was in the form of an instruction. He told Adam to teach his children that only those who tried to improve their lives and obey God's commandments could ever hope to inherit the kingdom of God. Salvation is not automatic. It is only available to those who strive throughout their lives to overcome evil and cleanse themselves of imperfection. None of us can achieve the highest level of absolute perfection in this life, but we must go as far as we can so that little preparation remains to be done in the spirit world. This self-improvement is called "repentance" and the Lord intimated that it must be a continuing process until eventually we do become perfect even as our Father in heaven is perfect. Otherwise we cannot return to the celestial kingdom of the Father "for no unclean thing can dwell there, or dwell in his presence."[12]

Then the Lord revealed something concerning God, the Father, which men ever since have found most difficult to believe or comprehend.

He revealed God's true name to Adam. In the pure language of Adam this name meant "Man of Holiness." Here was a revelation indeed! Behind this statement was one of the most searching, noble and inspirational concepts ever vouchsafed to humanity:

> As man is, God once was,
> As God is, man may become.

---

[12]*Ibid.,* 6:57

In other words, God Himself once followed the pattern of progress which we ourselves are now pursuing. He is a Man of Holiness—an exalted personality who once passed through a probationary estate just as we are now doing. Everything we experience, whether it be joy, sorrow, disappointment or success, is fully appreciated by our Heavenly Father for He, Himself, passed through similar scenes of testing and self-improvement. No wonder Jesus would later say: "The Son can do nothing of himself but what he seeth the Father do,"[13] and commenting on this, Joseph Smith states that if "the Son doeth what He hath seen the Father do then the Father hath some day laid down His life and taken it again."[14]

There are some who find this magnificent concept difficult to accept because they feel that it brings God down to the level of man; but, as a matter of fact, the very opposite is true. It verifies what God has taught His children from the beginning—that man is the offspring of God, made in His own image, and is potentially capable of rising to the same celestial heights of omnipotence and glory which our Heavenly Father has successfully attained before us. The Lord Himself has said of those who become His heirs: "They are they into whose hands the Father has given all things—They are they who are priests and kings, who have received of his fulness, and of his glory . . . wherefore, as it is written, *they are Gods,* even the sons of God—Wherefore, all things are theirs, whether life or death, or things present, or things to come, all are theirs and they are Christ's, and Christ is God's."[15]

From this it is clear that not only is God an exalted "Man of Holiness" but He aspires to have His children become just like Him. It is the goal for all those who follow the straight course which ascends up onto the highroad of eternal progression. Nothing could be plainer in the above scripture than the fact that "as God is man

---

[13]John 5:19
[14]*Teachings of Joseph Smith,* p. 312
[15]D. & C. 76:55-59

may become" by obedience to the principles and ordinances of the gospel.

Adam was also taught a great deal on this occasion concerning the mission of Jesus Christ. After explaining that the Father's true name meant "Man of Holiness," the Lord added, "and the name of his Only Begotten is the Son of *Man,* even Jesus Christ, a righteous Judge, who shall come in the meridian of time."[16] This scripture states that Adam was definitely given to understand that the reason he and Mother Eve could be forgiven their transgression in the Garden of Eden was because of the atoning sacrifice of Jesus Christ which would become efficacious in their behalf as soon as they had repented and made covenants with the Lord through baptism. Adam was told that Jesus Christ is the "only name which shall be given under heaven, whereby salvation shall come unto the children of men."[17]

At this early stage of his training Adam probably did not understand just how the atonement of Jesus Christ could make their repentance efficacious or bring salvation to the children of men, but at least he was comforted by the positive assurance from the Lord that it would do so.

ADAM LEARNS THE SIGNIFICANCE OF THE "NEW BIRTH"

The Lord also went on to explain to Adam that the sacrifice of Jesus Christ would not cleanse men from their sins unless, following repentance, they were willing to be baptized by water and receive the Holy Spirit. Then the Lord presented to Adam the symbolism of the initiatory ordinances of the gospel.

He explained that the natural birth of every human being into mortality is characterized by three things: *first,* the element of water in which the infant is cradled until the time of his birth, *second,* the presence of the human spirit which takes possession of the infant body and gives light and life to it, and *third,* the blood which character-

---

[16]Moses 6:57
[17]*Ibid.,* 6:52

izes the travail and suffering at birth. The Lord then explained that just as the water, spirit and blood are characteristics of our initiation or birth into mortality, so also they are symbolically employed to initiate us into the kingdom of God.

The candidate is first immersed and brought forth out of the *water* of baptism; he is then endowed with the *Spirit* of the Holy Ghost which thereafter leads him into all truth and justifies or testifies of his worthiness before the throne of God; and finally, the *blood* and suffering of Jesus Christ become effective as an atoning sacrifice for his individual sins.

Symbolism has a definite appeal to the mind of man, and God has employed it wherever it would aid us in remembering and understanding His eternal purposes and designs. The Lord impressed this fact upon Adam when He declared: "And behold, all things have their likeness, and all things are created and made to bear record of me."[18] Note that symbolism is endorsed by God as a teaching method, but He abhors mysticism. Mysticism is that ancient pseudo-scholasticism which loudly pretends to know great truths but somehow never gets around to disclosing them.

We see from the above scripture that the symbolical comparison between the natural birth and the "new birth" into God's kingdom has been used from earliest times. The Lord made free use of this symbolism in explaining the initiatory ordinances to Adam: "Inasmuch as ye were born into the world by water, and blood, and the spirit, which I have made, and so became of dust a living soul, even so ye must be born again into the kingdom of heaven, of water, and of the spirit, and be cleansed by blood, even the blood of mine Only Begotten; that ye might be sanctified from all sin."[19]

Similar words were later used by the Apostle John,[20] and when the Savior was upon the earth He continuously referred to being "born of the water and of the Spirit"

[18]*Ibid.*, 6:63
[19]*Ibid.*, 6:59
[20]1 John 5:1-9

although it was cause for considerable wonderment among His materialistic listeners.[21]

Now the Lord summarized for Adam the significance of the "new birth" in this classical declaration:

"By the water ye keep the commandment,
By the Spirit ye are justified,
By the blood ye are sanctified."

In these three statements may be found the real significance and meaning of the initiatory ordinances of the gospel. Here Adam was taught *first,* baptism is a token or sign by the candidate that he will obey God's commandments; *second,* the Holy Spirit evaluates the repentance and sincerity of the candidate and if he is worthy, justifies him;[22] *third,* the Son then intercedes in his behalf and through the efficacy of His blood and suffering on Calvary gains for the candidate a remission of his sins which sanctifies him and permits his name to be entered in the book of life.

In this interview with Adam, the Lord was also anxious that the first patriarch of the race should understand the work and mission of the Holy Ghost as well as that of the Savior. He therefore referred to the third member of the Godhead as follows: "It (the Holy Ghost) is given *to abide in you;* the record of heaven; the Comforter; the peaceable things of immortal glory; the truth of all things; that which quickeneth all things, which maketh alive all things, that which knoweth all things, and hath all power, according to wisdom, mercy, truth, justice, and judgment."[23]

In other words, the inspiring companionship of the Holy Ghost constantly blessing a man by abiding in him is the *gift* of the Holy Ghost. The Holy Ghost will temporarily inspire and enlighten all who seek light and truth,[24] but the *gift* of the Holy Ghost is when it is given "to abide in you" as a constant comforter and companion

[21]*Ibid.,* 3:4
[22]See also D. & C. 76:53
[23]Moses 6:61
[24]Moroni 10:4

of light, truth, peace, knowledge, mercy, justice and judgment.

<small>ADAM IS BAPTIZED AND RECEIVES THE HOLY GHOST</small>

Having taught Adam the significance and necessity of the initiatory ordinances, God prepared to introduce Adam into his first covenant. The scripture says: "Adam cried unto the Lord, and he was caught away by the Spirit of the Lord, and was carried down into the water, and was laid under the water, and was brought forth out of the water. And thus was he baptized."[25]

Adam had the honor of being instructed in the principles of the gospel by Jehovah in person and of being physically carried down into the waters of baptism by the Spirit of the Lord or the Holy Ghost who is the second counselor in the First Presidency of heaven. Not only Adam but several later prophets are also described as having enjoyed direct personal contact with this notable personality called the Holy Ghost.[26]

Immediately after his baptism, the Holy Ghost enveloped Adam so that he "was born of the Spirit and became quickened in the inner man."[27]

Today, as in ages past, when the gift of the Holy Ghost is conferred upon a candidate he is given this solemn injunction, "Receive the Holy Ghost." This is an instruction to the recipient of this great blessing to be receptive to the Holy Ghost which will thereafter seek to abide in him and quicken the inner man. The "inner man" is the spirit in each of us—which spirit is a literal offspring of God[28]—and which was born into its present temporal tabernacle, thereby becoming more or less subject to the instincts and dictates of the flesh.

The gift of the Holy Ghost quickens the spirit or the "inner man" and gives us the motivation to dominate our physical environment and mold it to conform to our spiritual needs as well as our temporal. It makes us "more alive" spiritually. After being thus quickened through

<hr>

[25]Moses 6:64-65
[26]1 Kings 18:12; 2 Kings 2:16; Ezekiel 3:12, 14; Acts 8:39
[27]Moses 6:65
[28]D. & C. 76:24; Hebrews 12:9; Acts 17:28

the gift of the Holy Ghost the human personality is often noticeably changed so that personal refinement, the comprehension of deep gospel themes and the manifestation of tenacious loyalty to ideals and principles become prominent attributes which replace gross fleshy weaknesses of the past.

It was for this very reason that the Savior later instructed His Apostles that they should tarry in Jerusalem "until ye be endowed with power from on high."[29] Jesus knew that once they had felt the power of the Holy Ghost they would be able to endure all things.

ADAM RECEIVES THE PRIESTHOOD AND TEMPLE ORDINANCES

Modern revelation specifically states that the order of the Priesthood was "instituted in the days of Adam."[30] Adam's possession of the Priesthood is referred to in the following verses: "He (Adam) heard a voice out of heaven saying: Thou art baptized with fire, and with the Holy Ghost. This is the record of the Father, and the Son, from henceforth and forever; *And thou art after the order of him who was without beginning of days or end of years,* from all eternity to all eternity. Behold, thou art one in me, a son of God; and thus may all become my sons."[31]

The "order of Him who was without beginning of days or end of years" is a unique and peculiar phraseology which has always referred to the Holy Priesthood after the order of the Son of God.[32] Although the actual ordination of Adam is not referred to, the fact that it had already taken place is clearly implied in this passage.

In the writings of Moses another verse strongly implies that some time during his training period Adam was also introduced into the endowment and possibly other temple ordinances. Moses says: "And thus the Gospel began to be preached, from the beginning, being declared

[29]Luke 24:49
[30]D. & C. 107:41
[31]Moses 6:66-68
[32]*Teachings of Joseph Smith,* p. 323

by holy angels sent forth from the presence of God,
and by his own voice, and by the gift of the Holy Ghost.
*And thus all things were confirmed unto Adam, by an holy
ordinance. . . .*"[33] Those familiar with the blessings to
be received in the temple will recognize in this statement
a likely reference to the endowment which could not be
more accurately described than as a "holy ordinance"
designed to confirm all things pertaining to the gospel
plan—the Fall, the influence of the adversary in the
earth, the preaching of the gospel to all mankind and the
necessity for repentance and obedience to the ordinances
and principles of the plan of salvation.

Baptism is also a "holy ordinance" but it would not
confirm "all things" unto Adam. It would have had to
be something much more illuminating than that. It seems
to point clearly to the endowment.

Adam Sees a Prophetic History of the World

At the conclusion of this magnificent revelation the
Lord climaxed it with a panoramic vision of the future
wherein Adam saw a prophetic view of "all the families
of the earth."[34] He prophesied concerning them. This
gave Adam a true perspective of his own role in life as
well as that of his children who would multiply and cover
the earth. It was almost more than he could comprehend.
As the reality of it all penetrated his conscious perception
he found himself scarcely able to contain himself for joy.
As he considered the great destiny of his children down
through the corridors of time he "blessed God and was
filled, and began to prophesy."[35]

In connection with his prophesying, Adam felt constrained to express to his Heavenly Father a prayer of
thanksgiving for the great new flood of knowledge which
had suddenly poured light and understanding into his
mind on this sacred and memorable occasion. Lifting his
face toward heaven he sang out his psalm of praise:

---

[33]Moses 5:58-59; *Teachings of Joseph Smith,* pp. 166-170
[34]*Ibid.,* 5:10
[35]*Ibid.*

"Blessed be the name of God,
For because of my transgression
My eyes are opened,
And in this life
I shall have joy,
And again in the flesh
I shall see God!"

(Moses 5:10)

CHAPTER ELEVEN

The Amazing Reaction of Adam's Children to God's Revelation

What was the first thing Adam did after he received his revelation on the plan of salvation?

Was Mother Eve able to understand the plan? What was her reaction?

Then what did Adam and Eve do?

Does it appear that there was a very urgent reason why Adam wanted his children to understand the gospel plan? What was it?

As the plan of salvation was explained to them how did they react?

Do you think it was natural for the children of Adam and Eve to want a revelation of their own?

Did they get a revelation?

What should this teach us?

After the children of Adam and Eve concluded that "their" angel was telling the truth and Adam was deceiving them how do you think this affected the social and psychological relationship between the first parents and these children?

Why do you think Lucifer was permitted to appear as an angel of light to deceive the children of Adam and Eve? Does this teach us a great new truth concerning the nature of the conflict between Lucifer and Jehovah?

Would you consider Lucifer's deception of these children to be a temporary or permanent victory in the battle for their souls?

Is righteousness to succeed in the earth because there is no evil or *in spite* of evil?

How is Lucifer to "be bound"?

ADAM'S REACTION TO THE "GOOD NEWS" OF THE GOSPEL

The psalm of praise with which Adam blessed the name of God at the close of His remarkable revelation on the plan of salvation clearly indicates the degree of rapture and relief which came to him when the Lord finally revealed the true purpose of this life and the reason for the Fall.

Adam had lived to be a grandparent in an atmosphere of sorrow, repentance and self-incrimination. Now he suddenly learned the real attitude of God toward the Fall. He learned that it was part of God's plan for the advancement of His children; that mortality was intended to be a probationary or testing period and that if men would live righteously this life could be made an estate of joy and achievement.

The greatest thing of all, however, was the declaration of the Lord that Adam and his posterity could eventually work out their salvation and return to the mansions of their Heavenly Father. Filled with this almost overwhelming burden of "good news"—which is what the word *gospel* means—Adam hastened to carry this glorious message of hope and salvation to his wife and children.

ADAM GIVES AN ACCOUNT OF THE REVELATION TO MOTHER EVE

The first person to whom Adam went with his treasure of knowledge was Mother Eve. In a quiet place where they could be alone, Adam poured out the exciting and wonderful news. At first, no doubt, it was almost incomprehensible. After so many dark years of totally eclipsed hope, how could there suddenly be so much light? Could it really be true that God had forgiven them? With the glory of the vision still fresh in his mind, Adam assured his beloved wife and companion that it was indeed true.

Here was the greatest discovery of new knowledge that man would ever make. Seldom in the history of the

race has there probably been so much genuine joy felt
by anyone as that which Adam and Eve now shared. In
a single day they had leaped from the dismal depths of
humiliating grief to exotic heights of heavenly happiness.

The joy with which Mother Eve received the message is specifically referred to in the scripture,[1] and the
depth of her understanding is vividly portrayed in this
joyful exclamation to Adam: *"Were it not for our transgression we never should have had seed, and never
should have known good and evil and the joy of our redemption and the eternal life which God giveth unto all
the obedient!"*[2]

Perhaps the true feelings of Mother Eve can be
appreciated only when it is recalled that she, more than
anyone else, had carried the blame for the sorrow and
spiritual excommunication which had resulted from the
Fall. She was the first one to partake of the forbidden
fruit. It was she who received the greater condemnation
from the Lord when He found them hiding fearfully
among the trees in their garden home. It was Eve who
had made the greatest sacrifice in physical travail and
sorrowful toil as a result of the Fall.

And who will doubt that during the long, lonely years
since the exile from Eden, there had not been occasions
when frustration, fatigue and hopelessness had induced
Eve's children to point the finger of accusation toward
Mother Eve and say, "Behold our condition! See what
calamity you have brought down upon us!"

Now, however, everything should be different. A
whole new horizon of light and knowledge had risen
before them. The words of Mother Eve not only convey
a remarkable insight into the meaning and purpose of the
plan of salvation but they also reflect a personal message
of humble vindication as she said: "Were it not for our
transgression we *never* should have had seed, and
never should have known good and evil and the joy of
our redemption and the eternal life which God giveth
unto all the obedient."

[1]Moses 5:11
[2]*Ibid.,* 5:11

Surely this was a moment of triumphant satisfaction for the mother of all men!

In their hearts both Adam and Eve felt a surging emotion of prayerful thanksgiving. The scripture says they raised their faces toward heaven and though they could not see their Heavenly Father, they spoke to Him and blessed His name for the joy and happiness that had come to them that day.[3]

ADAM AND EVE EXPLAIN THE GOSPEL TO THEIR CHILDREN

Adam and Eve were probably filled with thrilled anticipation as they made their way in all haste to the dwelling place of their children and grandchildren. There was deep significance in this journey.

Over the years the inquiring minds of their children had probably poured out a thousand questions concerning life and its meaning. And for two generations Adam and Eve had been forced to confess complete ignorance on the subject. This must have been a great trial to them because, human nature being what it is, this lack of knowledge undoubtedly resulted in a loss of respect and filial affection insofar as their children were concerned.

Now, however, everything would change. They had obtained the answers at last!

The scripture states that Adam and Eve hurriedly gathered their children about them and carefully explained to them all that had happened. As the message was slowly unfolded the first parents must have watched the faces of their children anxiously. They waited for the first reflection of animated appreciation. But nothing happened. The expressionless countenances of their children reflected nothing but cold and wary suspicion. Perhaps they were thinking: "Why has God waited so long to reveal this message? After so many years of darkness is it logical to believe that God has suddenly come to say that all is forgiven? Furthermore, if God had a message for all of us, why didn't *we* see Him? Why didn't *we* have a revelation?"

[3]*Ibid.*, 5:12

They probably suspected that Adam and Eve had falsely fabricated the whole revelation.

ADAM'S CHILDREN RECEIVE A REVELATION

Just beyond the veil a powerful personality stood watching this scene of domestic discord. The present course of events was wonderfully suited to the far-reaching plans which He had in mind for Adam's children. At this moment they openly doubted the revelation which God had given to Adam. And they wanted a revelation of their own. Very well! They should have one.

Suddenly a blazing light burst through the veil of eternity to reveal before the eyes of Adam and Eve and all their children a majestic being clothed in a brilliant and transcendent glory. In solemn and impressive tones he announced: "I am also a son of God!"

Then, as though he had come direct from heaven to bring a message of truth to the inquiring minds of Adam's children, he pointed toward Adam and Eve and in a commanding voice declared, "Believe it not."[4]

Immediately Adam and Eve knew the identity of this angelic messenger. He was their adversary, the leader of the rebellion in the spirit world, the prince of perdition —Lucifer.

To the amazement of Adam and Eve their children were awed into complete acceptance of this angelic impostor. When the vision had passed they could see that their children had been profoundly impressed. Adam and Eve tried to explain to them who Lucifer really was but they did not succeed. The fact that this was the being who first deceived Mother Eve in the Garden of Eden seemed to mean nothing. And the pleading of the first parents to beware of Satan lest he also mislead them was to no avail. Adam and Eve had the heartbreaking experience of seeing all of their children—from the eldest to the youngest—turn against them.

---

[4]Moses 5:13

Not only did these children and grandchildren disdainfully reject the glorious revelation which Adam had received, but their subsequent attitude toward the first parents was tantamount to a direct accusation that the whole thing was a lie. Had they not received a revelation of their own? Had not a glorious being appeared before them and specifically commanded them not to believe what Adam had told them?

"And," the scripture concludes, "they believed it not. ... They loved Satan more than God!"[5]

Why Was Satan Permitted to Deceive the Children of Adam and Eve?

It is desirable, perhaps, to pause for a moment and consider the reason why Satan would have been permitted by God to appear in this deceptive manner and frustrate the efforts of Adam and Eve to share the gospel with their children. Why didn't God hold Satan back?

We might go further and ask, "Why does God permit Satan to operate at all?"

When Lucifer rebelled in the pre-existence and led one-third of the Father's spirit children into open revolution, it might occur to some that God should have interfered and struck Satan from his kingdom. But God did not. In fact, during the "war in heaven" shown to John the Beloved on the Isle of Patmos, it does not appear that Elohim interfered in any way even though He was greatly concerned with the outcome. The scripture says that when Satan was ultimately cast out it was Michael and his angels who did it. It even describes *how* they did it: "by the word of their testimony."[6]

In other words, those of the Father's spirits who had determined to reject Lucifer's rebellion exercised their influence and freedom of expression until they had definitely won the open support of the majority of the spirits in heaven. And so unified did they become that the

[5]*Ibid.*, 5:13
[6]Rev. 12:11

scripture says the rebellious hosts of Lucifer "prevailed not; neither was their place found any more in heaven."[7] That is how Satan and his hosts were cast out. The Father left it to His children to decide for themselves whom they would follow.

Now the war continues here upon the earth. As a heavenly voice declared to John the Beloved: "Woe to the inhabitants of the earth and of the sea! for the devil is come down unto you, having great wrath, because he knoweth that he hath but a short time."[8] Lucifer is quoted as having declared: "I will exalt my throne above the stars of God: I will sit also in the mount of the congregation, in the sides of the north: I will ascend above the heights of the clouds; I will be like the most High."[9]

As in the pre-existence, Lucifer is still the challenger and accuser of those who are trying to make a success of this voluntary plan of salvation. The very name *Satan* is of Hebrew origin and signifies "an accuser."[10]

There is evidence that Lucifer sometimes goes before the Lord to opine that he is not getting a fair chance to show up the weaknesses of Jehovah's plan and the weakness of those who subscribe to it.[11]

He argues that if he were allowed to use as much influence to thwart the plan as Jehovah uses in fostering it, he could demonstrate the fact that men would rather follow Satan than God.

The majesty of the constitution of free government which prevails throughout God's cosmic universe requires that Satan have his opportunity to compete with Jehovah for the voluntary allegiance of the hosts of men. Otherwise, men could never be considered to have had the "chance to choose."[12]

Satan's war against Jehovah is terrible and real. Insofar as Lucifer is concerned it is a death struggle with impeachment and exile awaiting the day of his downfall.

[7]*Ibid.*, 12:8
[8]*Ibid.*, 12:12
[9]Isaiah 14:12-14
[10]Cruden's *Complete Concordance,* under "Satan"
[11]Job 1:6-11
[12]2 Nephi 2:16, 27

In the meantime, while men are tasting the fruits of their free agency, Satan presses hard for every advantage and belligerently demands equal opportunity with Jehovah in recruiting the souls of men. It is apparent from scriptural authority that, within limits, the theocratic government of heaven permits this freedom of expression—even when it takes the form of destructive satanical deception. God will not force Lucifer to be righteous any more than he will force men to be righteous. If the plan of Jehovah is to succeed, it must succeed *in spite* of Lucifer.

It is a significant characteristic of almost every dispensation of the gospel that whenever the celestial veil has been parted to permit a new communication between God and man, Lucifer has been right there to follow it very shortly with a revelation of his own. It was so in the days of Moses;[13] it was so in the days of Christ.[14] The same thing happened during the restoration of the gospel to Joseph Smith,[15] and we have seen that it occurred when the gospel was first given to Adam. It is interesting to observe that on several of these occasions Lucifer has been allowed to dramatize his deception by going so far as to appear as though he were "an angel of light."[16]

It will be seen from this that the deceiving of Adam's children by Satan at the very moment when Adam was so anxious to have them understand and appreciate the revelation which God had given him, was merely a preliminary skirmish—a foretaste of what men could expect during Lucifer's six-thousand-year war against Jehovah. It was a sample of the diabolical deception which Satan was capable of practicing when the furthering of his fiendish cause required it.

And for the moment, it appeared as though Lucifer had won a monumental victory.

[13]Moses 1:12-22
[14]Matt. 4:1-11
[15]D. & C. 128:20
[16]2 Cor. 11:14; D. & C. 128:20

CHAPTER TWELVE

Prelude To Disaster

When Adam and Eve were rejected by their first children where did they place their future hopes?

Eve was blessed with a son of whom she said: "I have gotten a man from the Lord; wherefore he may not reject His words." Who was this son? What did his name mean?

What kind of personality was Cain? Was he a strong leader? Is there any indication that he received the Priesthood? Did he receive open revelations from the Lord? Could he have become a son of perdition without the Priesthood and without revelation?

What were the three things which Cain apparently permitted to become stumbling blocks to his progress?

Who commanded Cain to make an offering of the fruit of the ground?

When Cain's offering was rejected and he turned wrathfully from the place of sacrifice what dramatic event occurred which should have helped him straighten out his crooked career?

Did Cain rebel in a spirit of deceived ignorance or did he choose the leadership of Lucifer with his eyes open?

Whom did Cain marry? Was this likely further to complicate his position?

Why did Lucifer want Cain to rule over him? Did Lucifer subsequently promise to allow Cain to rule over him?

Who was the inspiration for the first murder cult? How extensive was the conspiracy which resulted in the death of Abel?

What was the most significant thing about the oath which Lucifer administered to Cain and Cain administered to his brothers?

ADAM AND EVE PRAY FOR A WORTHY SON

Who will count the long frustrating months or years that followed the rejection of Adam and Eve by their children? No doubt the first parents must have made many attempts to reconcile them, to reason with them and to gain their confidence. But the scripture is very clear that these children cut themselves off from their parents.

In the lonely dark hours of the night Adam and Eve must have frequently discussed what course they would take. Everything possible must have been tried but when they failed to find any possible approach to their existing children, they finally focused their hopes on the children who might yet be born to them.

It was in this spirit that Adam and Eve approached the Lord with the desire that they would be blessed with another son. They wanted a son who would be a choice spirit, responsive to the gospel message and worthy of the Priesthood. And in due process of time the scripture says they had a son. He was a son on whom Adam and Eve could shower their affections and ambitions—a brilliant boy who showed great promise of leadership and was eventually ordained to the Priesthood of Adam.[1]

Mother Eve looked upon this lad as an answer to her prayer. When she first gazed into his infant countenance she joyfully exclaimed: "I have gotten a man from the Lord; wherefore *he may not reject his words!*" (Moses 5:16) The happy parents gave the child a name which meant "obtained" or "possessed" through the blessings of the Lord.[2]

The name was Cain!

From later developments we know that Cain was a strange combination of personality traits. His character was a coat of many colors. He was forceful, ambitious and zealous in whatever he undertook to accomplish. Perhaps, during the pre-existence, he was a great moving force for the cause of Jehovah. But with all of his good qualities, Cain's pattern of progress had probably been

[1]*Teachings of Joseph Smith*, p. 169
[2]Peloubet's *Bible Dictionary*, under "Cain"

accented with an occasional depth charge of explosive
personal pride. In many respects he was similar to Lucifer—a bright "star of the morning" and a leader among
the spirits of the Father, but only so long as it suited his
own personal convenience and designs. Deep within
were festering seeds of sedition and violence fed by the
flames of an all-consuming ambition and a self-centered
pride. Like a number of others who would be born in
later generations, Cain had become a prince in the cause
of God's righteousness but stood ready to scuttle the
whole kingdom for thirty pieces of silver or any other
trivia which happened to attract the whims of his can-
kered soul. However, this weakness must not have
blossomed into open rebellion until he was tested in
mortality.

THE COMPLEX QUALITIES OF A SON OF PERDITION

Technically and legally, Cain had probably made
himself eligible for many blessings during the First Estate.
Were it not so he would not have been born into such favorable circumstances in the second estate. He was born
at a time when the gospel was upon the earth, when he
could (and did) receive the Priesthood,[3] he even enjoyed
revelations direct from God. From the later pleadings
of the Lord with Cain it is apparent that he was legally
entitled to what he had received and would continue to
be so unless he perverted the course of his life.

God "knew all things from the beginning" and He
had observed Cain down through the eternities and knew
what he would do with his free agency when he came into
mortality. Beyond any shadow of doubt God knew that
although Cain had been enrolled in the cause of righteousness previously, he nevertheless had been harboring
a secret nest of serpents in his breast and as a result would
reveal his true character when put to the test in mortality.
The Second Estate is ingeniously designed to prove the
mettle of every man. It is the great final obstacle course
on the highway of eternal progression. It highlights our
strength and uncovers our weaknesses.

[3]*Teachings of Joseph Smith,* p. 169

Therefore, in the person of Cain—a man "gotten of the Lord"—God purposely presented Adam and Eve with a son whom He knew would ultimately break their hearts. But in the sadness of those subsequent years God was only sharing with the first parents the burden of sorrow which He Himself was forced to bear as Cain turned contemptuously from Jehovah to accept the ever-lasting embrace of perdition. It was understandable that God should wish to share this sorrow with two of His most beloved and trusted servants—Adam and Eve. Perhaps it was for this reason that He made Cain their son.

It does not say how long after he received the Priest-hood that Cain began to resist the laws of righteous liv-ing. Subsequent events indicate that he was in close association with his older brothers—the daughter of one apostate brother later became his wife—and it is possible that his pride and native inclinations toward unholy am-bitions found a responsive chord in the sarcastic cyn-icism of these older and more sophisticated relatives. It would also appear that Adam must have detected the growing infidelity of Cain and called the commandments of the Lord to his attention, for Cain is quoted as having sneeringly remarked: "Who is the Lord that I should know him?"[4] This must have come as a tremendous shock to Adam and Eve. They were forced to admit that the plague of apostasy had now contaminated even this choice son in whom they had planted their whole hope for the future.

The Birth of Abel

It appears to have been during this state of affairs and under these circumstances that Abel was born.[5] No doubt the first parents redoubled their efforts from the time of his infancy and raised him into adolescence with the deepest anxiety for his welfare. Their hopes for a righteous heir must have been fanned into a new flame as

[4]Moses 5:16
[5]*Ibid.*, 5:17

the sweet spirit of Abel began to reflect in his daily life the very epitome of the gospel's principles.[6]

As soon as he was of an eligible age, Adam was commanded by God to ordain him to the Priesthood, and Abel thereby became authorized to assist Adam in making the sacrifices and offerings unto the Lord.[7]

It is easy to see how such a development would have poured fuel upon the jealousy of Cain who was probably forbidden from assisting in the ordinances at the altar of sacrifice because of his rebellious attitude. Cain was further antagonized by the fact that even if he had been allowed to offer a sacrifice he would have had to obtain a lamb from his younger brother, for "Abel was a keeper of sheep, but Cain was a tiller of the ground."[8]

A third factor which alienated Cain and Abel was the fact that Cain coveted the flocks of Abel. In that early pastoral age, large flocks represented the most precious kind of wealth—providing not only food but skins and wool for clothing, tents and fabrics. It was not sufficient in Cain's mind that he himself should have the wealth of loaded granaries and other supplies of food stocks. He wanted also to have the flocks of Abel.[9]

With such thoughts racing through his brain, Cain presented an inviting prospect to the great adversary of the race. With all the sophistry and power he possessed, Lucifer stepped through the veil and stood before the astonished Cain.

Whether or not this was the first time Lucifer had appeared to Cain in person we do not know. But be that as it may, Cain undoubtedly possessed a knowledge of all the mysterious and exciting things which his older brothers said Satan had revealed to them and therefore Cain offered an attentive and respectful ear to everything the deceiver had to say.

[6]Matt. 23:35; 1 John 3:12
[7]*Teachings of Joseph Smith,* p. 169
[8]Moses 5:17
[9]*Ibid.,* 5:38

CAIN RECEIVES COMMANDMENTS FROM SATAN

Lucifer commanded Cain to offer up *Cain's* possessions of wealth—the fruit of the ground.[10] Why should Cain have to seek a lamb from his younger brother for sacrifice? Why wasn't the fruit of *his* labor as worthy as that of young Abel? This reasoning appealed to Cain and therefore, from that moment on, the scripture says "Cain loved Satan more than God."[11]

"And in process of time it came to pass that Cain brought of the fruit of the ground an offering unto the Lord."[12]

In solemn mockery Cain brought forth the fruits of his vanity and laid them on the altar. By some token which is not recorded, Cain discovered that his offering was completely unacceptable to the Lord. At the same time he learned that Abel's offering was sanctified and accepted. Cain was outraged! His egotistical vanity was prodded to the quick and his passionate anger boiled over—thereby making his mind a fertile field for the seeds of murder which Satan later proposed to plant.

CAIN RECEIVES A REVELATION FROM THE LORD

In blinded wrath Cain hastened from the scene of the sacrifices but he had not gone far before he was suddenly stopped in the way. A voice spoke to him out of the heavens. He knew the voice. It was the Lord. "Why art thou wroth? Why is thy countenance fallen? If thou doest well, *thou shalt be accepted.* And if thou doest not well, sin lieth at the door, and Satan desireth to have thee; and except thou shalt hearken unto my commandments, I will deliver thee up, and it shall be unto thee according to *his* desire. . . . Thou shalt rule over him!"[13]

What a jolt this revelation should have carried to the dark and disappointed heart of Cain. It should have pulled him up short. He was being duped! He was fall-

[10] *Ibid.,* 5:18-19
[11] *Ibid.*
[12] *Ibid.,* 5:19
[13] *Ibid.,* 5:22-23

ing for the luring trap of the adversary of the race. Lucifer wanted Cain to be a ruler in his own satanical kingdom. But why? The Lord knew the reason. Satan was fighting a losing battle against Jehovah. Satan was out of his environment. He was trying to tempt "men in the flesh" and compete with Jehovah for their allegiance. But he didn't know how to reach men in physical tabernacles. He hadn't had the necessary experience. He needed a brilliant and enterprising personality like Cain to fill the role of general manager in his kingdom— someone to originate schemes and plans which would trap the race, frustrate the purposes of the Second Estate and defeat the success of Jehovah's plan for the salvation of humanity.

Lucifer saw in Cain the ideal personality for such an assignment. And Lucifer would resort to anything to have Cain—even sacrifice his own position of leadership among the fiends of his unrighteous domain. Better to take this extreme action than lose the war! And without Cain or someone similar who had lived through mortality and knew best what to prescribe, Lucifer saw himself confronted by an early defeat.

It is apparent from subsequent passages which we will consider that Satan was already beginning to feel the pressure of Jehovah's success as the superintendent of the Second Estate. Lucifer had thought that his program of force, violence and deception would soon "destroy the world,"[14] but already he could feel the competition of Jehovah's superior wisdom out-maneuvering him. To be sure, he had deceived and weaned away all of Adam's first children, but there would be other children like Abel who would not be deceived—at least, not by anything Lucifer could conceive of. He needed a superior intellect like Cain who had tasted of mortality and knew what lies and trials would snare the souls of men. That was why he was willing to sacrifice so much to recruit Cain into his kingdom.

---

[14] *Ibid.*, 4:6

CAIN MAKES A DECISION

So Cain stood at the crossroads. Any ordinary Priesthood holder would have retreated quickly to the proffered protection of Jehovah's generous forgiveness. To learn the true significance of Lucifer's plans and the extreme danger of the course he was then pursuing should have have been enough. But not so with Cain. The fact that the mighty Lucifer would bargain for his soul and beg for his services fascinated Cain. It tickled his fancy and nurtured his ego. Therefore he made up his mind.

Although he had received a revelation from heaven, he determined never again to heed the voice of the Lord. The scripture says, "And Cain was wroth, and listened not any more to the voice of the Lord, neither to Abel, his brother, who walked in holiness before the Lord."[15]

From this it would appear that young Abel did all within his power to bring the proud Cain to his senses. But a man who would not accept a call of repentance from the Lord would be unlikely to accept it from his younger brother. In fact, the humble petitions of Abel were probably like sprinkling salt into the raw sores of Cain's conscience.

Now Cain did the very thing Satan probably hoped he would. It appears that he completely allied himself with his apostate older brethren. The latter must have gloried in this complete conversion of Cain to their way of life. And the scripture says: "Adam and his wife mourned before the Lord because of Cain and his brethren."[16]

Cain found this new arrangement very much to his liking, particularly since he enjoyed the sympathy and companionship of a young woman who was also a Satan-worshiper. She was the daughter of one of Cain's older brothers and therefore his niece. It was not long before their mutual affinity drew them together in marriage, and the scripture says, "They loved Satan more than God."[17]

[15] *Ibid.*, 5:26
[16] *Ibid.*, 5:27
[17] *Ibid.*, 5:28

The Founding of a Murder Cult

Now Lucifer was ready to lay the snare which he hoped would capture Cain. He therefore presented himself before Cain and began tantalizing him with the possibility of acquiring all of his brother's flocks. This was something Cain wanted more than anything else in the world. But how could he obtain Abel's flocks? Satan assured him there was a way: "Swear unto me by thy throat, and if thou tell it thou shalt die; and swear thy brethren by their heads, and by the living God, that they tell it not; for if they tell it, they shall surely die; and this *that thy father may not know it;* and this day I will deliver thy brother Abel into thine hands."[18]

It is apparent from this that Lucifer feared Adam and wanted to accomplish the next major step in his program without the father of the race being forewarned of it. The form of the oath which Lucifer administered to Cain was couched in terms which constitute the most solemn covenant that man can make. Notice the strange anomaly wherein Satan, the enemy of God, wanted Cain to swear "by the living God," that he would not disclose the great secret Lucifer was about to reveal to him. This reflects the secret respect which Satan continues to feel toward the God of the universe even though he is working day and night to destroy His kingdom.

Notice also that Satan did not dare to have Cain participate in this murder covenant alone. The great secret which Lucifer was about to reveal to Cain was how to take human life by stealth to "get gain." But what if some of the older brothers should discover what had happened to Abel and seek to revenge his blood? The violent death of young Abel might arouse latent sympathies among the older brothers even though they had opposed the lad during his lifetime. This had to be circumvented. Therefore Cain was commanded by Satan to bind all of his apostate brothers under the same oath. This would institute the first murder cult in the world.

[18]*Ibid.,* 5:29

It was a terrible and awe-inspiring step to take. To persuade Cain further that he had ample support in this new venture, Lucifer took an oath by all that either of them considered holy, that he, the fallen prince of heaven, would thereafter be subject to the commands of Cain. As the scripture says: "And Satan sware unto Cain that he would do according to his commands. And all these things were done in secret."[19]

Had there been the slightest vestige of righteousness left in the heart of this man who was the first of all the Judases, he would have spurned the plague of secret murder which Satan was proposing. But at that particular moment Cain had room for neither reason nor remorse. He saw nothing in the future for himself but unprecedented power and unprecedented wealth. He went forth unto his older brothers and lighted the flame of greed in each of their hearts with the selfsame torch that Lucifer had used to inflame Cain. One by one he placed them under the oath.

The stage was now set for the great and terrible drama Satan had inspired and planned.

[19]*Ibid.,* 5:30

CHAPTER THIRTEEN

Adam and Eve
Lose Their Favorite Son

The murder cult set up by Cain had a specific economic objective. What was it?

What was Cain's mental attitude as he went about spreading the Mahanite cult?

Was the slaying of Abel by stealth or did Cain come up to him in a friendly manner and then seize him when he was off guard? Was the crime accompanied by violence?

When the murder was completed Cain exclaimed: "I am free! Surely the flocks of my brother falleth into my hands." What does this reflect in the character of Cain?

What happened to Cain as he was leaving the murder scene?

What was Cain's response to the Lord's challenge?

Did Cain feel repentant for what he had done? Did he show any concern for the feelings of Father Adam or Mother Eve?

What did the Lord say would happen to Cain?

After the disclosure of his crime, what did Cain do?

The Lord said He would put a mark upon Cain. Did He also put a mark on his descendants?

Were there any neutrals in heaven?

Will the descendants of Cain ever have the opportunity of receiving the Priesthood?

Does the scripture indicate that Cain lost his position as Master Mahan? What does Josephus say happened to Cain?

Does the scripture indicate that some of the seed of Cain were very talented and could have made a great contribution to human happiness?

CAIN BECOMES THE FIRST MASTER MAHAN

It has always been Lucifer's supreme ambition to destroy human life. The whole design of the oath-bound fraternity which Satan had suggested to Cain was for the purpose of motivating men to commit murder. It must be kept in mind that the Second Estate was engineered and planned as a profitable school and probation for those of the Father's children who were loyal in the pre-existence. The program requires that an important work be accomplished by the human family during this life. It can best be done with a large population of righteous people working together as in the days of Enoch—building schools, temples, homes and industries; cultivating and beautifying the earth; exploiting the natural resources provided; bringing all things under dominion.

Lucifer's strategy involves a two-pronged thrust against humanity: *first*, to keep the population at a minimum by inspiring war, murder and race-suicide and *second*, to use ignorance, deception, jealousy, greed and strife to spread wickedness among whatever population survives so that humanity will not be effective in accomplishing the work which earth life was designed to achieve. The whole panorama of history reveals a continuous campaign on the part of the adversary to destroy human life either by violence or by corruption.

Lucifer's alliance with Cain was designed to launch this satanical program almost at the very commencement of human history. Lucifer knew that the secret society which Cain would organize among his older brothers would be the spawning place for many murders. Inflamed by the prospect of unearned spoils, he knew they would conspire together to kill "and get gain." Later this same motivation would drive these antediluvian Gadiantons to commit mass murder in open warfare. In fact, during Cain's lifetime we shall see that his descendants mobilized their forces and spread terror across the land—massacring men, women and children, annihilating whole nations.[1]

---

[1]Moses 7:7

Lucifer must have looked up toward heaven and laughed as he watched Cain secretly selling each of his older brothers on the new cult and then exercising his devilish priestcraft in administering the oath to each of them according to the pattern which Satan had taught him. As for Cain, he gloried in it. It gave him a tremendous sense of power. His apostate brothers rallied round him with indulgent expressions of devotion and loyalty. It caused Cain to cry out with triumphant exultation: "Truly I am Mahan, the master of this great secret. . . . *I may murder and get gain!*"[2] Then the scripture adds, "Wherefore, Cain was called Master Mahan and he gloried in his wickedness."[3]

Now Cain was filled with a sense of security which the secret protection of his oath-bound brethren provided. He was ready for his first act of violence. He therefore called upon Satan to deliver Abel into his hands.

It is clear from the scripture that the manner in which Cain was tutored to slay Abel was by betrayal. Cain was to go into the field and approach Abel as his friend and brother. Then, when Abel was unprepared and off guard, Cain was to rise up and slay him.

Abel Becomes the First Human Being to Suffer Death by Violence

This was precisely the pattern which Cain followed: "And Cain went into the field, and Cain talked with Abel, his brother. And it came to pass that while they were in the field, Cain rose up against Abel his brother and slew him."[4]

This was a cold, calculated murder. Subsequent verses state that the blood of Abel was spilled out upon the ground, indicating that Cain had thrown himself upon his younger brother with great physical violence. When the struggle was over and Cain looked down upon his brother who lay dying at his feet, there was not the slightest qualm of sympathy or pity. Cain looked out

---

[2] *Ibid.*, 5:31
[3] *Ibid.*
[4] *Ibid.*, 5:32

over the fields and meadows with lust and greed written across his countenance. Raising his face toward the skies he cried out: "I am free; surely the flocks of my brother falleth into my hands!"[5]

The completed crime of shedding the blood of a human being sometimes shocks the perpetrator into a horrified recognition of the enormity of the offense. Concerning Cain, however, the scripture simply says: "Cain gloried in that which he had done."[6]

Hebrew tradition has it that Cain carefully concealed the body of young Abel so that his act of fratricide would not be detected. He then strode confidently from the scene. As he was leaving, however, his moment of triumph was suddenly interrupted. The voice of the Lord stopped him. "Cain, where is Abel, thy brother?"

The thoughts which raced madly through Cain's mind must have been typical of those which flood the mind of any cornered felon. What could he say? After such careful planning the scheme was undone! Now the whole world would know.

Pulling himself together, he instinctively reached for the nearest lie. With pretended indifference he mumbled, "I know not. Am I my brother's keeper?"

The righteous indignation of the Lord flowed out upon Cain. Jehovah had been required by the fundamental laws of heaven to allow Cain to express his free agency, but now that the terrible deed was completed, He made no effort to conceal the wrath of His indignation as He stood over Cain to pronounce judgment.

"Cain . . ." He said, "What hast thou done? The voice of thy brother's blood cries unto me from the ground. And now thou shalt be cursed from the earth which hath opened her mouth to receive thy brother's blood from thy hand. When thou tillest the ground it shall not henceforth yield unto thee her strength. A fugitive and a vagabond shalt thou be in the earth!"[7]

[5]*Ibid.,* 5:33
[6]*Ibid.*
[7]*Ibid.,* 5:34-37

As Cain listened to the Lord his triumph turned to gall within him. Like the lying malefactor that he was, he determined to shift the blame for the crime he had committed. He whined out: "Satan tempted me because of my brother's flocks. And I was wroth also; for his offering thou didst accept and not mine."[8] Then, in a final burst of anguish and self-pity he exclaimed: "My punishment is greater than I can bear. Behold thou hast driven me out this day from the face of the Lord, and from thy face shall I be hid; and I shall be a fugitive and a vagabond in the earth; and it shall come to pass, that he that findeth me will slay me, because of mine iniquities, *for these things are not hid from the Lord.*"[9]

It seems to have been a surprise to Cain to realize suddenly that nothing is hidden from the Lord—not even the secret meetings of his Satan-sponsored murder cult nor the surreptitious slaying of his younger brother.

Notice the phrasing of Cain's plea. There is not a scintilla of repentance in the whole petition—nothing but remorse for having been caught and the fearful prospect of the consequences. There is no concern for Abel, for Father Adam or Mother Eve, for the Lord or anyone else whom he had offended. His plea is nothing but a series of lamentations:

"My punishment is greater than I can bear!"
"Thou hast driven me out!"
"From thy face shall I be hid!"
"I shall be a fugitive and a vagabond!"
"He that findeth me will slay me!"

Now the Lord exhibited a token of mercy to Cain which Cain had refused to manifest to Abel. Said He: "Whosoever slayeth thee, vengeance shall be taken on him sevenfold." Then the Lord placed a mark upon Cain so that anyone finding him should not kill him because of the Lord's decree concerning him.

[8]*Ibid.,* 5:38
[9]*Ibid.,* 5:38-39

THE CURSE OF CAIN

The previous prophecy which the Lord had pronounced upon Cain, was now in full force and effect. This is what the Lord had said would happen to Cain if he continued in his course of rebellion: "From this time forth thou shalt be the father of his (Lucifer's) lies; thou shalt be called Perdition; for thou wast also before the world. And it shall be said in time to come—That these abominations were had from Cain; for he rejected the greater counsel which was had from God."[10]

So Cain became the first son of perdition among men. The Lord says the incomprehensible depths of sorrow to which such personalities sink is in consequence of their "Having denied the Holy Spirit after having received it, and having denied the Only Begotten Son of the Father, having crucified him unto themselves and put him to open shame."[11] This is what Cain had done. He had held the Priesthood,[12] partaken of the gospel ordinances,[13] walked and talked with God, drunk of heavenly knowledge and then—in spite of all this—gone braying into the wilderness, plotting murder, renouncing righteousness and defying God. It is understandable why this should be called the "unpardonable sin."

When Cain had heard the Lord's decree he stole back to the sinister haunts of his Mahan headquarters where his Satan-worshiping wife and his oath-bound brethren waited anxiously for the news that the slaughter was done. But Cain's heart was like a cinder. The blood on his hands had cost him his soul. Never again would he see God. Never again would he know true happiness. The light that "lighteth the lives of all men" had gone out of him.

He could not stand living any longer in this vicinity. The sight of his father and mother must have been abhorrent to him. Their sorrow-stricken faces and their bodies stooped by grief must have been like fire and

[10]*Ibid.*, 5:24-25
[11]D. & C. 76:35
[12]Smith, J. F., *Way to Perfection*, p. 98
[13]Brigham Young, *Journal of Discourses*, 2:142

brimstone in his brain. Cain therefore announced he
was going to move. He took all his possessions—his
spoils, his household goods, his wife, his brothers and
the paraphernalia of the secret society—and moved to
a new province east of Eden.[14] Like a nomad he must
have dragged his caravan from place to place. His restless, remorseful spirit probably robbed him of sleep and
the will to settle. As a result the whole land through
which he passed was named "Nod" which meant
"wandering."[15]

At this point Josephus, the Jewish historian, has the
following observation concerning developments:

"And when Cain had travelled over many countries,
he, with his wife, built a city named Nod, which is a place
so-called, and there he settled his abode; where also he
had children. However, he did not accept of his punishment in order to amendment, but to increase his
wickedness; for he only aimed to procure everything that
was for his own bodily pleasure, though it obliged him
to be injurious to his neighbors. He augmented his household substance with much wealth, by rapine and violence;
he excited his acquaintances to procure pleasure and
spoils by robbery, and became a great leader of men into
wicked courses. He also introduced a change in that
way of simplicity wherein men lived before. . . . He
changed the world into cunning craftiness. He first of
all set boundaries about lands; he built a city and fortified
it with walls, and he compelled his family to come
together to it."[16]

The scripture states that it was in this new land that
Cain and his wife had their first son and after that they
"begat many sons and daughters."[17] Ironically enough,
they named their first son Enoch—not to be confused by
any manner of means with the famous patriarch, Enoch,
who lived much later and whose city was eventually
translated.

[14]Moses 5:41
[15]Peloubet's *Bible Dictionary* under "Nod"
[16]*Antiquities of the Jews*, Book I, Ch. 2.2
[17]Moses 5:42

A further coincidence is the fact that when Cain built the first city in the world and established his Mahan headquarters in it, he named it after his son Enoch so that Cain's capital was called "The City of Enoch." But this had nothing to do with the later community of righteousness which was called after the patriarch, Enoch, and was translated. The two cities must not be confused.

The Seed Of Cain

Because God knew all of His children "from the beginning" and knew what would be best for them during the Second Estate He deliberately planned the time and place and circumstances where various types of personalities would best fit in. This is clearly referred to by Moses wherein he states that from "days of old" the Lord has limited the growth and expansion of various nations so as to maintain a proper proportion of righteous leadership in the earth.[18] In other words, He has all classes of beings to deal with. Some are superior in one way, some in another. Some are outstanding in material things, some are predominant in things of the spirit. Some are a happy combination of each. In planning the Second Estate the Lord had to be sure that those personalities who were particularly suited to positions of righteous leadership should be sprinkled judiciously throughout all peoples in all ages so as to promote the welfare of the *whole* human family.[19] This power of leadership is God's Priesthood.

There was a certain group of spirits, however, who for some reason not yet revealed to us, were not to be given the powers of the Priesthood during this life. That this was for *their* benefit as well as for the welfare of humanity in general is evident from the fact that *it is only a temporary restriction.* Often the Lord postpones a blessing until the individual is in a position to use that blessing properly. Eventually these spirits will receive all the opportunities that the rest of the human family have received. For the time being, however, the Lord has

[18]Deut. 32:7-8
[19]Abraham 3:22-23

decreed that they shall not possess or exercise the powers of presidency which are contained in the Priesthood.

This is the group of spirits who have come to the earth through the lineage of Cain.

DESCENDANTS OF CAIN WERE NOT NEUTRAL SPIRITS IN HEAVEN

Some have suggested that perhaps this postponement of blessings which are enjoyed through the Priesthood was imposed upon this group because they were neutral during the great war with Lucifer in the pre-existence. Joseph Smith, however, stated that this is not a true doctrine. His position on this question was quoted by Brigham Young on December 25, 1869, wherein he stated that Joseph Smith had declared that the descendants of Cain were not neutral in heaven, for all spirits took sides.[20]

The leaders of the Church have clearly taught that this segment of the Father's children will eventually receive every opportunity that other nations have received. Joseph Smith taught this doctrine[21] and Brigham Young summarized the position of the Church on this matter when he said:

"The Lord said, I will not kill Cain, but I will put a mark upon him, and that mark will be seen upon the face of every Negro upon the face of the earth; and it is the decree of God that that mark shall remain upon the seed of Cain until the seed of Abel shall be redeemed, and Cain shall not receive the Priesthood, until the time of that redemption. Any man having one drop of the seed of Cain in him cannot receive the Priesthood; *but the day will come when all that race will be redeemed and possess all the blessings which we now have.*"[22]

Brigham Young was very specific in promising the seed of Cain that in their proper time they would receive the Priesthood if they would live to be worthy of it. Said he:

---

[20]Smith, J. F., *Way to Perfection*, p. 105
[21]*Ibid.*
[22]*Ibid.*, p. 106

"Why are so many of the inhabitants of the earth cursed with a skin of blackness? It comes in consequence of their fathers rejecting the power of the holy Priesthood, and the laws of God. They will go down to their death. And when all the rest of the children have received their blessings in the holy Priesthood, *then that curse will be removed from the seed of Cain, and they will then come up and possess the Priesthood.*"[23]

Early History of the Seed of Cain

Within five generations Cain's descendants developed into a flourishing community. In spite of their founding father's wickedness many of them exhibited unusual talents and a desire to improve their condition. One of these was named Jabal who "was the father of such as dwell in tents, and they were keepers of cattle; and his brother's name was Jubal, who was the father of all such as handle the harp and organ."[24] A half-brother of these men was named Tubal Cain, "an instructor of every artificer in brass and iron."[25]

During this brief period of growth which included the first five generations of Cain's children it appears that Lucifer's murder cult had been perpetuated as a secret fraternity. Since they were all fairly close relatives and the element of competition was not yet pronounced there is no record of any use of the fraternity to "murder and get gain."

In fact, the scripture states that by this time Cain had lost his position of leadership in the fraternity and his great-great-great-grandson, Lamech, had become the Master Mahan.[26] It was under these circumstances that the murder cult suddenly flourished into activity again.

Lamech heard that Irad, his own great-grandfather, had been revealing the secret signs, ceremonies and mysteries to some of "the sons of Adam" who apparently did not belong to the society and were not under the solemn oath. "Wherefore Lamech, being angry, slew him, not

---

[23]*Ibid.*, p. 107
[24]Moses 5:45
[25]*Ibid.*, 5:46
[26]*Ibid.*, 5:49

like unto Cain, (who slew) his brother Abel, for the sake
of getting gain, but he slew him for the oath's sake."[27]

Later Lamech felt a deep remorse of conscience for
the thing he had done and so he confessed the murder to
his two wives: "Hear my voice, ye wives of Lamech,
hearken unto my speech; for I have slain a man to my
wounding, and a young man to my hurt."[28]   Note that
he calls his great-grandfather a "young man," which,
according to the longevity of those early days, was really
so.

The wives of Lamech were horrified to learn that he
had slain Irad, his own great-grandfather.   Therefore
they spread the news abroad and Lamech was forced to
flee into exile.   All available records indicate that during
this early period women were not admitted to the secret
society of Mahan,[29] therefore these women probably had
not known that Lamech was the chieftain or Master
Mahan of Satan's secret society.   His weakness in con-
fessing his crime to his wives carried the death penalty
under the Mahan oath, "Wherefore Lamech was despised, and cast out, and came not among the sons of men,
lest he should die."[30]

This incident impressed upon all the Satan-worshipers that they must guard the secrets of their society more
carefully.   At the same time it seemed to have sparked the
fraternity into murderous activity once again.   From this
time forward "their works were abominations, and began
to spread among all the sons of men."[31] Thus a great curse
settled down like a blight over the earth.   Among these
wicked conspirators no honest man was safe.   At any
moment his wealth, his house, his wife or his daughters
might become the object of desire for some grasping
Mahanite whose membership in the secret society would
be known to none save those who belonged to the cult.
In the subterranean darkness of the Mahan temple the

[27]*Ibid.*, 5:50
[28]*Ibid.*, 5:47
[29]*Ibid.*, 5:51
[30]*Ibid.*, 5:54
[31]*Ibid.*, 5:52

murder would be plotted and in the nighttime the spoils would be seized.

Like the burning sulphurous lava from a diabolical volcano, the cult began to spread its curse among all the children of men. Within a few years it turned the people of Cain into a savage, bloodthirsty nation of predatory raiders.[32]

And somewhere in that land of sorrow and degenerate humanity a great dark figure lurked among the crags and hilltops overlooking the inhabited valleys. It was Cain. No longer was he Master Mahan. No longer was he rich. No longer did he chant the devilish ritual of the Mahan cult. Prophecy had been fulfilled. The once proud Cain had found the low road that leads to perdition. From him the earth had withheld its strength. And as God had said, "A fugitive and a vagabond shalt thou be in the earth!"[33]

[32]*Ibid.*, 7:7
[33]*Ibid.*, 5:37

CHAPTER FOURTEEN

The Patriarchal Line Becomes Established

The tragedy of Abel's death was accentuated in the minds of Adam and Eve by several circumstances which would not have been present in the death of any of their other children. What were these circumstances?

Up to this time would you say that the efforts of Adam and Eve to raise up an honorable posterity had been practically a complete failure?

The birth of their next child marked the beginning of the happy and abundant life for Adam and Eve. What was the child's name?

How old was Adam when this heir to the Priesthood was born?

As this boy reached maturity what was there about his appearance that gave Adam cause for astonishment?

What kind of education did Seth receive? Could he write? What language did he speak? Did he write any books? Were his sermons recorded?

How old was Seth when he received the Priesthood? Is there a hint as to why Adam became reluctant to ordain his descendants until they had proved themselves valiant beyond any shadow of doubt?

Is it true that every person living on the face of the earth today is a descendant of Seth? What age did he attain?

Only one of Seth's sons is named in history although he had many children. Why are the others not named?

Does it appear that Enos was the oldset son of Seth? How old was Seth when Enos was born? When did Enos receive the Priesthood?

During the ministry of Enos the whole body of the Church moved to a "promised land." Who led the people there? What was the new land called? What appears to have happened to Adam and Seth at the time of this move?

When the Church wanted to meet with Adam three years before his death where did the meeting take place? Is this significant?

How old was Enos when he died?

News of Abel's Death Comes to Adam-ondi-Ahman

Having pursued the experiences of Cain and the immediate developments following Abel's death, let us now return to conditions at Adam-ondi-Ahman where the stark reality of this first murder left a burden of grief and sorrow such as few parents have ever been required to bear.

The slaying of Abel probably occurred out among the fields and pasture lands located on the plains of Olaha Shinehah. These plains surrounded the homestead of the first parents.[1] Abel, as a keeper of sheep and cattle, would probably be away from home on frequent occasions and it may have been quite some time before the first parents became alarmed at Abel's absence. When Adam first went looking for the boy he probably conjured up in his mind all of the things which most parents begin to imagine when a member of the family fails to return at the expected time. Was he ill and unable to return? He could have been hurt. Perhaps he had been attacked by wild beasts, or the more difficult animals in his own flocks might have given him trouble.

But no matter what Father Adam may have imagined in those long frantic hours of fruitless searching, nothing could have prepared him for the impact of the shock which must have struck his heart when he finally found his son. As he tenderly lifted the crumpled, blood-

---

[1]D. & C. 117:8

stained body from the hiding place where Cain had flung
him, Adam probably felt a passion of emotion sweep
through him that brought a cry of anguish to his lips and
sent a flood of tears coursing down his cheeks.

Few fathers have had to walk through the shadows
of this particularly dark valley of death and discover in
it the broken body of a dead son killed by the brutal and
violent hands of his own brother.

It was a never-to-be-forgotten moment in the life of
the first patriarch of the race. He probably gazed intently upon the scene for a long time as he painfully visual-
ized in his mind what had happened. Adam's next
problem was the task of breaking the news to Mother
Eve. How could he bring himself to tell her? What
could he say? As he carried the quiet, lifeless form of
their favorite son back to the family home where the
boy's mother waited in such anxiety, what words could
he use to soften the blow?

It must have been a deeply poignant moment when
that meeting took place.

And the heavens themselves must have wept a short
time later as these two parents stood lonely and broken-
hearted at the brink of an open grave and consigned the
mortal remains of their best-beloved son to the enveloping
embrace of the silent earth. For Adam and Eve it was
as though the work of a lifetime had been suddenly swept
away.

Into that grave went not only the body of youthful
Abel but all of the hopes, dreams and plans of his grief-
stricken parents. He was the heir to all they possessed,
not only the heir to their worldly goods so frugally gar-
nered but their heir to the Priesthood, the gospel plan
and a whole new cultural pattern of righteous living.
He would have been the future presiding high priest
over the kingdom of God on earth!

In the lonely years that followed it would have been
only human and natural for Father Adam to have sometimes found it necessary to restrain his instinctive inclinations to go forth and revenge the inexcusable slaying

of this boy. Adam, however, kept his feelings in abeyance. He not only had the strength of his own self-discipline to carry him past the crisis of this temptation but perhaps he also had the reassurance of a direct revelation which verified what the Lord had previously declared to Cain—that the life of that Master Mahan and the punishment for his murderous act were to be left to the judgments of God.

Prior to this time Adam and Eve had experienced what they must have believed were the deepest fathoms in the labyrinth of sorrows. But now they had felt the overwhelming blackness of the deepest sorrow of all. It must have taken years to smooth the cutting edges of the dark memories which sometimes came darting back into their minds to torture them with thoughts of righteous Abel and all that his loss had meant to them.

The Birth of Seth

Although the first parents did not know it, they had now navigated the most narrow and turbulent rapids in the stream of life which the Lord had expected them to follow. Through their hardships and sorrows God's purposes had been accomplished according to plan. Now he was able to reward them partially for their integrity and faithfulness. Golden years of happiness were looming up at last on the horizon.

But at this particular stage of their lives it would have been very easy for the first parents to have concluded that there was nothing but heartache in rearing a family and that they should therefore decline to have any more children. Already they had raised a great many children and not a single one of them had matured into a man or woman of whom they could be proud; none, that is, except Abel, and now he was dead.

Like multitudes of parents who would live after them, they could have easily decided to shed any future worries or responsibilities and devote the rest of their lives to the acquisition of personal comforts and the exploitations of personal satisfactions.

But if Adam and Eve had followed this course of conduct they would have cut themselves off from a marvelous blessing.   They did not know it, but the Lord was now ready to give them a brilliant and righteous spirit who would be a source of comfort and joy to them forever.   Because they had the faith to have another son they received the blessing.   The beginning of happy and abundant living for Adam and Eve commenced with the birth of Seth.

Adam was 130 years old when this baby boy was born.[2]   As the Lord knew it would, his coming inspired new hopes and new plans in the minds of his parents. During his early childhood the tutoring of Seth was supervised with the greatest care.   He was taught the same science of righteous living that Abel had been given and as the years passed by Adam and Eve saw him grow in strength and stature and saw him increasing the powers of his mind and spirit.   Finally, when Seth began to reach maturity, Adam noted with astonishment that his own youthful appearance of a century before was mirrored in the figure and countenance of this lad.   There was great pleasure in this wonderful son, for he was as righteous as Abel and, at the same time, so closely resembled his father that he appeared to have been made in the very image of Adam.[3]

This remarkable fact is referred to by the Lord in a modern revelation wherein He says that "Seth was a perfect man, and his likeness was the express likeness of his father . . . and could not be distinguished from him only by his age."[4]

SETH IS ORDAINED TO THE PRIESTHOOD

During his training period, one of the most important things which Seth had to acquire was the ability to read and write in the fluent and expressive language of Adam.[5] He also learned how to keep the historical records or

[2]Moses 6:10
[3]*Ibid.*
[4]D. & C. 107:43
[5]Moses 6:5-6

books of remembrance which God had commanded that they should maintain from generation to generation.[6]

It is interesting to observe that Father Adam apparently became most conservative in ordaining any of his descendants to the Priesthood after his soul-searing experience with Cain. The fact that a son should commence his life in righteousness was not enough. There had to be time for testing. Only after a man had proved himself faithful and valiant throughout the course of many tribulations did Father Adam seem to feel justified in favoring him with the keys, powers and blessings of divine authority. Even with righteous Seth, Adam waited until this favored son had reached the age of sixty-nine before he ordained him to the holy order of the Priesthood. Never again, except in the case of Enoch—who was chosen by the Lord through direct revelation while he was still very young—did Adam give the Priesthood to any of his heirs until they had reached a very substantial age. One of his heirs was not ordained until he was 200 years old, and another was not ordained until he was 496![7]

Seth appears to have been highly favored by the Lord throughout his long life. "God revealed himself unto Seth," the scripture states, and he "offered an acceptable sacrifice like unto his brother Abel."[8] In fact, his approval by the Lord was so pronounced that the scriptures say "Adam glorified the name of God; for he said: God hath appointed me another seed, instead of Abel, whom Cain slew."[9]

Altogether Seth lived a total of nine hundred and twelve years,[10] and during his long ministry he saw the Church of God become a great organized power for good among the children of men. He also witnessed the growth of licentious abominations among the wicked but rejoiced in the number of men and women who responded to his preaching and expressed a desire to forsake all evil

[6]D. & C. 107:43
[7]*Ibid.,* 107:46
[8]Moses 6:3
[9]*Ibid.,* 6:2
[10]*Ibid.,* 6:16

and enter the waters of baptism so as to become citizens
in the kingdom of God. Seth prophesied and preached
repentance over 840 years. As a result, many who would
have otherwise grown up in wickedness caught the vision
of faith which his daily conduct and sermons portrayed.[11]

Gradually, as the work progressed, Seth was joined
by other righteous Priesthood bearers. He lived to see
the building of the City of Enoch but died just ten years
before that singular community of righteousness was
translated.

Seth's sermons and inspired writings were included
in the holy scriptures of that day. In the not too distant
future all these will be restored and modern men will be
able to read them.[12]

Three years before the death of Adam—when Seth
was 797 years old—he received a patriarchal blessing at
the hands of his aged and illustrious father.[13] At that
time the Lord promised Seth through the voice of Adam
that Seth's posterity would be preserved unto the end
of the earth.[14] He was further promised that among his
descendants would be the chosen vessels of the Lord
who would perpetuate the Priesthood.[15] Today, every
human being upon the face of the earth carries in his veins
the blood of righteous Seth and the direct patriarchal
descendants of this great man have constituted the principal prophets in every dispensation.

BIOGRAPHICAL SUMMARY OF THE LIFE OF SETH

Before leaving Seth, let us catalogue the highlights of
his life. He was born approximately 3,870 B.C. when
Adam was 130 years old.[16] He was in the exact image
of his father[17] and could only be distinguished from
Adam by his age.[18] He was ordained to the Priesthood

[11]Moses 6:23
[12]2 Nephi 31:16-18
[13]D. & C. 107:42
[14]Ibid., 107:42
[15]Ibid.
[16]Moses 6:10
[17]Ibid.
[18]D. & C. 107:43

by Adam when he was 69[19] and enjoyed revelations direct from God.[20]   He prophesied and preached repentance throughout his life.[21]   He received his patriarchal blessing when he was 797 which was three years before Adam's death and was promised that his seed would remain in the earth forever.[22]   He was a scholar in the reading and writing of Adam's language[23] and helped in maintaining the sacred scriptures of the patriarchs.[24] He had a numerous posterity and died in 2,958 B.C. after attaining the remarkable age of 912![25]

Seth Chooses Enos As His Patriarchal Heir

According to holy writ Seth raised up a numerous posterity of "many sons and daughters,"[26] but only one of his sons is named in the scriptures.   This is because the records which we now have were originally written as a *history of the patriarchs* and those who were responsible for these books deliberately refrained from cluttering up the space with the names of any persons not directly connected with the patriarchal descent of the Priesthood.   It is for this reason that the only son of Seth named in the scripture is "Enos."

It would appear that Enos accompanied his father, Seth, throughout his long ministry and during this long association the scripture says that Seth "taught his son Enos in the ways of God."[27]

It is very unlikely, however, that Enos was the oldest son of Seth.   This becomes apparent when it is discovered that Enos was not born until Seth was 105 years old.[28]   Available evidence indicates that by the time Adam and Eve were that old they had become great-grandparents.   We know that they had two generations

---

[19]*Ibid.*, 107:42
[20]Moses 6:2
[21]*Ibid.*, 6:23
[22]D. & C. 107:42
[23]Moses 6:5-6
[24]D. & C. 107:43
[25]Moses 6:16
[26]*Ibid.*, 6:11
[27]*Ibid.*, 6:13
[28]*Ibid.*, 6:13

of descendants before Cain and Abel,[29] and by the time
Cain and Abel had matured there would have been time
for a third generation—which would have made Adam
and Eve great-grandparents. We know all of this transpired before Adam was 130.[30] This gives us a reliable
standard of family growth during those early times and
applying this standard to Enos we can see that if he were
born when his father was 105, he was in all probability a
younger son.

Of course, it may be argued that perhaps his father,
Seth, did not marry until after he had passed one hundred, but this is extremely unlikely when it is realized
that marriage at an early age for the purpose of "raising
up seed unto the Lord" was a fundamental tenet of the
gospel, and Seth would have been encouraged by Adam
and Eve to take this step early in life.[31]

The fact that a patriarchal heir did not have to be the
oldest son or "legal heir" is very significant. It shows
that just as Father Jacob would later reach down and
give his first blessing or the patriarchal rights of the
Priesthood to his *eleventh* son, Joseph,[32] so also Seth felt
at liberty to choose Enos from among many of his older
brethren. Seniority was not the controlling criterion in
selecting a patriarchal heir. It was worthiness. A patriarch therefore chose his oldest *worthy* son to perpetuate
the patriarchal Priesthood.

THE MINISTRY OF ENOS

But even after Enos had been preferred above his
brethren and was being trained for his calling, Seth still
refrained for many years from openly naming him his
heir. In fact, Seth trained Enos for 134 years before he
finally took him to Father Adam to receive the Priesthood![33] However, this careful training paid marvelous
dividends. In later years Enos gained equal standing

29*Ibid.*, 5:3
30*Ibid.*, 6:10
31*Ibid.*, 2:28; 3:24
32Genesis 49:26
33D. & C. 107:44

with his father as a prophet of the Lord.[34] He united his prayers with Seth and received revelations from the Lord which were incorporated in the book of remembrance—the scripture maintained by Adam and his sons.[35]

Enos was learned in the language of Adam so that he could read and write this marvelous medium of expression which the scripture says was "pure and undefiled."[36] He used this same perfect language while preaching "and spake and prophesied and called upon all men everywhere to repent."[37]

PEOPLE OF GOD SETTLE IN A LAND OF PROMISE CALLED "CAINAN"

It was during the ministry of Enos that adverse social conditions became extremely acute. The human family had been upon the earth for several hundred years and had multiplied to the point where they were "numerous upon all the face of the land."[38] This congested population was extremely unsatisfactory to the patriarchs because "in those days Satan had great dominion among men, and raged in their hearts; and from thenceforth came wars and bloodshed; and a man's hand was against his own brother, in administering death, because of secret works, seeking for power."[39]

It therefore became desirable to move the principal body of the Saints of that dispensation to a new location where their children would be less likely to be ensnared or contaminated by the cancer of greed and murder which was capturing the hearts of men. We learn that the land where the Saints had been maintaining their headquarters was called "Shulon"[40]—which was probably very near to Adam-ondi-Ahman. The scripture then says that "Enos and the residue of the people of God came out from the land, which was called Shulon, and dwelt

---

[34]Moses 6:13
[35]*Ibid.*, 6:3-5; 46
[36]*Ibid.*, 6:6; See *Way to Perfection*, pp. 60-76
[37]Moses 6:23
[38]*Ibid.*, 6:15
[39]*Ibid.*, 6:15
[40]*Ibid.*, 6:17

in a land of promise, which he called after his own son, whom he had named Cainan."[41]

It is significant that this new land should be called a "land of promise." In the scripture this phrase has always referred to a territory which has been discovered or settled through the divine guidance of the Lord.[42]

It is also desirable to note here that this land of Cainan was named after the son of Enos and was not related in any way to Cain as the name might seem to imply. In a later chapter we shall see that the people of Cain settled in the land of *Canaan*. Great confusion may result from a study of certain parts of the scripture unless the distinction between "Cainan" and "Canaan" is constantly kept in mind.

It should also be remembered that the geographical locations of the lands we are now discussing were located in some portions of the Western Hemisphere. After the Flood these same names were given to lands on the Eastern Hemisphere.

When the body of the Church moved from Shulon to Cainan, Adam and Seth apparently did not go with them. They may have remained behind to continue their missions. If Adam and Seth had been with Enos when this important move was made the scripture would surely have mentioned their names instead of simply saying "Enos and the residue of the people of God. . . ." It is apparent from this that while Adam and Seth still retained their patriarchal presidency over Enos, they nevertheless allowed this young man to take over the general administrative leadership of the "people of God" in order to move them to a new location.

Adam and Seth no doubt maintained frequent communication with these people but personal association must have been rare because the son of Enos (whose name was Cainan) is described as meeting Adam while he was on a journey to Shedolamak. The fact that this meeting between Cainan and Adam is carefully mentioned in scripture would lead one to conclude that it was

[41]*Ibid.*, 6:17
[42]1 Nephi 2:20; Deut. 27:3

an historic highlight. Certainly it would not be singled out for reference if Adam were living in the same place as Cainan and had occasion to meet Cainan often.

We also know that when the members of the Church wanted to receive their last blessing from Adam just before his death they went back to Adam-ondi-Ahman.[43] All these known facts seem to point to the conclusion that Adam (and probably Seth) remained in the vicinity of the original homestead and did not move to Cainan when Enos did. They may have desired to remain close to the original centers of population where the more wicked segments of society needed their dynamic message of repentance.

BIOGRAPHICAL SUMMARY OF THE LIFE OF ENOS

The above includes practically all of the known biographical data concerning Enos. Let us summarize it for future reference. Enos was born 3,765 B.C. when his father, Seth, was 105 years old[44] and his grandfather, Adam, was 235. Enos was taught "in the ways of God" by his father and was ordained to the Priesthood by Adam when he was 134 years old.[45] He became a prophet of renown and traveled extensively calling upon men everywhere to repent. He was a scholar of the Adamic tongue and assisted in writing the book of remembrance.[46] He supervised the migration of the members of the Church to a new location which he named after his son, Cainan.[47] The ministry of Enos was carried on during a period of extreme wickedness among the general population.[48] He raised up a family of "many sons and daughters" and died in 2,860 B.C. after having lived a long and profitable life of 905 years duration.

---

[43]D. & C. 107:53
[44]Mises 6:13
[45]D. & C. 107:44
[46]Moses 6:5
[47]*Ibid.*, 6:17
[48]*Ibid.*, 6:15

CHAPTER FIFTEEN

Problems of Longevity, Population, Growth and Geography

Do the scriptures indicate that the ancient patriarchs had sufficient knowledge to set up a scientific calendar?

Has the Lord verified the long lives of the ancient patriarchs in any of His modern revelations?

Was there ever a time in history when the long lives of patriarchs from the pre-flood period could be compared with the shorter lives of the patriarchs who lived after the Flood? In other words, was there ever a time when both groups overlapped and lived together at the same time so their longevity could be compared?

Do you think there has been a tendency to overlook the population pressure which probably expanded civilization very rapidly during the pre-flood period? The scripture says that during the life of Enos the population had increased until "the children of men were numerous upon all the face of the land." (Moses 6:15) Do you think this could have been literally true?

The scripture indicates that the fertility of parents was up to twenty-four times longer than it is today. Do you think it is unreasonable to assume that the average family during that period was ten children (who reached maturity and married)? Do you think a population of a billion or more would push its frontiers around the entire earth during the 1,656 years which preceded the Flood?

What unusual condition characterized the geography of the earth during the pre-flood period? Was there a Pacific Ocean? Do we have any indication that there might have been a great sea where the Atlantic Ocean now is?

Might this knowledge be of some assistance in evaluating the discoveries of artifacts belonging to primitive peoples who appear to have lived in Europe, Africa and some part of Asia prior to the Flood?

Since we know that the Western Hemisphere saw the beginning of civilization in the pre-flood period is it possible that these faraway places in Africa and Eurasia only saw the vestigial endings of civilization during this period?

DID THE PATRIARCHS REALLY LIVE SO LONG?

Few statements contained in the scripture have taxed the credulity of the average student quite as much as the alleged length of life attributed to the antediluvian patriarchs; for example, the nine patriarchs from Adam to Noah (Enoch is not included because he was translated) lived an average of 912 years!

Some will say that perhaps the length of the year was different in those days and that this may account for the apparent longevity of these people. However, the year has always been a four-seasoned phenomenon of nature which repeats the same cycle with clocklike regularity. And while the particular season or date which fixed the beginning of the new year has been changed a great many times in history the length of the calendar year has always been substantially the same.

Furthermore, we now know that the ancient patriarchs had scientific knowledge available which would have permitted them to set up their calendars as accurately as we do in modern times. Through the writings of Abraham we learn that "the fathers" received revelations direct from God on the wonders of astronomy and were therefore well acquainted with the relationship of the "planets and the stars."[1] Abraham describes the details of a revelation which he himself received similar to those received by the patriarchs of old, and he points out that

---
[1]Abraham 1:31

he was told the "set time of reckoning" for the earth, the moon and the sun.[2] Obviously, this is all the patriarchs would have needed to set up the most accurate type of calendar.

That this is precisely what they did may be gathered from their own scriptural history wherein it is recorded that before the flood the patriarchs had divided the year into months and had established a system for the recording of all important historical events in terms of an annual calendar.[3] In fact, it would have been impossible for them to have properly maintained the book of remembrance and the genealogies of the patriarchal line (showing dates of birth and death, total length of each life, etc.) without having a scientific method of fixing dates and measuring time. A careful reading of Genesis, chapters seven and eight, will reveal that the year was divided into twelve months and while the beginning of the year is said to have been fixed by the autumnal equinox,[4] nevertheless, the total length of the year was calculated the same as it is now.

This is further borne out by the Lord's disclosure to His prophets that the history of the race has been divided into seven periods of a thousand years each.[5] When the genealogies are added up for the antediluvian period they do not account for the requisite number of years unless full credence is given to the precise number of years attributed to each of the patriarchs by the scriptures.

The literal longevity of the early patriarchs may be further demonstrated by the fact that the long lives of Noah, Shem, Ham and Japheth (who lived both before the Flood and after the Flood) were chronicled by the historians of that day, side by side with the shorter lives of the postdiluvian patriarchs. In fact, after the Flood, Noah is said to have outlived nine generations of his descendants, and Genesis clearly records how the degree of longevity was gradually shortened after the Flood

---

[2]*Ibid.,* 3:6
[3]Genesis 7:11
[4]Josephus, *Ant. of the Jews,* Book I, 3:3 and note
[5]D. & C. 77:6-7; 88:108-110

from generation to generation.⁶ The contemporary historians of the period who knew Noah and his sons as well as the post-Flood patriarchs, would certainly have used the same year-measurement for the long-lived Noah as they were using for the shorter-lived prophets of their own generation.

The famous Jewish historian, Josephus, warns his readers not to misinterpret the discrepancy which appears to exist between the span of life before the Flood and the span of life after the Flood. Said he: "Let no one, upon comparing the lives of the ancients with our lives, and with the few years which we now live, think that what we have said of them is false; or make the shortness of our lives at present an argument that neither did they attain to so long a duration of life; for those ancients were beloved of God . . . and because their food was then fitter for the promulgation of life . . . and besides, God afforded them a longer time of life on account of their virtue and the good use they made of it in astronomical and geometrical discoveries. . . . Now I have for witnesses to what I have said, all those that have written Antiquities . . . that the Ancients lived a thousand years."⁷

But, as with all things which we have not personally experienced, the unusual length of the life-span during these early generations is indeed difficult for modern man to comprehend. Consider, for example, the fact that the missionary work of Enos extended over 750 years. If he had begun his mission when the Magna Charta was signed he would just be finishing his mission now. Or, to illustrate it another way, if Enos had been born in 972 A.D.—almost a century before the Normans invaded the British Isles—he would have died the same year Brigham Young did—1877!

THE POPULATION BEFORE THE FLOOD

With men and women living for so many years it can be quickly appreciated how rapidly the land would have filled up with human beings. In fact, during the lifetime

⁶Genesis 11:10-28

⁷Josephus, *op. cit.,* Book I, 3:9, (*Op. cit.* indicates the title of the book has appeared previously.)

of Enos the scripture says that the population had increased until "the children of men were numerous *upon
all the face of the land.*"[8]

Based upon our previous observations concerning the
family of Adam and Eve it can be seen that a new generation of children was added to the population about
every 35-50 years just as it is today. However, the remarkable difference between population rates in those
days as compared to the present time is found in the fact
that today the reproduction period for the average parents is completed in about twenty years. In the antediluvian period it is known to have been at least *twenty-
four times that long!* The scripture refers to parents who
were capable of bearing children for as long as 500
years.[9]

Undoubtedly population rates were reduced to a certain extent by the same factors which militate against
population growth today—factors such as infant mortality, disease, wars, accidents and so forth. Nevertheless, when it is considered that those who survived lived
ten to twelve times longer than we do and when we consider that very large families appear to have been the
rule rather than the exception, it can be appreciated how
the population potential could have risen much faster
than it would under modern conditions.

For example, let us take the above factors into consideration and roughly estimate the increase in population
during a period of 650 years. Let us assume that Adam
and Eve had ten sets of parents descend from them.
From the scripture it would appear that they had many
more but for the purpose of this illustration let us assume
that their surviving children combined to make ten
couples. If each of these couples had ten children who
survived and married and they in turn had ten children
per couple, here is what would have happened in 650
years:

8Moses 6:15
9Genesis 5:32

Number of Years	*Population Growth*
50 years	If, during the first fifty years, Adam and Eve had ten sets of parents descend from them, and each of these couples had ten surviving children during the following fifty years it would make:
100 years	100 surviving children. If these combined to make 50 couples and each couple had a family of ten during the next fifty years it would make:
150 years	500 surviving children. If these combined to make 250 couples and each couple had a family of ten during the next fifty years it would make:
200 years	2,500 surviving children. If these combined to make 1,250 couples and each couple had a family of ten during the next fifty years it would make:
250 years	12,500 surviving children. If these combined to make 6,250 couples and each couple had a family of ten during the next fifty years it would make:
300 years	62,500 surviving children. If these combined to make 31,250 couples and each couple had a family of ten during the next fifty years it would make:
350 years	312,500 surviving children. If these combined to make 156,250 couples and each couple had a family of ten during the next fifty years it would make:
400 years	1,562,500 surviving children. If these combined to 781,250 couples and each couple had a family of ten during the next fifty fifty years it would make:
450 years	7,812,500 surviving children. If these combined to make 3,906,250 couples and each couple had a family of ten during the next fifty years it would make:

500 years	39,062,500 surviving children. If these combined to make 19,531,250 couples and each couple had a family of ten during the next fifty years it would make:
550 years	195,312,500 surviving children. If these combined to make 97,656,250 couples and each couple had a family of ten during the next fifty years it would make:
600 years	976,562,500 surviving children. If these combined to make 488,281,250 couples and each couple had a family of ten during the next fifty years it would make:
650 years	4,882,812,500 surviving children.

By this time Enos would be in the midst of his ministry and already the population of this last generation would be nearing five billion—more than twice the population of the earth today. And this figure of nearly five billion does not represent the total population but only the number of offspring in the last generation. Because nearly all of the ancestors of these 4,882,812,500 children would still be alive, they must be added together to compute the total population. This would make 6,103,515,-610!

It should be emphasized that this tabulation does not pretend to be an estimate of the actual number of people living on the earth during this period because we have no accurate way of knowing, but it is designed to demonstrate how rapidly the population *could* have increased in a short period of time and literally fulfilled the scriptural statement that the people covered "all the face of the land."

Such a population or even a substantial percentage of such a population would have rapidly extended the boundaries of civilization in every possible direction. In the past we have probably underestimated the population pressure which undoubtedly pushed the pioneers of the antediluvian period far from the original cradle of the race at Adam-ondi-Ahman. The vast majority of these have left no record of history for us to study.

The sacred history which the Lord commanded His prophets to write only concerns itself with the nations and peoples directly related to the lives and ministries of the great patriarchs. It does not pretend to represent the history of all the nations which finally came into existence during this period. Just as the Bible makes no mention of the Chinese, the Jaredites and many other large population groups which existed contemporaneously with the Hebrews, so also the scripture we are now studying may have completely ignored large segments of humanity which gradually isolated themselves over a period of several centuries in the nethermost corners of the earth.

The Geography of the Earth before the Flood

This expansion of the population would have been facilitated by the fact that the land was not divided into islands and continents during this early period but was "one land." In fact, the "division" which separated America from the rest of Eurasia did not take place until the days of Peleg which was several generations *after* the Flood.[10]

However, this does not necessarily mean that the land formed a complete band around the earth. In fact, it appears from the writings of Enoch that there was always a channel of sea in the region of our present Atlantic Ocean which probably connected the Arctic and Antarctic Oceans together. Enoch refers to this as the "Sea East,"[11] and during his lifetime a great peninsula of land "came up out of the depths of the sea"[12] and many people went out upon it. This would indicate a very large body of water for the "Sea East" and since the patriarchs are known to have had their civilization in the central and eastern part of the United States, a body of water which they describe as being a Sea *East* would place it in the approximate location of the Atlantic Ocean.

This being the case, the global continent or "one land" would have extended west from the American con-

---

[10]Genesis 10:25
[11]Moses 6:42
[12]*Ibid.,* 7:14

tinent and encircled the earth to the Atlantic coast of
Europe. This would mean that during this early period
there was no Pacific Ocean to "divide" the land with
thousands of miles of salt water waste. In the patriarchal
period apparently this was all arable land which was high
enough to be above sea level. The scriptures clearly
infer that the great cataclysm which isolated the western hemisphere by dividing the land, was actually caused
by the sea sweeping down from the north to inundate the
sinking terrain which now lies at the bottom of the Pacific
Ocean.

Just before the millennium when the land will become united into a single continent again "like as it was
in the days before it was divided" we are told that these
waters will be forced back again "into the north countries,
and the islands shall become one land."[13] The manner
in which the continents and islands are to become "one
land" by forcing back the seas seems to identify the manner in which they were divided in the first place.

It is from all of these various scriptures that we conclude that originally the great continent of "one land"
almost completely encircled the earth—a circle possibly
broken only by the "Sea East." This would make the
present territory which we call the United States, the
eastern end of this global continent and Europe and
Africa the western end. Perhaps this explains why the
Lord described the location of the Garden of Eden
(which we know was located in America) as "eastward."[14]

And since this land "eastward" was the cradle of the
race, the current of migration would have been toward
the west. Population pressure and exploratory adventure probably pushed the tide of humanity farther and
farther west until eventually they crossed the vast territory presently covered by the Pacific Ocean and reached
the borders of what is now the Orient. In later centuries
they probably struggled to the western borders of the

[13]D. & C. 133:23
[14]Cowley, M. F., *Wilford Woodruff*, p. 481; Moses 3:8

continents which are the Europe and Africa of our own day.

Scientific diggings have disclosed the crude artifacts of some very early primitive peoples who seem to have lived in rather large numbers throughout Eurasia prior to the arrival of mankind in these regions after the Flood. It would be reasonable to assume that if these people did live in this area before the Flood and were the isolated descendants of those who had migrated over a period of centuries from the refinements and civilization of the land "eastward," then in all probability they would have degenerated into a stone-age type of civilization much as the Lamanites after the Nephite civilization was destroyed.

When all of the facts are known, we may learn that the crude implements which we find deposited here and there throughout Eurasia were made by groups of isolated humanity who, during a period of more than 1,500 years, wandered thousands of miles from their original ancestral home and degenerated into primitive tribal societies throughout these regions. Archaeological students who have stumbled upon the caves and other protected areas where these people lived have assumed that these were the beginnings of man's civilization, when, as a matter of fact, we see from the scripture we are presently studying that these may have been the *vestigial endings of civilization!*

CHAPTER SIXTEEN

From Cainan to Enoch

During the early youth of Cainan what social conditions were conducive to delinquency and crime?

Why did the Mahanite murder cult have secret signs and passwords? What advantages were supposed to accrue to people who joined the cult? Do we have anything like it in modern times?

What special recognition came to Cainan to perpetuate his name throughout the pre-flood period? How old was he when he received the Priesthood? What unusual event occurred while he was "journeying to the place Shedolamak"? (D. & C. 107:45)

How old was Cainan when Mahalaleel was born? Do you think there must have been some special reason why Mahalaleel was not ordained to the Priesthood until he was 496? How old was Mahalaleel when he died?

When Mahalaleel was 65 he had a son born to him who was named "Jared." What is the significance of this name? What is the one outstanding thing for which Jared is remembered in ancient scripture? Who received the Priesthood first, Jared or his patriarchal heir?

How old was Jared when Enoch was born? Where was Enoch born? What tribute does Enoch pay to his father?

Enoch suffered from a physical defect in his youth. What was it? Did it cause him to feel embarrassed and inferior?

Enoch had left his own country and was on a journey at the time of his first heavenly manifestation. What geographical landmark was he near?

In this revelation why did the Lord say He was angry with the children of men? Why was Enoch shocked by his divine calling? What did he say to the Lord? What did the Lord promise Enoch if he would fulfil his duty?

Why do you think the Lord showed Enoch "the spirit world" at this particular time? Did the knowledge which he received through this revelation give him prestige and authority as he went forth to preach? Do you think his youth was an advantage or disadvantage in fulfilling his mission?

The Rise of an Evil Generation

Now let us return to the history of the patriarchs. In chapter fourteen we had just completed the life of Enos. Next we will consider the biography of his son whose name was Cainan.

Cainan was born in 3,675 B.C. when his father, Enos, was ninety years of age.[1] It was during the early lifetime of Cainan that Satan succeeded in winning a great social conquest among the children of men. Political assassinations, rapine, robbery and fraud spread across the face of the land. The Satan-worshiping Mahanites plagued the more thrifty and industrious citizenry with extortion and bloodshed wherever they had organized contingents of their murder cult. Feuding, reprisal and corruption of government must have followed, for the scripture says that during this terrible period "a man's hand was against his own brother, in administering death, because of secret works, seeking for power."[2] In fact, the contagion of this sordid spirit of suspicion and aggression finally spawned into open warfare among the people. "Satan had great dominion among men, and raged in their hearts; and from thenceforth came wars and bloodshed."[3]

A more detailed description of the Mahan murder cult is furnished us by the Prophet Helaman who had a

---

[1]Moses 6:17
[2]*Ibid.*, 6:15
[3]*Ibid.*

similar secret society to contend with in his day. He
said many of the people "did unite with those bands of
robbers, and did enter into their covenants and their oaths,
that they would protect and preserve one another in
whatsoever difficult circumstances they should be placed,
that they should not suffer for their murders, and their
plunderings, and their stealings. And it came to pass that
they did have their signs, yea, their secret signs, and their
secret words; and this that they might distinguish a
brother who had entered into the covenant, that whatsoever wickedness his brother should do he should not be in-
jured by his brother, nor by those who did belong to his
band, who had taken this covenant. And thus they might
murder, and plunder, and steal and commit whoredoms
and all manner of wickedness, contrary to the laws of
their country and also the laws of their God."[4]

Cainan was therefore raised to maturity in a day
when evil men stalked the earth. Few parents have the
privilege of raising their children in an "ideal" environment, but on the other hand, some parents have had
particularly bitter elements to combat in order to save
their children from the influences of their time. Such
was the case with Mormon, for example, who raised
Moroni during the pitched campaigns of a sixty-year
race war. Such was the case with the parents of Daniel.
the parents of Moses, the parents of David. And it was
also true of Cainan. Enos, his father, must have watched
over him anxiously as he approached adulthood and his
personal habits and philosophy of life began to take final
form.

But Cainan was a choice spirit and responded to his
training. He even received revelations from the Lord
before he was ordained to the Priesthood. The scripture
says that it was in the fortieth year of his life that "God
called upon Cainan in the wilderness."[5] This was a great
honor and it may have influenced Enos in selecting
Cainan for his heir. Enos himself had received the
Priesthood only four years previously and undoubtedly

---

[4] Helaman 6:21-23
[5] D. & C. 107:45

he was studying his sons for the purpose of selecting a worthy candidate to carry on the Priesthood powers in the following generation.

For reasons which we have previously mentioned, a son born to Enos when he was ninety years of age would not, in all probability, be his eldest son. Outstanding worthiness would have been required of Cainan to give him preference over his older brothers. The quality of his life may be properly judged by the fact that he was selected by Enos from among "many sons"[6] to receive the sacred keys of patriarchal authority.

It was in the early days of Cainan that the great migration of the Church to the new "promised land" appears to have taken place. As we have previously seen, his father, Enos, was assigned the responsibility of directing this mass movement of the "people of God" from the land of Shulon near Adam-ondi-Ahman to a new territory, and when the people had settled in it, Enos named it in honor of Cainan.[7] This shows that the move took place after Cainan was sufficiently mature to be recognized as the prospective heir of Enos—possibly sometime after he received his revelation from the Lord at the age of forty.

It would appear further that Cainan's ordination to the Priesthood many years later had to wait until there was an opportunity to receive it from Father Adam. It was the custom in those days to have the oldest surviving patriarch ordain each new heir to the Priesthood. But as was indicated in a previous chapter Adam and Seth apparently did not go to the new land of promise with Enos and the rest of the Saints, therefore modern revelation makes special mention of the important event in Cainan's life when "he met Adam in journeying to the place Shedolamak."[8]

In the very next sentence it says that Cainan was ordained to the Priesthood and that he was eighty-seven years of age when it was conferred upon him. From this we assume that he was ordained by Adam and

[6]Moses 6:18
[7]*Ibid.,* 6:17
[8]D. & C. 107:45

that it was the singular coincidence of this unexpected meeting between Adam and Cainan which permitted the ordination to take place at that time.

Cainan lived a long and profitable life. He was trained in the reading and writing of the Adamic tongue[9] and his inspired sermons and revelations were included in the book of remembrance.[10] He lived a total of 910 years and during that time raised up a large family.[11] He died 2,765 B.C. which was 248 years after the City of Enoch had been translated and 423 years before the commencement of the Great Flood.

Biographical Summary of the Life of Mahalaleel

It was 3,605 B.C. when Cainan was seventy years of age that a son was born to him whom he named Mahalaleel.[12] This name is said to have meant "praiser of God."[13]

Mahalaleel was probably born and raised in the land of Cainan shortly after the people of God settled in that new location.

One of the strange facts connected with Mahalaleel's life was the unusually long period of time which elapsed before Father Adam ordained him to the Priesthood. When it did occur it was such a significant event that the scriptures fix it in chronological history to the very day: "Mahalaleel was four hundred and ninety-six years and *seven days* when he was ordained by the hand of Adam."[14] Why his ordination was postponed until he was 496 we are not told, but it is obvious that it was for some substantial reason and not merely an accident. This becomes particularly apparent when it is realized that Mahalaleel did not receive the Priesthood until 231 years after his son Jared, 244 years after his grandson Enoch and 104 years after his great-grandson Methuselah.

[9]Moses 6:6
[10]*Ibid.,* 6:5
[11]*Ibid.,* 6:19
[12]*Ibid.,* 6:19
[20]Peloubet, *op. cit.,* under "Mahalaleel"
[14]D. & C. 107:46

At the time Mahalaleel received this ordination, Adam was a very old man, in fact, it occurred just thirty-nine years before Adam's death. Adam therefore took occasion not only to confer the Priesthood upon Mahalaleel but also to give him his patriarchal blessing at the same time.[15] This blessing, like all others of its kind, was to encourage Mahalaleel to carry out his important mission in life.

Mahalaleel outlived Adam by 360 years and died in 2,710 B.C.[16] The scripture says he "begat sons and daughters. And all the days of Mahalaleel were eight hundred and ninety-five years, and he died."[17]

Biographical Summary of the Life of Jared

Now we come to the life of a man who became famous because he was the father of a remarkable son. Who will say, however, which is the greater role—to thrust one's self upon the pages of history or to dedicate one's life to the molding of a child who finds a place in history. This man chose the latter course. His name was Jared, and his famous son was Enoch.

Jared was born in 3,540 B.C. when his own father, Mahalaleel, was 65 and Adam was 460. The name Jared signifies "Descending"[18] and probably had reference to his position in the patriarchal line through which the Priesthood descended.

Concerning the early life of Jared there is not a single sentence recorded, but when he was 162 he welcomed into his family a baby boy who was to become one of the greatest social and religious leaders of all times. This was Enoch. However, in the beginning there was no way by which Jared might have known of the special attributes of this young lad, for, as subsequent events demonstrated, Enoch was a humble and unpretentious boy with no apparent desire for either power or leadership. Nevertheless, Jared went out of his way to share

[15]*Ibid.*, 107:46
[16]Moses 6:20
[17]*Ibid.*
[18]Peloubet, *op. cit.*, under "Jared"

with Enoch the same knowledge of the gospel which he had given all of his children.   Jared is given full credit by the scripture for having taught Enoch "in all the ways of God."[19]

This fact takes on particular significance when it is realized that during the formative years of Enoch's childhood—when Jared was instructing him in all the ways of God—Jared did not yet hold the Priesthood.   In fact, he did not receive it until he was 200 years of age.[20]   However, pending the receipt of this great blessing he went right ahead exercising the light within him by humbly teaching his children to walk in the paths of truth and righteousness.

Jared must have gained great personal satisfaction from the achievements of Enoch.   After Enoch had received his revelations and become one of the most famous spiritual leaders in the entire country, he built a city which was eventually translated because of its righteousness.   But it must have been a sobering experience for Jared and the other patriarchs to see this entire city translated and taken from the earth while they, themselves, were left.   Their mission was to remain on the earth and follow the course of mortality down to the portals of the grave.

Life for Jared and the remaining patriarchs probably became extremely complex after the precipitous departure of Enoch and his city.   They no longer possessed the prestige and honor of being citizens of the most famous city in the world.   The city was gone and so were its people.   With them went the prestige of the patriarchs.   They now became a handful of ostracized and possibly persecuted "Sons of God" among the general population which was growing in wickedness with every generation.

The latter years of Jared's life were probably spent amidst mounting adversity as he and his associates sought to dam the tide of almost universal apostasy.   Jared's mortal mission endured until 2,578 B.C. which gave him

[19]Moses 6:21
[20]D. & C. 107:47

a life span of 962 years—next to the longest life recorded in scripture.

He lived to see the early part of the life of Noah— in fact, when Jared died Noah was already 366 years of age, and because of the tidal wave of licentious wickedness, the ominous cataclysm of the terrible Flood had already been foreshadowed in prophecy.[21]

The Life Of Enoch

But let us go back now and consider the remarkable life of Jared's son, Enoch. Enoch was born in 3,378 B.C. when Jared was 162 years of age and when Father Adam was 622. Enoch was born in the land of Cainan among the people of righteousness and according to his own account he was brought up in the strict tradition of the gospel plan. As Enoch later testified: "My father taught me in all the ways of God."[22]

Enoch was handicapped in his early youth by an impediment of speech. It was difficult for him to express himself and as a result he was ridiculed and rejected by certain groups of cruel and ill-mannered people. Enoch was very sensitive to this deficiency and reacted just as any normal child might have done. When absent from his own immediate family he felt that he was unwanted and a social outcast.

While in his youth—probably in his teens—Enoch had an experience which changed the course of his whole life. He had left his home in Cainan and was traveling toward the Sea East. Suddenly it happened. "The Spirit of God descended out of heaven, and abode upon him."[23] As he felt this quickening influence envelop him he became aware of a voice speaking to him:

"Enoch, my son, prophesy unto this people, and say unto them—Repent, for thus saith the Lord: I am angry with this people, and my fierce anger is kindled against them; for their hearts have waxed

[21]Moses 7:43
[22]*Ibid.,* 6:41
[23]*Ibid.,* 6:26

hard, and their ears are dull of hearing, and their eyes cannot see afar off; And for these many generations, ever since the day that I created them, have they gone astray, and have denied me, and have sought their own counsels in the dark; and in their own abominations have they devised murder, and have not kept the commandments, which I gave unto their father, Adam. Wherefore, they have foresworn themselves, and, by their oaths, they have brought upon themselves death; and a hell I have prepared for them, if they repent not!"[24]

Young Enoch was overwhelmed with this sudden call to the ministry. Did not the Lord know of his inability to speak—his bound tongue that required the greatest effort to say the simplest things? In trembling humility he bowed himself to the ground and pleaded with the Lord: "Why is it that I have found favor in thy sight, and am but a lad, and all the people hate me; for I am slow of speech; wherefore am I thy servant?"[25]

The Lord admonished Enoch and said: "Go forth and do as I have commanded thee, and no man shall pierce thee. Open thy mouth, and it shall be filled, and I will give thee utterance, for all flesh is in my hands, and I will do as seemeth me good. Say unto this people: Choose ye this day, to serve the Lord God who made you. Behold, my Spirit is upon you, wherefore all thy words will I justify; and the mountains shall flee before you, and the rivers shall turn from their course; and thou shalt abide in me, and I in you; therefore walk with me!"[26]

The Lord instructed Enoch to anoint his eyes with clay and then wash them. As soon as he obeyed this commandment the veil was lifted from his eyes so that he was able to see the spirit world and all those things which are "not visible to the natural eye."[27]

In connection with this revelation the Lord plainly indicated that He desired a revitalization of the mis-

[24]*Ibid.,* 6:27-29
[25]*Ibid.,* 6:31
[26]*Ibid.,* 6:32-34
[27]*Ibid.,* 6:36

sionary work of His kingdom. For this purpose Enoch was being suddenly raised up in his youth—almost as a prophet out of season—to lift up a higher standard of vigorous warning to the wicked than some of the other Priesthood holders had been accustomed to doing. The news of Enoch's unusual communication from heaven soon spread abroad in the land. His name was passed about in awe and wonder as each man exclaimed to his neighbor: "A seer hath the Lord raised up unto his people!"[26]

[26]*Ibid.,* 6:36

CHAPTER SEVENTEEN

The Ministry of Enoch

Enoch received the Priesthood at an earlier age than any other of the patriarchs except Noah. How old was Enoch when he was ordained?

What miraculous healing did Enoch receive in his youth? Could he have fulfilled his mission without it?

As a missionary Enoch went forth to make friends for the cause of righteousness. What deduction do you draw from the statement that when he first began speaking "all men were offended because of him"? (Moses 6:37)

There is nothing in the scripture to indicate that Enoch was unusual or eccentric. Why then do you think the people said: "We go yonder to behold the seer, for he prophesieth . . . a wild man hath come among us." (Ibid., 6:38)

What did Mahijah ask Enoch? What effect did Enoch's spirited reply have upon the people who were listening? Was Enoch teaching "Christianity"? Did he preach in one or many nations?

What great tragedy did Enoch predict which involved the seed of Cain and the people of Shum? Why didn't he preach to the seed of Cain?

What did Enoch do with the people who repented and asked to join the Church? Where would they probably go?

What international crisis was created as a result of Enoch's mission? Is it likely that the members of the Church could have defended themselves if they had tried to? Would they have become well established in their new homes in so short a time?

Although a number of prophets have been given permission to use the full power of the Priesthood they have seldom done so. On this occasion Enoch felt justified in saving his people through this means. What did he do? What was the result?

What happened to the land of the people who came to seize the land of Enoch's people? The City of Enoch flourished for 365 years. Was it ever attacked again by a military force? Does the scripture explain why?

ENOCH RECEIVES THE PRIESTHOOD AND A MIRACULOUS HEALING

When Father Adam learned that Enoch was approved of God and had received a glorious revelation concerning the secrets of heaven, he hastened to ordain him to the Holy Priesthood. Enoch was only twenty-five years of age at the time.[1] It was extremely unusual for Adam to ordain any of his heirs in their youth. After his heartbreaking experience with Cain, Adam appears to have required that a man be old enough to prove his complete worthiness before receiving divine authority. But with Enoch it was different. Already he had been called of God to go forth and preach repentance unto the people. To complete his preparation the Priesthood needed to be conferred upon him. Adam therefore did not hesitate. If Enoch was approved of God, certainly he was acceptable to Father Adam.

Enoch therefore had the unprecedented distinction of being ordained to the Priesthood long before his father or grandfather. Jared, his father, was not ordained by Adam until thirteen years later, and Mahalaleel, his grandfather, was not ordained until 244 years later.

Immediately Enoch went forth to perform his divine calling. Sometime in those early days of his ministry —perhaps even at the very beginning—a miracle occurred. Suddenly Enoch could speak freely. As God had said, "Open thy mouth, and it shall be filled. . . . I will give thee utterance!"[2] This was only the first of many miracles which occurred during the ministry of

[1] D. & C. 107:48
[2] Moses 6:32

Enoch. It must have been a moment of personal triumph as Enoch stood forth among the same identical people who had formerly ridiculed him, and poured forth his message of repentance with powerful and expressive eloquence.

"And it came to pass that Enoch went forth in the land, among the people, standing upon the hills and the high places, and cried with a loud voice, testifying against their works."[3]

This was no petty prattling of an itinerant preacher. Here was a brilliant young prophet—a polished shaft from the quiver of the Lord—whose words pierced like needles of Macedonian steel the calloused hearts of the crowds who came to hear him. The mobs surrounded the hills and high places from which he spoke and the scripture says "all men were offended because of him."[4] But at least he had their attention. In fact, his reputation spread like the east wind before him. The people anticipated his arrival in each new locality and as messengers brought word that he drew near the people exclaimed: "We go yonder to behold the seer, for he prophesieth, and there is a strange thing in the land; a wild man hath come among us!"[5]

And when they heard him speak openly of their sins and secret oaths and murders and immorality they were greatly offended but "no man laid hands on him for fear came on all them that heard him" and they whispered one to another, "He walked with God!"[6]

Finally, a man named Mahijah approached young Enoch and demanded to know more specifically who he was. "Tell us plainly," said Mahijah, "who thou art and from whence thou comest?"

Enoch responded with an eloquence which clearly demonstrated that he had been completely healed of his former impediment of speech. Said he, "I came out from the land of Cainan, the land of my fathers, a land of righteousness unto this day. And my father taught me

[3]*Ibid.,* 6:37
[4]*Ibid.,* 6:37
[5]*Ibid.,* 6:38
[6]*Ibid.,* 6:39-40

in all the ways of God. And it came to pass, as I journeyed from the land of Cainan, by the sea east, I beheld a vision; and lo, the heavens I saw, and the Lord spake with me, and gave me commandment; wherefore, for this cause, to keep the commandment, I speak forth these words. . . .

"The Lord which spake with me, the same is the God of heaven, and he is my God, and your God, and ye are my brethren, and why counsel ye yourselves, and deny the God of heaven? The heavens he made; the earth is his footstool; and the foundation thereof is his. Behold, he laid it, an host of men hath he brought in upon the face thereof. And death hath come upon our fathers; nevertheless, we know them, and cannot deny, and even the first of all we know, even Adam. For a book of remembrance we have written among us, according to the pattern given by the finger of God; and it is given in our own language." (Moses 6:41-46)

The scripture says that while Enoch was talking to the people they suddenly seemed to appear weak and faint.' They began to tremble and sit or lie upon the ground as though their bone and sinew had turned to water. But this did not affect Enoch's sermon. With the power of God blazing in his eyes the young prophet looked down upon them as though he would consume them with his very words.

"Behold, Satan hath come among the children of men, and tempteth them to worship him; and men have become carnal, sensual and devilish and are shut out from the presence of God. But God hath made known unto our fathers that all men must repent!" (Ibid., 6:49-50)

Then Enoch went back into the book of remembrance to retell the detailed circumstances surrounding the first glorious vision given to Father Adam by the Lord. It is the most complete account in any scripture of the dispensation of the gospel to Adam. Enoch reminded his listeners that the Fall was designed as a blessing. God had said to Father Adam that in this earth life men "taste the

---

'Ibid., 6:47

bitter, that they may know to prize the good."⁸ The Lord had also said: "And it is given unto them to know good from evil, wherefore they are agents unto themselves."⁹

Young Enoch reminded his audience of Satan-worshipers that Jesus Christ would come in the flesh and provide the means whereby men could again return to their Heavenly Father if they would only repent and hold fast to the things which they knew from their own experiences were good. Enoch told them of their need for faith in the true and living God, their need for repentance from their blasphemous and corrupt lives, their need for baptism by immersion in water and then promised them that if they would obey these instructions they would receive the Holy Ghost.

As Enoch neared the end of his sermon he cried out to the multitude at his feet: "Behold, our father Adam taught these things, and many have believed and become the sons of God, and many have believed not, and have perished in their sins, and are looking forth with fear, in torment, for the fiery indignation of the wrath of God to be poured out upon them."¹⁰

With such sermons as this it was no wonder that the reputation of Enoch spread like wildfire up and down the land.

Enoch Predicts a Violent Race War to Be Launched by the Seed of Cain

Not only did Enoch call the people to repentance, but like the true prophet that he was, he opened the eyes of their understanding to future events of tremendous political and social importance which were about to take place among them. One of his prophecies related to a war of annihilation which the seed of Cain would launch against the people of Shum.

"I was clothed upon with glory;" said Enoch, "and I saw the Lord; and he stood before my face, and he talked with me, even as a man talketh one with another, face

⁸*Ibid.,* 6:55
⁹*Ibid.,* 6:56
¹⁰*Ibid.,* 7:1

to face. And he said unto me: Look, and I will show unto thee the world for the space of many generations."[11]

Enoch said that he beheld a panoramic vision which stretched before him, and he saw "a great people which dwelt in tents, which were the people of Shum." Then, "I looked towards the north, and I beheld the people of Canaan, which dwelt in tents. And the Lord said unto me: Prophesy; and I prophesied, saying: Behold the people of Canaan, which are numerous, shall go forth in battle array against the people of Shum, and shall slay them that they *shall utterly be destroyed.*"[12]

After annihilating the people of Shum, Enoch was shown that the Canaanites would divide the land among their own people and dwell in the fields that belonged to those whom they had slaughtered. Enoch was able to predict further that the wrath of God would be poured out upon this conquered land so that it would be cursed "with much heat, and the barrenness thereof shall go forth forever!"[13] He saw also that the people of Canaan were cursed with "blackness" and "were despised among all people."[14] This blackness identifies the people of Canaan as being of the seed of Cain. As Enoch later stated: "The seed of Cain were black, and had not place among them."[15]

After this Enoch says, "I looked, and I beheld the land of Sharon, and the land of Enoch, and the land of Omner, and the land of Heni, and the land of Shem, and the land of Haner and the land of Hanannihah, and all the inhabitants thereof. And the Lord said unto me: Go to this people, and say unto them—Repent, lest I come out and smite them with a curse, and they die. And he gave unto me a commandment that I should baptize in the name of the Father and of the Son."[16]

---

[11]*Ibid.,* 7:3-4
[12]*Ibid.,* 7:6-7
[13]*Ibid.,* 7:8
[14]*Ibid.,* 7:8
[15]*Ibid.,* 7:22
[16]*Ibid.,* 7:10-11

Enoch Completes His Mission

Everywhere that Enoch went his message divided the populace. He demanded that the people take inventory of themselves. From nation to nation he carried his dynamic declaration: "Choose ye this day to serve the Lord God who made you!" As with the great Apostle Paul who would preach a similar message thirty-three centuries later, Enoch discovered that the people separated into clear-cut camps for or against him. The few who accepted his message responded to the spirit of gathering and collected in a central place—probably in Cainan—while the remainder swore in their wrath somehow to destroy Enoch.

It must have taken several years to complete this particular mission, for Enoch made his personal plea to all of the people in all of the lands God had shown him in vision—the land of Sharon, the land of Enoch, the land of Omner, the land of Heni, the land of Shem, the land of Haner and the land of Hannanihah. In fact, the scripture states that he called upon "all the people, save it were the people of Canaan, to repent."

The people of Canaan were excluded for the very good reason that they were a nation of murderers and anarchists. Those who shed innocent blood and sin against the light deliberately exclude themselves from the circumference of the plan of salvation. The gospel is only for those who have not committed the heinous crime of destroying human life in cold blood. There is nothing in the plan of salvation for the murderer. The scripture says he cannot gain forgiveness for that sin either in this life or the life to come because the atoning sacrifice of Jesus Christ does not cover it![17] That is why Enoch did not preach to the people of Canaan. Like Cain, their forefather, these people gloried in what they had done. They had gone so far in the perversion of righteousness that preaching the gospel in Canaan at this time would have been tantamount to casting precious pearls of truth in the mire of a swine pen.

[17]D. & C. 42:18, 79

Enoch and the Members of the Church Are Attacked by Force of Arms

It is apparent from the scripture that Enoch not only converted as many of the people as he could, but he also preached "the gathering" to them, so that they could be saved temporally as well as spiritually. Undoubtedly the command of God to Enoch was similar to the one received in our own dispensation when the Lord declared: "Ye are called to bring to pass the gathering of mine elect; for mine elect hear my voice and harden not their hearts; Wherefore the decree hath gone forth from the Father that they shall be *gathered in unto one place* upon the face of this land, to prepare their hearts and be prepared in all things against the day when tribulation and desolation are sent forth upon the wicked."[18]

Scarcely had Enoch arrived home from his mission and settled the newly converted members of the Church before a cry of alarm spread throughout the land. Mighty armies of conquest were marching in upon them! Enoch had realized that his campaign for reformation had been a cause of offense among the proud and wicked multitudes who had assembled to hear him, but just *how* deeply they were offended now became apparent. For the first time in the recorded annals of sacred history the people of God were subjected to direct attack by their enemies. Being a peace-loving people they were probably caught completely unawares. This is apparent from the unusual manifestation of heavenly power which was interposed to save them.

At this time the Church in Cainan had five of the patriarchs living in their midst—Enos, Cainan, Mahalaleel, Jared and Enoch. Enoch was still a very young man, but it was he who was sustained—both by the people and God—to lead the members of the Church in this moment of peril.[19]

Instead of organizing large armies and building moats and trenches, Enoch went forth alone to meet the savage

[18]*Ibid.,* 29:7-8
[19]Moses 7:13

and vengeful hosts which came pouring over the hills and plains to slaughter the people and seize the land. At exactly the precise moment when it would have the greatest effect, Enoch exercised the power of the Priesthood he possessed and solemnly spoke "the word of the Lord" in accordance with the divine instructions he had received. Immediately the convulsions of the earth roared forth in a mighty wave of grinding stone and trembling terrain which split the crust of the earth into gaping seams and turned the blood of the invading hosts to water. Mountains slipped from their foundations and slid across the path of the would-be conquerors. Rivers left their courses and sent a wall of churning destruction down upon the cringing legions of foot soldiers and chariots. In the hills and forests the terror of the hour gripped both man and beasts, and the scripture says the "roar of the lions was heard out of the wilderness."[20]

This almost unbelievable display of power which the enemies of Enoch were close enough to hear him call down from heaven was so impressive that they who escaped fled fearfully to their own lands and spread the news of all they had witnessed. And they probably found ready listeners, for the quaking in the depths of the earth had been no small or local affair. Its violence had been felt over a vast area. During the quake a great peninsula of land had even sprung up out of the depths of the sea.[21]

And another thing which was especially impressive at the moment was the fact that the great nation of strong and large-statured men who were referred to as "giants" —and who were undoubtedly feared above all other peoples because of their fierceness and strength—behold, these were no more anxious to be pitted against Enoch than the rest of his enemies. In fear of their lives, the scripture says these giants fled from their own land and "stood afar off."[22]

[20] *Ibid.*, 7:13
[21] *Ibid.*, 7:14
[22] *Ibid.*, 7:15

Then a strange thing happened. All these people who had been formerly allied together by their common hatred of Enoch and the principles for which he stood, now turned upon each other and poured out the venomous rage of their dammed-off frustration. "From that time forth there were wars and bloodshed among them," the record states.

But never again during the long period of more than three centuries that Enoch and his people occupied this territory did a single nation dare to trouble or antagonize the people of God. "The fear of the Lord was upon all nations so great was the glory of the Lord, which was upon his people. And the Lord blessed the land, and they were blessed upon the mountains, and upon the high places, and did flourish."[23]

---

[23]*Ibid.*, 7:17

CHAPTER EIGHTEEN

The Founding of a Golden Age

Why does congested city life have a tendency to breed crime, graft and social degeneration?

What was the most singular thing about the layout of "the City of Zion"? Did it allow for natural expansion?

Do we have any basis for believing that the City of Enoch had a temple?

Is the "Order of Enoch" simple to operate or complex? Does it require a carefully prepared people to make it successful or could any community make it work?

Can you explain the basic framework of the Order of Enoch? Did it emphasize the stewardship principle or community ownership of property? Did any of the people have "private" property? How important was the individual under this system?

The bishops in the Order of Enoch tried to teach each person how to become self-sustaining. Do you think this was the reason they finally had no poor among them?

When a person joined the Order of Enoch who decided how much that person would be given as his stewardship? Was it important for the steward to feel satisfied with the fairness of the arrangement? What procedure was followed to make sure there was harmony and good will? Could a person leave the Order of Enoch whenever he wanted to?

Have you ever compared the details of the Order of Enoch with the principles of communism? Do they have anything in common? Would you class the Order of Enoch as a system of communism or a system of free enterprise?

Did the early Christians practice communism? Is there any evidence that they practiced the stewardship principle? Do you know whether or not there have been any attempts to make "Christian Communism" work? Do you know why these attempts failed? What did Joseph Smith say about "common stock" or communism?

THE CITY OF ZION BECOMES ESTABLISHED

Peace is the parent of prosperity. As soon as the enemies of Enoch had left the people of God to themselves they began to flourish throughout the land.[1] As we have previously indicated, this great gathering of early-day Saints probably took place in the land of Cainan since we know it was the territory specifically designated as "a land of promise" and was the place where all the righteous people had been led to settle since the days of Enos.[2]

Up to this time the members of the Church appear to have engaged almost entirely in pastoral occupations. In fact, it was traditional with the patriarchs both before and after the Flood to discourage any congested concentration of population. All previous references to city life and industrial occupations (which, of course, usually thrive only in large population centers) are those attributed to the unrighteous segment of humanity.[3]

This does not mean, however, that God frowns upon industry and city life as such. It simply means that unless a people are particularly well disciplined they cannot afford to risk the social hazards of being concentrated in a closely confined area just for the meager economic advantages it might bring. Under such conditions a whole people have been known to degenerate through crime, graft, fraud and corruption within a single generation. However, God himself is a builder of cities, but His design and His manner of administering the affairs of such cities are far different from those which have prevailed among the cities of men, either ancient or modern.

[1]Moses 7:17
[2]*Ibid.*, 6:17
[3]*Ibid.*, 5:42, 46

It was during the particular period which we are now
studying that God saw fit to raise up what appears to
have been the first city of divine sanction in the history
of the world.   The scripture says that in anticipation of
this great organized effort to build a city unto the Lord,
"Enoch continued his preaching in righteousness unto the
people of God."[4]   He was seeking to prepare them social-
ly, economically and spiritually.   And it describes the
results of this labor: in process of time "The Lord called
his people Zion, because they were of one heart and
one mind, and dwelt in righteousness; and there was no
poor among them."[5]

Then the scripture continues: "And it came to pass
in his (Enoch's) days, that he built a city that was called
the City of Holiness, even Zion."[6]   No detailed description of this city exists, but we may perhaps assume that
it resembled closely the revealed pattern for "The City
of Zion" to be built in modern times.   In this pattern the
city was divided into blocks of ten acres each.   City
streets were all of the same width, 132 feet, making allowances for sidewalks and parking of twenty feet.   The
center blocks were all reserved for temples, schools,
places of worship, public buildings and storehouses.   The
surrounding blocks were divided into lots sixty-six feet
wide and 330 feet deep, making each lot one-half acre.
"Not one lot in this city is to contain more than one house,
and that is to be built twenty-five feet back from the
street, leaving a small yard in front ... the rest of the lot
for gardens; all of the houses are to be built of brick and
stone."[7]

Concerning supplies for the city, the revealed pattern
indicated that "On the north and south are to be laid off
the farms for the agriculturist, and sufficient quantity of
land to supply the whole plot; and if it cannot be laid off
without going too great a distance from the city, there
must also be some (land for agriculture) laid off on the
east and west."[8]

[4]*Ibid.*, 7:19
[5]*Ibid.*, 7:18
[6]*Ibid.*, 7:19
[7]*Doc. Hist. of Church*, Vol. I, pp. 358-9
[8]*Ibid.*

Concerning livestock, the pattern designated a certain place just outside the city limits "to be laid off for barns, stables, etc. for the use of the city so that no barns or stables will be in the city among the houses."[9]

The most unusual thing about this pattern for a city was its method of expansion. The original city plat was designated to cover only one mile square and was intended to accommodate only fifteen to twenty thousand persons. Concerning the time when this space would be filled up and there would be need for expansion, the instructions read: "When this square is thus laid off and supplied, *lay off another in the same way,* and so fill up the world . . . let every man live in the city, for this (i.e. the whole cluster or group of independent communities) is the City of Zion."[10] In other words, the economic, educational and social advantages of city life were to be enjoyed by all but as the community grew it would be *automatically* decentralized so as to avoid the confusion, congestion and social irresponsibility which too often typify city life in the average modern metropolis.

Did the City of Enoch Have Temples?

Because the scriptures include no details concerning the City of Zion we of course find no reference to the building of temples. Nevertheless we have every reason to believe that a temple would be one of the first sacred buildings which Enoch would be instructed to construct just as the Lord commanded the Church to do in our own dispensation. When one contemplates the purpose and design of the temple and considers the fact that the ordinances to be received therein are as eternal and universal in their application as the basic ordinances of baptism and confirmation, then it can be appreciated that just as Adam and the early patriarchs were the first to receive baptism and the gift of the Holy Ghost, so also they would be the first to be instructed in the ordinances of the temple.

---

[9]*Ibid.*
[10]*Ibid.*

The fact that Enoch's dispensation would be required
to build a temple in the same manner as the dispensations
which followed may be clearly drawn from the Lord's
own statement: "How shall your washings be acceptable
unto me, except ye perform them in a house which you
have built in my name? For, for this cause I commanded
Moses that he should build a tabernacle, that they should
bear it with them in the wilderness, and to build a house
in the land of promise (Solomon's Temple), that those
ordinances might be revealed. . . ."[11] Then He concludes
by stating that temples are something "which my people
are always commanded to build unto my name."[12]

This clearly shows the established pattern for both
ancient and modern times. Joseph Smith says the temple service is "the order pertaining to the Ancient of
Days," or Adam, which demonstrates the antediluvial
antiquity of these sacred ordinances .

Enoch was sixty-five years old when the foundations
for the City of Zion were first laid.[13] This was a momen-
tous year for Enoch. He was not only blessed with the
vision of this great new society which he was to be instru-
mental in establishing but this was also the year that his
son and heir to the Priesthood, Methuselah, was born.[14]

For reasons which we have previously discussed,
Adam does not appear to have been dwelling with the
people in this part of the land but continued to maintain
his residence at Adam-ondi-Ahman. Nevertheless, the
wise and benevolent first patriarch must have required
frequent reports from his children in Cainan, and no doubt
he found unbounded joy in the valiant work of Enoch.
We know that he was in close communication with this
new young leader of the Saints and visited with him, for
in the year that the great city of Zion was founded,
Adam laid his hands upon Enoch's head and gave him
his patriarchal blessing.[15]

[11]D. & C. 124:37-38
[12]Ibid., 124:39
[13]Compare Moses 7:68 with Moses 8:1
[14]D. & C. 107:48
[15]Idem

The "Order Of Enoch"

One of the most outstanding features of the society which Enoch established was the manner in which the Lord instructed him to combine the religious ideals of the people with certain divinely inspired economic principles. The successful practice of these principles resulted in a golden age of prosperity which continued throughout the earthly existence of this community—a total of three hundred and sixty-five years.[16] We know from modern revelation that this economic system which was called "The Order of Enoch"—was built on the willingness of the people to refine themselves to that point where they could accept the "whole law of consecration."

Each man consecrated himself and all he possessed to the welfare of his fellow men and the work of the Lord. He became his brother's keeper, loving his neighbor as himself and working with every fiber within him to improve the security and happiness of both himself and the community. This did not come easy. As previously indicated, this program evolved gradually and required time and constant zeal on the part of all these people (which were taken out of many nations) to achieve the singleness of purpose which the whole law of consecration required.

The basic principles which made the Order of Enoch workable are better understood today than they have been for many centuries. This is because these principles were re-revealed when the gospel was restored a little over a hundred years ago. Although the Church has never been permitted to practice the Order of Enoch except on a limited basis,[17] nevertheless, sufficient is known about the over-all program to appreciate its fundamental precepts. Briefly, the Order of Enoch requires that those who become members in it accept the following precepts as being true and self evident:

First, that all things in the earth belong to the Creator and that men are only the *custodians* of these resources and riches which He has placed upon

[16] Moses 7:68
[17] D. & C. 105:34

the earth for the welfare of mankind. (D. C. 104:15-17; 55-57)

Second, that the fatherhood of God and the brotherhood of man require that human beings look upon one another as members of the same family— the family of God, and that they are directly responsible for one another's welfare. (D. C. 104:18)

Third, that in this family relationship every person is expected to do his share. Each shall give what he has (labor, skills, art, management, goods, services) and in return, receive what he needs. All have a place in the program except one type of person—the idler. Under the Order of Enoch the managers of the system were forbidden to give the fruits of others' labors to any person who could, but would not work. (D. C. 42:42)

Fourth, that the members of the Order of Enoch shall take the responsibility of giving education and assistance to those who are lacking in the ability or capacity to provide for themselves. This was not just charity for the poor but a program to provide the poor with the necessities of life *and then* aid them in becoming self-sustaining members of the order. The ultimate object—and one which the people of Enoch attained—was to have "no poor among them." (Moses 7:18)

Fifth, that private property and the dignity of the individual must be preserved. The private property of each member of the order was to be "according to his family, according to his circumstances and his wants and his needs," (D. C. 51:3) "inasmuch as his wants are just." (D. C. 82:17) Everything he could produce over and above the needs of himself and family was to be donated to the common treasury of the Order for the welfare of others less fortunate. (D. C. 42:33, 34, 55; 70:7-10) As for the dignity and independence of the individual, Dr. John A. Widtsoe points out that in this Order, "every man must be respected as a free agent. He may enter the Order at his pleasure. Once in the

Order, he must be allowed to use, fully, and as he pleases, any properties placed in his hands. He may leave the Order at his pleasure." (*Church News*, 15 May 1949, p. 23)

It is interesting to observe the mechanics which were followed in setting up the system. A man who wished to enter the order deeded everything he owned by an irrevocable deed to the Presiding Bishop of the Church who had charge of the affairs of the Order. The Bishop then deeded back to the individual, as a stewardship, all that the man's abilities and requirements warranted, and placed any surplus in the common treasury of the Order.

During this transaction it was most important that the Bishop and the applicant have a meeting of the minds as to just how much the man should have deeded back to him as a stewardship. Concerning this, Joseph Smith stated: "The matter of consecration must be done by the mutual consent of both parties; for to give the Bishop power to say how much every man shall have, and he be compelled to comply with the Bishop's judgment, is giving the Bishop more power than a king has; and, upon the other hand, to let every man say how much he needs, and the Bishop be compelled to comply with his judgment is to throw Zion into confusion and make a slave of the Bishop. The fact is, there must be a balance or equilibrium of power between the Bishop and the people; and thus harmony and good will may be preserved among you.

"Therefore, those persons consecrating property to the Bishop in Zion, and then receiving an inheritance back, must reasonably show to the Bishop that they need as much as they claim. But in case the two parties cannot come to a mutual agreement, the Bishop is to have nothing to do about receiving such consecrations; and the case must be laid before a council of twelve High Priests. . . ."[18]

From this it will be seen that the Order of Enoch was placed on a sound, practical and businesslike basis. A man received full title to his stewardship

---

[18]*Doc. History of the Church*, Vol. I, pp. 364-5

and it was thereafter expected that he would take pride in showing how much he could do with it so as to multiply his resources and thus prove worthy of being assigned more. It was strictly a merit system with the greatest possible emphasis being placed upon individual initiative.

There are many details concerning the administrative procedures in the Order of Enoch which have not yet been revealed but we have sufficient information to help us understand the basic constitution of the Order and appreciate the blessings it gave to those who refined themselves to that point where they could live in such a society.

The Order of Enoch and Communism Compared

It should be clearly apparent from the foregoing that the Order of Enoch and the principles of modern Marxian Communism are as far apart as the poles. There has been a tendency, however, to confuse the two, and therefore a brief restatement of each system is being set forth as an aid in comparing them.

ORDER OF ENOCH	MARXIAN COMMUNISM
PROPERTY: Privately owned except for certain community services such as public utilities.	State owned, state operated and state controlled.
PROFITS: Retained by the individual "according to his family, according to his circumstances and his wants and his needs." Surplus to be voluntarily donated to the common treasury of the Order. (D. C. 42:33, 55; 70:7)	No private profits permitted.
PARTICIPATION: Voluntary. Each man owns his individual stewardship and may discontinue his affiliation at any time by withdrawing his stewardship property from the Order. (D. C. 51:5)	Forced. In Soviet Russia, for example, the penalty for attempting to leave the system and flee from the country is death. (Edict of November, 1929, and paragraph 58 of penal code, 1943 edition) with five years in Siberia for one's family (edict of June, 1934).

THE FAMILY: Made the basic social unit of the Order. Fixed upon family members the reciprocal obligation of looking after the material needs of each other. The Order took over *only* when the family failed for some reason to fulfil its function. (D. C. 83:2-5)

The Communist Manifesto states: "Abolition of the family! . . . The bourgeois family will vanish as a matter of course . . . with the vanishing of capital." (P. 26) Marriage and filial relations were to be outlawed. The Manifesto continues: "The Communists . . . desire to introduce . . . an openly legalized community of women." (p. 28) Children born through "free love" unions were to be raised by the state.

PERSONAL SECURITY: Made paramount. Right to possess legal title to all property held in a stewardship permitted each man to enjoy full independence *even to the point of taking his stewardship out of the system if he so desired.*

Completely subordinate to the representatives of the state. In Soviet Russia each community consists of a large "company town" with all lodgings owned by the government. The factory supervisors can eject the worker from his h o m e for breaches of labor discipline (such as tardiness, inefficiency, etc.) and he can get no other home. (Edict of Dec. 4, 1932)

COMPETITION: Encouraged. Each man attempts to prove himself "a profitable servant" and the more ingenuity and efficiency he manifests, the more profitable he is considered to be.

Forbidden. Workers are permitted to make suggestions but if the idea is rejected, no one is allowed to go out and "show" that it can be done better and cheaper than the way the government is doing it.

SUPERVISION: Decentralized. Each man is given a wide latitude as to the manner in which he will develop his own particular stewardship to the greatest possible advantage. The judgment by the Bishop is on the final results.

Highly centralized. Each man is frozen to his job and must perform according to a continuous flow of instructions which emanate from government administrators.

MORALS AND RELIGION: These were the foundation of the order. Respect for God and his Priesthood was the soil in which the Order of Enoch sank its roots, and the high moral precept which made each man his brother's keeper was the secret of its success.

Marx coined the phrase: "Religion is the opium of the people," and then wrote in the Communist Manifesto: "Communism abolishes eternal truths; it abolishes all religion, and all morality, instead of constituting them on a new basis; it therefore acts in contradiction to all past historical experience."

The reason why so many have confused the Order of Enoch or so-called "United Order" with Communism is because many students of the Bible have misunderstood the economic order of the early Christians and have assumed that they were "pure communists." This misconception is based on Acts 2:43-44: "And all that believed were together, and had all things common; And sold their possessions and goods, and parted them to all men as every man had need." Also Acts 4:32: "And the multitude of them that believed were of one heart and of one soul: neither *said* any of them that ought of the things which he possessed was his own; but they had all things common."

DID THE EARLY CHRISTIANS PRACTICE COMMUNISM?

Notice, however, that this description in Acts of the economic society which the early Christians established, is not a treatment of the legal structure of this arrangement but of the spirit which prevailed over their cooperative enterprise. Thus, in keeping with the spirit of the new gospel, they looked upon all they possessed as being the property of God which they were permitted to enjoy in common. But notice that they did not lump their property together in a common stock. Each man just simply "said" that the things which he possessed were not his own. This was an "attitude" of unity and mutual brotherhood which they were attempting to build up among themselves in keeping with the principles Jesus had taught them. But they continued to enjoy legal title to their property and only sold whatever they felt was necessary in order to provide for the needs of the poor. This is clearly demonstrated in the next chapter of Acts.

Ananias and Sapphira sold a possession to make a contribution to the Church and then held back part of the money. Peter criticized them for pretending that the money they contributed to the Church was the whole price of the property. Then he said: "While it (the property) remained, was it not *thine own?* and after it was sold, was it not in thine own power? why hast thou conceived this thing in thine heart? thou hast not lied unto men, but unto God."[19]

In other words, property remained legally in the hands of each member as his own and he had complete control over its disposition. He contributed it or withheld it as he desired. It was a *voluntary* contribution. The sin of Ananias and Sapphira was their false declaration that they were contributing all that the sale of the property had brought them. As Peter reminded them, "After it was sold, was it not in thine own power?" They didn't have to contribute any more than they wished, but they should not have pretended that they were giving the whole price when it was really only part.

Dummelow's *Bible Commentary* has the following to say concerning the verses previously quoted: "The Church of Jerusalem recognized the principle of private property. A disciple's property really was his own, but he did not say it was his own; he treated it as if it were common property."[20]

Joseph Smith wrote in his diary: "I preached on the stand about one hour on the 2nd chapter of Acts, designing to show the folly of common stock. In Nauvoo everyone is steward over his own."[21]

The idea of community ownership of property such as that advocated by Marxian Communism is opposed to the "stewardship" principle which is a basic Christian concept both in the New Testament and the Doctrine and Covenants. The verses in Acts have been misun-

---

[19]Acts 5:4
[20]Dummelow's *Bible Commentary*, p. 824
[21]*Doc. History of the Church*, Vol. VI, p. 37

derstood. As the incident concerning Ananias and
Sapphira demonstrates, the early Christians held their
property as a personal possession but made voluntary
contributions to the "common good" wherever they were
able.

It is also interesting to observe that communal ownership violates every instinct of human nature. It de-
stroys initiative, nullifies free agency, suppresses
inventive exploration, minimizes the dignity of the individual and makes a god out of an abstract thing called
"The State"—to which is delegated complete, unre-
stricted control over life, liberty and property. During
the lifetime of Karl Marx his principles were put to
work on a brotherhood basis in practically every country of the world. Although he, himself, was violently
atheistic and said his purpose in life was to "dethrone
God and destroy Capitalism," nevertheless, many
thought they saw in his program the elements of a
Christian Utopia. Literally hundreds of communities
were therefore organized by well meaning people to
make Marxian Communism work. But in not one single
instance did they succeed. Only when the professional
revolutionary, V. I. Lenin, put a whole nation under the
sword was he able to force any appreciable number of
human beings to endure the practice of communist theory
for any length of time. Like so many other weak systems of government, it can survive only in an atmosphere
of a slave state, ruled by a king or dictator.

The inspired Order of Enoch therefore had nothing
in common with the social or economic principles advocated by Karl Marx. The Order of Enoch was designed
to fit human needs, not destroy them. It encouraged
initiative, stimulated healthy competition, cultivated the
proper exercise of free agency, gave each man pride of
ownership in his personal stewardship and personal development. It was designed to give each member a
partnership with God in the enjoyment of the wealth of
the earth.

CHAPTER NINETEEN

The Vision of Enoch
and the Death of Adam

What is the "second comforter" which was given to the entire City of Enoch? What does the Lord mean when He promises to come and "dwell" with a people? Were there a few people in the City of Enoch who didn't receive the "second comforter" or did they all finally qualify?

How influential did the City of Enoch become?

Did Enoch know his city and people were going to be translated? When the Lord showed Enoch a vision of the rest of the people why did the Lord weep?

How wicked were the people who lived in the days of Noah? When the Lord showed Enoch a personal, intimate view of their lives, what effect did it have on Enoch?

What was Enoch's reaction when the Lord showed him that practically the entire human race would be destroyed in a great flood? What did Enoch ask the Lord to do?

Did Enoch see a vision of the coming of Jesus Christ in the flesh? Then what was Enoch shown which came as a great shock to him?

What was Enoch shown concerning the last days? The Lord declared that the entire City of Enoch will someday return to the earth. When will that be?

Three years before the death of Adam, Enoch attended a great conference. Where was it and what was the occasion? Who was the clerk of that conference? A most unusual event occurred at this conference. What was it?

How old was Adam when he died? How old was Enoch
at that time? How old was Enoch when his people
were translated? Were any of the other patriarchs
translated with him? Do the people of Enoch still
have to go through another change to become resurrected beings? What is their present status? What
is their mission?

The Lord Dwells with the People of Enoch

The scripture records a most unusual circumstance
which occurred during the ministry of Enoch. It states
that the "Lord came and dwelt with his people, and they
dwelt in righteousness."[1] The intimacy of the association between the Lord and the people of Enoch at this
time was such that they could call upon Him for continuous guidance and instruction. It was the promised
Second Comforter—given, as it were, to a whole city!

As Joseph Smith explained: "What is this other Comforter? It is no more nor less than the Lord Jesus Christ
Himself; and this is the sum and substance of the whole
matter; that when any man obtains this last Comforter,
he will have the personage of Jesus Christ to attend him,
or appear unto him from time to time, and even He will
manifest the Father unto him, and they will take up their
abode with him, and the visions of the heavens will be
opened unto him, and the Lord will teach him face to face,
and he may have a perfect knowledge of the mysteries
of the Kingdom of God; and this is the state and place
the ancient Saints arrived at when they had such
glorious visions. . . ."[2]

The Saints in the days of Enoch had this great privilege. It is certain, however, that the appearance of the
Lord to the people would not be a promiscuous event such
as would occur on the streets or in public. It was a sacred
occasion probably reserved for the Holy of Holies in
the temple.[3] Being a personage of spirit at this time,
the only way the Lord would manifest Himself to the

---

[1]Moses 7:16
[2]*Teachings of Joseph Smith*, pp. 150-151
[3]Exodus 25:22 plus 26:34

people would be "in glory"⁴ and no doubt such appearances were reserved for special occasions and to fulfil specific needs. The Lord probably said unto the people of Enoch as He later said to the Israelites through Moses: "Let them make me a sanctuary; *that I may dwell among them.* . . . And there I will meet with the children of Israel, and the tabernacle shall be sanctified by my glory. . . . And I will dwell among the children of Israel, and will be their God."⁵

So undoubtedly it was there—in the sanctuary of a house "built unto God"—that the glory of God was manifest, and it was only on very sacred and solemn occasions that the servants of the Lord were permitted to enter into His presence. It is believed that similar circumstances prevailed in the days of Enoch and that when the scripture states that the "Lord came and dwelt with his people," it means that He appeared on many occasions in the sanctuary of the temple which they built for that very purpose.

After Enoch and the leaders had been perfected and could enter into the presence of God, they labored with their might until eventually all the people of that great city became worthy of the same privilege.⁶

During the 365 years that the City of Enoch was in existence its citizens gradually became the most influential of all peoples. The scripture says: "The fear of the Lord was upon *all nations,* so great was the glory of the Lord, which was upon his people. And the Lord blessed the land, and they were blessed upon the mountains, and upon the high places, and did flourish."⁷

Enoch Sees the History of the World in Vision

So frequently and intimately did Enoch enjoy communications from the Lord that the scripture speaks of Enoch as having "walked with God." The Lord appears to have revealed things to him which perhaps had

⁴*Teachings of Joseph Smith,* p. 162
⁵Exodus 25:8; 29:43, 45
⁶Moses 7:69
⁷*Ibid.,* 7:17

never been revealed before. One of the greatest visions opened to the gaze of Enoch was the future history of the world.

First, Enoch was shown his own city and he beheld that in process of time it would be taken from the earth to a place which had been especially prepared for it. As Enoch pondered the scene the Lord said: "Behold mine abode forever!"[8] Then Enoch looked and saw all of those who yet remained upon the earth. "And they were a mixture of all the seed of Adam save it were the seed of Cain, for the seed of Cain were black, and had not place among them."[9]

Then Enoch saw that even though he and the righteous inhabitants of Zion would be taken from the earth, nevertheless the gospel would continue to be preached and many would accept the plan of salvation. He also saw that some of these righteous converts would be translated and caught up to join the inhabitants of the City of Zion.[10]

Enoch saw the wicked who would reject the gospel. He saw that they would not countenance the truth— neither in their philosophies nor in the conduct of their daily lives. As the Lord looked upon these hosts, He wept. Enoch was astonished and said: "How is it that thou canst weep, seeing thou art holy, and from all eternity to all eternity? And were it possible that man could number the particles of the earth, yea, millions of earths like this, it would not be a beginning to the number of thy creations . . . how is it that thou canst weep?"[11]

And the Lord said: "Behold these thy brethren; they are the workmanship of mine own hands, and I gave unto them their knowledge, in the day I created them . . . And unto thy brethren have I said, and also given commandment, that they should love one another, and that they should choose me, their Father; but behold, they are without affection, and they hate their own blood; And the

[8]*Ibid.,* 7:21
[9]*Ibid.,* 7:22
[10]*Ibid.,* 7:27
[11]*Ibid.,* 7:29-31

fire of mine indignation is kindled against them; and in my hot displeasure will I send in the floods upon them, for my fierce anger is kindled against them. *Behold, . . . among all the workmanship of mine hands there has not been so great wickedness as among thy brethren.* But behold . . . Satan shall be their father, and misery shall be their doom; and the whole heavens shall weep over them, even all the workmanship of mine hands; wherefore should not the heavens weep, seeing these shall suffer?"[12]

These wicked multitudes of the future whom Enoch beheld were those who would be the contemporaries of Noah, and although he saw the civilization of their day he did not know the nature of their wickedness which caused the Lord as well as all eternity to weep over them. Therefore the Lord opened to the gaze of Enoch a presentation of the vicious and degenerate practices which would prevail among them and make these people abominable above the wickedness of all other creatures whom God had created. And as Enoch "looked upon their wickedness, and their misery" he "wept and stretched forth his arms, and his heart swelled wide as eternity."[13]

Then he saw Noah and his sons laboring with the people, calling them to repentance. He saw their utter rejection by the hissing, ridiculing crowds of listeners so that finally, in keeping with the commandments of God, they built an ark in which their lives could be saved. And as Enoch saw the vision of the whole earth being submerged in a cleansing baptism—swallowing up entire nations and their civilizations—he wept with great bitterness of soul and said: "I will refuse to be comforted." But the Lord softened the shock of what he had seen by showing him how rapidly the earth would be filled up again with the descendants of Noah.

Then Enoch asked to be shown the day when the Lord would come. As the vision of Christ's ministry appeared the Lord said: "It shall be in the meridian of

[12]*Ibid.,* 7:32-37
[13]*Ibid.,* 7:41

time." And "Enoch saw the day of the coming of the Son of Man, even in the flesh; and his soul rejoiced."[14]

At the conclusion of this scene, Enoch looked upon the earth and he heard a voice come out of it saying: "Wo is me, the mother of men; I am pained, I am weary, because of the wickedness of my children. When shall I rest, and be cleansed from the filthiness which is gone forth out of me? When will my Creator sanctify me, that I may rest, and righteousness for a season abide upon my face?"[15]

As Enoch heard this voice of lamentation he besought the Lord and said: "Wilt thou not have compassion upon the earth? Wilt thou not bless the children of Noah? ... I ask thee, O Lord, in the name of thine Only Begotten, even Jesus Christ, that thou wilt have mercy upon Noah and his seed, that the earth might never more be covered by the floods."[16]

So great was the fervor of Enoch that the scripture says: "The Lord could not withhold; and he covenanted with Enoch, and sware unto him with an oath, that he would stay the floods; (and) that he would call upon the children of Noah."[17] He also further comforted Enoch by sending forth "an unalterable decree, that a remnant of his (Enoch's) seed should always be found among all nations, while the earth should stand."[18] This prophecy was literally fulfilled. Every human being now living upon the face of the earth possesses some of the blood of Enoch in his veins. Enoch was the great-grandfather of Noah and through Noah all of us are made descendants of Enoch.

The vision of the wickedness of men so stimulated the spirit of anxiety in Enoch that in spite of these wonderful promises previously made to him, he still felt constrained to inquire further. Said he: "When the Son of Man cometh in the flesh, shall the earth rest? I pray thee, show me these things."[19]

[14]*Ibid.*, 7:47
[15]*Ibid.*, 7:48
[16]*Ibid.*, 7:48-50
[17]*Ibid.*, 7:51
[18]*Ibid.*, 7:52
[19]*Ibid.*, 7:54

In reply the Lord said: "Look!" Enoch could hardly believe the sight of his own eyes. Instead of the ministry of Jesus Christ bringing peace to the world he beheld that wicked men would drive spikes into the hands and feet of the Messiah and lift Him up on a cross of crucifixion after the manner of heathen Rome. "And he heard a loud voice, and the heavens were veiled; and all the creations of God mourned; and the earth groaned; and the rocks were rent." Then Enoch saw the glory of the resurrection—not only of Christ but of the Saints. Among men, however, wickedness continued unabated. "And again Enoch wept and cried unto the Lord, saying: When shall the earth rest?"[20]

The vision continued. Enoch was shown that after the resurrection Jesus would leave the earth and go to His Father. And as "Enoch beheld the Son of Man ascend up unto the Father . . . he called unto the Lord saying, Wilt thou not come again upon the earth? . . . And the Lord said, As I live, even so will I come in the last days, in the days of wickedness and vengeance, to fulfil the oath which I made unto you concerning the children of Noah. . . . But before that day the heavens shall be darkened, and a veil of darkness shall cover the earth; and the heavens shall shake, and also the earth; and great tribulations shall be among the children of men, but my people will I preserve."[21]

The Lord further comforted Enoch by saying that in the last days the righteous would be gathered "from the four quarters of the earth, unto a place which I shall prepare, an Holy City, that my people may gird up their loins, and be looking forth for the time of my coming; for there shall be my tabernacle, and it shall be called Zion, a New Jerusalem."[22]

At this point in the vision, Enoch was shown that when the City of Zion or New Jerusalem was set up in the last days it would be the signal for the return of Enoch and his people to the earth after an absence of five thousand years! Said the Lord: "Then shalt thou and all

[20]*Ibid.,* 7:58
[21]*Ibid.,* 7:59-61
[22]*Ibid.,* 7:62

thy city meet them there, and we will receive them into our bosom, and they shall see us; and we will fall upon their necks, and they will fall upon our necks, and we will kiss each other. And there shall be mine abode, and it shall be Zion, which shall come forth out of all the creations which I have made; and for the space of a thousand years the earth shall rest."[23]

Enoch then beheld the Second Coming of Christ and the inauguration of the millennium "even unto the end of the world." He saw the sanctification of the earth, the establishment of righteousness and the hour of redemption. Thus concluded the vision of Enoch and as he looked and beheld the successful culmination of the divine program which was framed and planned by the Lord from before the foundation of the world, he "received a fulness of joy."[24]

Enoch Is Made Clerk at a Special Conference Called by Father Adam

In the year 3,073 B.C., when Enoch was 305, a great conference of the Church was called by Father Adam. It was not held in the City of Enoch nor any part of the land of Cainan but convened in the valley of Adam-ondi-Ahman, the ancient home of the first patriarch, which was located about forty miles north of the original Garden of Eden. There must have been a great stir among the people of God when word came that the aged Adam desired to meet with all "the residue of his posterity who were righteous." They probably migrated in a great body to participate in this historic family reunion, and possibly at no time in the history of the world—either before or since—has there been a conference of the Saints to compare with this one.

At this time Adam was in his 927th year and was "bowed down with age."[25] The purpose of the conference was to give him the opportunity of bestowing upon his righteous posterity a final blessing, for he knew he

[23]*Ibid.*, 7:63
[24]*Ibid.*, 7:67
[25]D. & C. 107:53, 56

was about to die. Enoch was appointed clerk of the conference and recorded in detail the thrilling events which transpired upon this occasion.[26] Among those present, special mention is made of those who were direct heirs to the Priesthood, including: Seth, Enos, Cainan, Mahalaleel, Jared, Enoch and Methuselah, "who were all high priests."[27] We are not told why Lamech, son of Methuselah, was not present. He had been called to the Priesthood twenty-one years before and had been ordained by Seth, but he is the only heir to the Priesthood who is not given credit for having been present at this conference. Perhaps he was called away by some special mission which prevented his attendance.

The first part of the conference was taken up by Father Adam who called his sons forth to give them his final father's blessing. Then, as a mighty climax to the meeting, the glory of the Lord was suddenly shown forth in their midst and the personage of the omnipotent Jehovah stood before them to honor the Ancient of Days. This testimonial of the Lord's love for this first man of all men so stimulated the enthusiasm of the congregation that they all rose up together and blessed the name of Adam, calling him Michael, the mighty prince and archangel— their valiant leader of the pre-existence.

Then Jehovah pronounced His blessing upon this faithful pioneer of the first dispensation. Said He: "I have set thee to be at the head; a multitude of nations shall come of thee, and thou art a prince over them forever!"[28]

"And Adam stood up in the midst of the congregation; and, notwithstanding he was bowed down with age, being full of the Holy Ghost, predicted whatsoever should befall his posterity unto the latest generation."[29]

ADAM DIES

Thus ended a glorious conference. As the vast assembly adjourned and prepared to return home they must have cast their eyes upon the greatly beloved Adam with

---

[26]*Ibid.,* 107:57
[27]*Ibid.,* 107:53
[28]*Ibid.,* 107:55
[29]*Ibid.,* 107:56

mixed emotions of love and sorrow. They must have
known that for most of them, this was the last time they
would ever behold this ancient patriarch in mortality.
The once perfect stature "made in the very image of
God," had been withered by time. In all probability the
strong arm which formerly wielded its strength now
trembled on a crutch. The eyes were dimmed, the shoul-
ders bent. The voice quavered and the countenance reflected the occasional pain which shot through the frame
of this long enduring tabernacle. The sands of time
were running out, and the seeds of death which Adam
had taken into his system in the Garden of Eden were
exacting their toll.

In warning Adam concerning the fruit from the tree
of knowledge, the Lord had said: "In the day thou eatest thereof thou shalt surely die."[30] At the time this statement was made the earth was "after the Lord's time, which
was after the time of Kolob, for as yet the Gods had not
appointed unto Adam his reckoning."[31] And the Lord
explained that the reckoning of one day according
to the reckoning of Kolob is "one thousand years" of the
time appointed to the earth in its present fallen condition.[32] Therefore the word of the Lord had restricted
the life of Adam to something less than a thousand years.
That period of time was nearly up.

It was three years after the great conference at Adam-
ondi-Ahman, that the first patriarch of the race termi-
nated his earthly mission. He was 930 years old when
he died.[33] This was in the year 3,070 B.C. Seth was
now exactly 800, Enos was 695, Cainan was 605, Mahalaleel was 535, Jared was 470, Enoch was 308,
Methuselah was 243, and Lamech was 56.

These patriarchal descendants of Adam probably
stood in thoughtful silence as the mortal mission of Adam
came to a close. Each of them must have reflected
upon this great last experience which is the way of all
flesh—an experience which would likewise come to all

[30]Moses 3:17
[31]Abraham 5:13
[32]Ibid., 3:4
[33]Moses 6:12

of them some day; all of them, that is, except Enoch. For him the Lord had provided another way.

THE CITY OF ZION IS TRANSLATED AND REMOVED FROM THE EARTH

In 2,948 B. C. when Enoch was 430 years old,[34] he and the population of the entire City of Zion were translated and removed from the earth to another planet. This quickening process was a remarkable physical metamorphosis whereby the seeds of death were neutralized within them and their bodies became subject to a higher system of physical laws. When this same experience occurred to three of the Nephite disciples they said the change within them was so great that at first they could not tell but what they had been released from their bodies entirely.[35] Then they realized that they still had their bodies but they were no longer a burden to them, nor were they subject to the biological requirements to which they were accustomed. "It did seem unto them like a transfiguration of them, that they were changed from this body of flesh into an immortal state, that they could behold the things of God. . . . And they were cast into prison by them who did not belong to the church. And the prisons could not hold them, for they were rent in twain. And they were cast down into the earth; but they did smite the earth with the word of God, insomuch that by his power they were delivered out of the depths of the earth; and therefore they could not dig pits sufficient to hold them. And thrice were they cast into a furnace and received no harm. And twice were they cast into a den of wild beasts; and behold they did play with the beasts as a child with a suckling lamb, and received no harm."[36]

This same sudden refinement was given to all of the people in the City of Zion. It also extended to their possessions. As President Brigham Young commented: "He (Enoch) obtained power to translate himself and

---

[34]D. & C. 107:49
[35]3 Nephi 28:15
[36]*Ibid.,* 28:15, 19-22

his people, with the region they inhabited, their houses, gardens, fields, cattle and all of their possessions."[37]

But while from all appearances they had assumed the characteristics of immortal beings, they nevertheless had *not* attained that degree of refinement which is enjoyed by resurrected beings. As Joseph Smith explained in a very enlightening discourse on this subject: "Now the doctrine of translation is a power which belongs to this Priesthood. There are many things which belong to the powers of the Priesthood and the keys thereof, that have been kept hid from before the foundation of the world; they are hid from the wise and prudent to be revealed in the last times. Many have supposed that the doctrine of translation was a doctrine whereby men were taken immediately into the presence of God and unto an eternal fullness, but this is a mistaken idea. Their place of habitation is that of the terrestrial order, and a place prepared for such characters (whom) He held in reserve to be ministering angels unto many planets, and who as yet have not entered into so great a fullness as those who are resurrected from the dead."[38]

The people of Enoch are therefore fulfilling a very important mission. "Translation obtains deliverance from the tortures and sufferings of the body, but their existence will prolong as to the labors and toils of the ministry, before they can enter into so great a rest and glory as that which they will receive in the resurrection."[39]

In modern revelation the Lord refers to the fact that "Enoch and his brethren . . . were separated from the earth and were received unto myself—a city reserved until a day of righteousness shall come."[40] That "day of righteousness" will be at the beginning of the millennium.[41] At that time Enoch and his people will return to the earth and join with the Saints of the latter days at the City of Zion or New Jerusalem which will be built during this present dispensation.[42] This will occur in-

[37]*Disc. of Brigham Young*, p. 162
[38]*Teachings of Joseph Smith*, p. 170
[39]*Ibid.*, p. 171
[40]D. & C. 45:11-12
[41]Moses 7:62-64
[42]D. & C. 84:2-5

cidental to the Second Coming of Christ and immediately after that the people of Enoch will undoubtedly receive the same blessing which was promised to the Three Nephites and John the Beloved. The Lord said: "When I shall come in my glory ye shall be changed in the twinkling of an eye from mortality to immortality. . . . to be received into the kingdom of the Father to go no more out, but to dwell with God eternally in the heavens!"[43]

It must have been a most impressive item of news that spread among the people after the translation of Zion. The saying went abroad everywhere: "Zion is fled!"[44] The abbreviated Bible version simply says: "And Enoch . . . was not; for God took him."[45] This passage has always perplexed scholars and it was not until we received the restoration of Genesis that the thrilling details concerning the translation of Enoch and Zion became known.

---

[43] 3 Nephi 28:8; 29:40; D. & C. 7:3
[44] Moses 7:69
[45] Genesis 5:24

CHAPTER TWENTY

From Methuselah to Noah

What great event took place the year Methuselah was born? How old was his father at the time of Methuselah's birth? Who was his father?

What do the authorities say the name of Methuselah means? Was this meaning literally fulfilled? How old was Methuselah when he died?

How old was Methuselah when Lamech was born? Lamech was the first patriarch to receive the Priesthood from someone other than Adam. Who ordained him? Did he outlive his father? How close did he come to seeing the year of the great Flood?

How long had the City of Enoch been translated when Noah was born? What prophet saw him in vision and had been told his name several centuries before he was born? How old was Noah when he received the Priesthood?

Is there a hint as to what might have happened to the early children of Noah and also the families of the other patriarchs?

In what order were Shem, Ham and Japheth born? Which of them held the Priesthood? Which of them were called "Sons of God"? Which of them "walked with God"?

What unusual event occurred at the time Noah was called on his 120-year-mission? How many times does the scripture indicate that an attempt was made to assassinate Noah during his mission?

What kind of message did Noah preach? What was the argument of the men who came with the claim that they were also the "sons of God"?

Except for the murder cult of the Mahanites we do not have any description of the "wickedness" which characterized the pre-flood period. Do we have any indication that their practices were similar to the abominations of Babylon, Egypt, Sodom and Gomorrah? Have you ever known a person whose life was "evil continuously"? Can you visualize a generation where "every man" was evil continuously?

How much significance do you attach to the Lord's statement that "the earth is filled with violence"?

The Patriarch Methuselah

Among those left on the earth after the translation of Zion there were a few who ordinarily would have been taken also, but apparently the Lord had other missions for them. Therefore they stood patiently by and watched the departure of Enoch and his people with heart-stirring feelings of astonishment, gladness and some sorrow. Among those who remained were all of Enoch's immediate forefathers except Seth and Adam. There was his father, Jared, age 592; his grandfather, Mahalaleel, age 657; his great-grandfather Cainan, age 727; and his great-great-grandfather, Enos, age 817. Seth had passed away just ten years before at the age of 912, and Adam had been gone for 122 years.

Not only did Enoch leave behind four of his paternal ancestors, but also his son and heir to the Priesthood, Methuselah. His grandson, Lamech, was left behind as well.

Methuselah was born 3,313 B. C. As before stated, his birth was in the same year that the City of Zion was begun. When Methuselah was one hundred years old, Adam ordained him to the Holy Priesthood.[1] Methuselah was 243 when Adam died, and 365 when his father and the City of Zion were translated. The scripture is plain in stating that the reason Methuselah did not accompany his father was because the Lord desired that he should be the one through whom the lineage of the patriarch

[1] D. & C. 107:50

and the powers of the Priesthood should be perpetuated: "Methuselah, the son of Enoch, was not taken, that the covenants of the Lord might be fulfilled, which he made to Enoch; for he truly covenanted with Enoch that Noah should be of the fruit of his loins."[2]

In the long life of Methuselah he undoubtedly performed a great mission, for otherwise he would not have been counted worthy of his position in the patriarchal line. Nevertheless, like all mortal beings, he had his weaknesses and the scripture refers to one specifically. He was tremendously impressed by the fact that it would be through him that the human race would be perpetuated; that is, among his descendants, the patriarch Noah would be raised up who would survive the Flood and thus, all the people of the earth after the Flood would carry the blood of Methuselah in their veins. This caused a surge of personal gratification to sweep through him each time this future event came to mind. It even crept into his preaching and because he boasted of it the scripture refers to it as though the Lord were displeased: "And it came to pass that Methuselah prophesied that from his loins should spring all the kingdoms of the earth (through Noah), and he took glory unto himself."[3]

It was during the ministry of Methuselah that the first recorded famine took place. It appears to have been extremely severe, for large numbers of the people died in consequence of it.[4]

Methuselah lived to see the passing of every other patriarch of the Adamic dispensation. He was 453 when Enos died, 548 when Cainan died, 603 when Mahalaleel died, 735 when Jared died. Even his own son, Lamech, preceded him to the grave by five years.[5] Methuselah, therefore, lived upon the earth longer than any other human being of whom we have any record. He lived until 2,344 B.C. which permitted him to fulfil the prophecy contained in his name. "Methuselah" is said to mean:

[2]Moses 8:2
[3]Ibid., 8:3
[4]Ibid., 8:4
[5]Ibid., 8:10

"At his death, the sending forth of waters."[6] This was literally fulfilled, for Methuselah died in the very year that the great Flood came. He was 969 years old—just thirty-one years less than a millennium!

THE PATRIARCH LAMECH

We do not know a great deal concerning Lamech. He was born of Methuselah when the latter was 187 years old.[7] At the age of thirty-two he was ordained to the Holy Priesthood under the hands of Seth.[8] This made Lamech the first patriarch to receive the Priesthood from someone other than Adam. By this time Adam was 906 years old and his feebleness may have forced him into comparative retirement. However, Lamech was able to receive his patriarchal blessing from Adam at the age of fifty-three,[9] and he was fifty-six when Adam died. Lamech lived during a considerable part of the golden age which characterized the City of Zion and was 178 when that remarkable civilization was removed from the earth. He was 182 when his son, Noah, was born and lived to observe the long ministry of Noah during 595 years. During this time he saw the collapse of nearly everything for which he and his fathers had labored. The decay of morals, ethics, social standards and spiritual refinement was so gross and flagrant that his son, Noah, even expressed regret that God had ever permitted the face of the earth to be contaminated by such degenerate creatures.[10]

Nevertheless, Lamech joined with his son, Noah, and with his father, Methuselah, to garner the souls of the few who would respond to the gospel plan. The scripture implies that as fast as these converts were perfected in righteousness they were translated and permitted to join the City of Zion.[11] This may have also been granted to qualified members of the families of the patriarchs.

[6]Clarke, op. *cit.*, Vol. I, p. 66
[7]Moses 8:5
[8]D. & C. 107:51
[9]*Ibid.*, 107:53
[10]Moses 8:25
[11]*Ibid.*, 7:27

Lamech lived to see the growing tidal wave of wickedness engulf every living human being upon the earth save himself, his father, his son, his three grandsons and their wives. He heard the last warning call of Noah as he went forth in the spirit of prophecy and testimony to seal up the licentious mockers among all nations unto complete destruction. He watched intently as Noah and his sons performed the herculean task of building the Ark. He watched the whole drama of the age drawing toward a terrible and awe-inspiring climax. Then suddenly, just five years before the cataclysmic deluge descended upon the earth, Lamech died. He was 777 years of age.[12]

THE PATRIARCH NOAH

Now we come to one of the greatest personalities of all time. Noah had been seen in vision by his great-grandfather, Enoch, many years before he was born.[13] Enoch knew what his name would be and also the importance of his mission.[14] Methuselah was so proud of the fact that Noah would be his descendant that he fell into temptation and boasted of it, taking "glory unto himself."[15] This may be better appreciated when it is realized that of all the spirits who had been born into the earth since Adam, none were of more excellent standing and prestige in the eyes of God than Noah. Noah was "Gabriel" in the pre-existence,[16] and after he was born he was placed "next in authority to Adam in the Priesthood; he was called of God to this office, and was (made) the father of all living in this day, and to him was given the dominion."[17]

Noah was born in the year 2,944 B.C. which was four years after the City of Zion was translated. At that time his father, Lamech, was 182 years old. From the beginning it was known that Noah would become one of the greatest prophets of any dispensation in history

[12]*Ibid.*, 8:11
[13]*Ibid.*, 7:42
[14]*Ibid.*
[15]*Ibid.*, 8:3
[16]*Teachings of Joseph Smith*, p. 157
[17]*Idem*

and therefore the Priesthood was conferred upon him while he was still a child. Methuselah ordained him at the unprecedented age of ten![18]

In his early life Noah observed the ministry of Methuselah and Lamech and heard the gospel taught by Enos, Cainan, Mahalaleel and Jared. All of these patriarchs were contemporaries of Noah.

It is interesting to note that each of these patriarchs had "many sons and daughters" in addition to the ones which are specifically mentioned in the genealogies of the Bible.[19] What happened to all these children? And what happened to the many sons and daughters of Noah who were probably born before Japheth, Shem and Ham?

Since none of them are listed among those who survived the Flood we cannot help wondering if these choice children of the covenant were also victims of apostasy and died in the roaring tides of the great deluge. One passage suggests a hopeful alternative. It states that during this period: "the Holy Ghost fell on many, and they were caught up by the powers of heaven into Zion!"[20] By the time Noah began his special mission at the age of 480 the City of Zion had already been gone nearly five centuries. Nevertheless, this passage would indicate that all those who joined the Church (and were not appointed unto death such as Methuselah and Lamech) were gradually perfected and then caught up to join the Saints of Enoch in their new terrestrial home. We can hope that among these righteous members of the Church, the numerous posterity of the patriarchs was included.

BIRTH OF JAPHETH, SHEM AND HAM

As with the other patriarchs, none of Noah's earlier children are mentioned. The scripture begins its account with three sons who were born to him in his later years and who were selected to perpetuate humanity after the Flood. It states that when Noah was 450 years old

[18]D. & C. 107:52
[19]See Moses 6:11, 14, 18, 20; 8:6,10
[20]Moses 7:27

Japheth was born.[21] Forty-two years later, when Noah
was 492, Shem was born.[22] Although Shem was the
younger of the two, he was later selected as Noah's first
heir to the Priesthood. Eight years later, when Noah
was 500, Ham was born. The scripture specifically states
that Japheth and Shem had the same mother.[23] This implies that Ham had a different mother and was therefore
only the half-brother of Shem and Japheth.

These three sons were born at a time when apostasy
and moral disintegration had engulfed the whole earth.
Violence, murder, war, theft, rapine, fraud and graft
characterized civilization everywhere. According to the
Lord, this society of mankind during the dispensation of
Noah was worse than anything before or since—worse
than Babylon where they offered human sacrifices, worse
than Greece where they subjected young children to degenerate orgies, worse than Sodom, worse than Gomorrah. In fact, the Lord declared: "Among all the workmanship of mine hands there has not been so great
wickedness" as that which prevailed in this age of which
we are speaking. It was a day when "the power of Satan
was upon all the face of the earth."[24] So successful was
Satan that the scripture says the earth seemed veiled with
a terrible chain of darkness and Lucifer "looked up and
laughed, and his angels rejoiced."[25]

But in spite of this environment, Noah succeeded in
surrounding his three sons with the mantle of the gospel
and the scripture says they "hearkened unto the Lord,
and gave heed, and they were called the sons of God."[26]
This title "The sons of God," is reserved for those who
receive the Priesthood,[27] therefore we know that these
three sons were all honored with divine callings. Ham's
calling to the Priesthood is specifically mentioned by
Abraham,[28] and Shem established the line through which

[21]*Ibid.*, 8:12
[22]*Ibid.*, 8:12
[23]*Ibid.*
[24]*Ibid.*, 7:24
[25]*Ibid.*, 7:26
[26]*Ibid.*, 8:13
[27]D. & C. 76:57-58
[28]Abraham 1:27

the Priesthood descended to all the postdiluvian patriarchs.[29] All three sons are described as having "walked with God'"[30]

When these three sons matured and married they each had daughters born unto them. Apparently, no male offspring were born to any of them until after the Flood. These daughters finally grew up and no doubt Japheth, Shem and Ham labored diligently to impress upon their minds the importance of the Lord's plan for happy living. But no matter how successful they might have been in getting them to accept the basic doctrines, there was one place where they failed completely. None of these men could dissuade their daughters from marrying outside the Church. In fact, it may have been that there were no righteous men whom they *could* have married. In any event, all of these daughters eventually rebelled against the warnings of their parents and the pleadings of Noah and took unto themselves husbands among the wicked.

Immediately the word of the Lord came unto Noah: "The daughters of thy sons have sold themselves; for behold mine anger is kindled against the sons of men for they will not hearken to my voice!" The "sons of men" referred to the wicked of that generation who rejected the gospel and were therefore not worthy of the Priesthood through which they could become the "sons of God."[31]

All of this occurred right at the time when Noah was doing his utmost to inspire a spirit of repentance among the people. Some time before, when he was 480, Noah had been called on a 120-year-mission to preach a message of "repent or perish" to the depraved and licentious inhabitants of the earth.[32] So important was this mission that the Lord had personally laid His hands upon the head of Noah and reaffirmed the Priesthood in him. The scripture says: "And the Lord ordained Noah after his own order, and commanded him that he should go forth

[29] I Chronicles 1:24-27; Abraham 1:3, 18
[30] Moses 8:27
[31] D. & C. 76:57-58
[32] Moses 8:17

and declare his Gospel unto the children of men, even as it was given unto Enoch."[33]

NOAH MARKED FOR ASSASSINATION BY HIS ENEMIES..

This was no command to give to a man of weak or timid temperament. Already Noah had been the object of an assassination plot conjured up by a tribe of men whom the people referred to as "giants" because of their size and strength. They had been greatly offended by Noah's preaching and they "sought Noah to take away his life; but the Lord was with Noah, and the power of the Lord was upon him."[34]

Noah continued to carry out his new calling with courage and fixed purpose. But Lucifer attacked him from another direction. He inspired the wicked to recall that they too were descendants of men who were originally entitled to be called "Sons of God." Therefore they leaped forward to challenge Noah with diabolical glee: Said they, "Behold, we are the sons of God; have we not taken unto ourselves the daughters of men? And are we not eating and drinking, and marrying and giving in marriage? And our wives bear unto us children, and the same are mighty men, which are like unto men of old, men of great renown!"[35] Here was the fallacious philosophy of the pragmatist: "Anything which succeeds is good, anything which fails is bad." And these wicked descendants of once righteous men had much to boast of. At the moment they were in physical possession of the earth. Now that the commonwealth of Enoch was gone they had spread their tyrannical power everywhere. They robbed the earth of her treasures, lived riotously, and scornfully pointed out to Noah that it was they who were enjoying the "good and abundant life." What could Noah offer them? They had everything!

It is interesting to note that the gospel preached by Noah—which is described as being the same as the gospel of Enoch—is identical with the message preached in

[33]Moses 8:19
[34]*Ibid.,* 8:18
[35]*Ibid.,* 8:21

the days of Christ and also in our own dispensation: "It came to pass that Noah continued his preaching unto the people, saying: Hearken, and give heed unto my words; Believe and repent of your sins and be baptized in the name of Jesus Christ, the Son of God, even as our fathers, and ye shall receive the Holy Ghost."[36]

Note the similarity between the words of Noah and the words of Peter. When the chief of the Apostles was preaching to the multitudes in Jerusalem he said: "Repent, and be baptized every one of you in the name of Jesus Christ for the remission of sins, and ye shall receive the gift of the Holy Ghost."[37] This clearly demonstrates that in every dispensation the gospel message has been fundamentally the same.

Now the enemies of Noah not only continued to reject his message but they set about with real intent to destroy him through the machinations of their murder cult. Noah knew he was in great danger and he pleaded with the Lord for protection. As the Lord later said: "He hath called upon me; for they have sought his life."[38] This was the second time that Noah had been in danger of assassination by his enemies. In his fervent communications with Jehovah, Noah apologized for the very existence of these decadent off-scourings of humanity who polluted every phase of life through their corruption. "His heart was pained that the Lord had made man on the earth, and it grieved him at the heart."[39]

As the Creator looked down upon the debauchery of this depraved generation of humanity He weighed them in the balance and pronounced judgment. He found that because of them the whole earth was "filled with violence,"[40] and "all flesh had corrupted its way upon the earth."[41] When God organized the earth and provided physical tabernacles for His sons and daughters He set up a pattern of life which would make this experience

[36]*Ibid.,* 8:23-24
[37]Acts 2:38
[38]Moses 8:26
[39]*Ibid.,* 8:25
[40]*Ibid.,* 8:28
[41]*Ibid.,* 8:29

profitable to them. He knew that the emotional rapture and other sensory experiences which the physical body was engineered to provide would be a source of deeper insight and greater joy than mankind had ever known in the pre-existence. The Master Technician also knew that the human body is a precision instrument designed to function within the limitations of comparatively strict specifications. These specifications for wise and wholesome living had been revealed to men. Jehovah had counseled men to think of their physical tabernacles as "temples of God" in a very literal sense. Their bodies reflected the engineering genius of a most wise and skilful Creator.

Adam had honored his earthly body and his physical environment for what God had intended them to be. So had Seth and Enoch. So had all the righteous from the very beginning.

But now a generation had risen in the earth which took a different view of life. With them, luxurious, pleasure-loving extravagance and lewd, licentious dissipation had become the entire object of existence. Frayed nerves and tired bodies were flagellated with stimulants: Narcotics to inflame the brain, obscene lewdness to pamper the senses and boiling fermentation from the vinegar vats of the wine presses to stifle judgment and cover the wild debaucheries of the people under the soggy cloak of alcoholic amnesia.

Not only did they reject the counsel of God but through reckless experimentation the masses of the people staggered down a steep road which spiraled into the depths of all-consuming darkness. They tasted every forbidden thing, seeking always for the *ultimate* thrill in some new indulgence. They made of life a continuous orgy of unleashed emotional frenzy which filled the earth with perversion, exploitation and degeneracy. Instead of seeking happiness, security and personal improvement the Lord says that "Every man was lifted up in the imagination of the thoughts of his heart, *being only evil continuously!*"[42]

---

[42]*Ibid.,* 8:22

And God said unto Noah: "The end of all flesh is come before me, for the earth is filled with violence, and behold I will destroy all flesh from off the earth."[43]

This was the end of Noah's great mission. For over 100 years he had labored to save the remnants of this generation. Now there was barely time to save his family and himself.

---

[43]*Ibid.,* 8:30

CHAPTER TWENTY-ONE

The Greatest Catastrophe in History

Where did Noah get the necessary information to build the Ark? How would the size of the Ark compare with a modern ocean liner? How many decks did it have? How was the Ark made "tight like a dish"?

What important event happened in the family of Noah five years before the Flood? Up to what point did Noah have the counsel of his grandfather, Methuselah?

Did Noah have difficulty herding the various animals into the Ark? How many of each clean species did he take? How many of the unclean species? How many days were apparently needed to get the animal life loaded into the pens of the Ark?

Has scientific research made it possible to understand more easily how Noah accomplished his task?

Do we know the exact date when the great Flood began? Apparently how many days was it before the flood waters reached the Ark and lifted it? How many more days did the storm last?

Did Noah's sons leave any of their children behind? Why?

Was the destruction of the Flood caused by anything besides rain. Was it a universal flood or just a local flood? Did the flood waters cover the earth? Do we know specifically that the Flood included the Western Hemisphere?

The Bible says the Ark had a window a cubit below the roof? Is this all the ventilation the Ark had?

As the Ark began to move across the deep did Noah have any way of knowing where he was going?

Building The Ark

The detailed revelation which God gave to Noah concerning the construction of the Ark is not included in the scriptures. However, we know from other revelations that whenever the Lord has commanded a prophet to build any structure after a divine blueprint He has always revealed the necessary instructions and frequently included the most minute details such as the design of curtains, arches, pillars, windows and doors.[1]

Take, for example, the revelation given to David concerning the plans for the temple which Solomon was to build. The scripture says: "Then David gave to Solomon his son the *pattern* of the porch, and of the houses thereof and of the treasuries thereof, and of the upper chambers. . . . And the pattern of all that he had by the spirit. . . . All this, said David, the Lord made me understand in *writing* by his hand upon me, even all the works of the *pattern.*"[2]

Probably Noah received his revelation on the Ark in this same manner and when he saw the form of it in vision he no doubt could say of the Ark what Nephi later declared concerning the ship which God commanded him to build. Nephi declared: "And the Lord did show me from time to time after what manner I should work the timbers of the ship. Now, I, Nephi, did not work the timbers after the manner which was learned by men, neither did I build the ship after the manner of men; but *I did build it after the manner which the Lord had shown unto* me, wherefore, it was not after the manner of men."[3]

A strong indication that Noah likewise followed a revealed blueprint from the Lord is borne out by the Bible where it refers to the construction of the Ark and says: "Thus did Noah; *according to all that God had commanded him,* so did he."[4]

The dimensions of the Ark as given in the Bible would indicate that it was far different from any ship

---

[1]Exodus, Ch. 26; Ezekiel, Ch. 40-41
[2]I Chr. 28: 11-19
[3]I Nephi 18: 1-2
[4]Genesis 6:22

which we would expect to be built in that early day. The authorities state that the dimensions given in the Bible would make the Ark about as large as the modern Italian liner, the *Rex*, which has a displacement of about 50,000 tons.[5]

The Ark is described as being 300 cubits long, 50 cubits wide and 30 cubits high.[6] Using the accepted minimum length for a cubit of 18 inches, the Ark would be 450 feet long, 75 feet wide and 45 feet high. Some authorities have pointed out, however, that a larger unit of measurement for the cubit was often used. But even if the minimum cubit measurement is used, the fact obviously remains that the Ark was an extremely large vessel for those times.

It had three decks,[7] and many windows located just below the roof.[8] Each of the decks was divided into compartments or rooms,[9] and the entrance to the Ark was by way of a door located high up on the side of the ship. This entrance apparently led onto the first deck.[10] We also know that the Ark was coated with pitch or tar both within and without, so that it was "tight like a dish." In fact, the scripture later compares the barges of the Jaredites with the Ark in this language: "And it came to pass that when they (the barges of the Jaredites) were buried in the deep there was no water that could hurt them, their vessels being tight like unto a dish, and also they were *tight like unto the ark of Noah;* therefore when they were encompassed about by many waters they did cry unto the Lord and he did bring them forth again upon the top of the waters."[11]

From this we may perhaps assume that the Ark, like the barges of the Jaredites, was so well constructed that when the door and windows were sealed shut, it was capable of weathering extremely rough seas—even to the extent of surviving brief periods of complete submersion.

---

[5]Free, J. P. *Archaeology and the Bible*, p. 41
[6]Genesis 6:15
[7]*Ibid.*, 6:16
[8]Insp. Version, Genesis 8:21
[9]Genesis 6:14
[10]*Ibid.*, 6:16
[11]Ether 6:7

The strength of the Ark is further indicated by the fact that the Lord told Noah to build this ship exclusively of "Gopher wood."[12] This word appears nowhere else in scripture. "Gopher wood" is said to have referred to a specie of cypress or cedar which was rot-resistant and which was also impervious to the attack of wood worms.[13]

THE DEATH OF LAMECH AND METHUSELAH

As the construction of the Ark neared completion, Noah lost the encouragement, guidance and companionship of his father and his grandfather. Lamech, his father, passed away just five years before the advent of the Flood. Methuselah, his grandfather, died sometime during the very year in which the Flood began. This was when Noah was 600 which would be 2,344 B.C.

As we have previously pointed out the name of Methuselah was prophetic in that it is said to have meant: "At his death, the waters come forth." It is significant that he lived right up to the time when the great deluge was about to engulf the earth, and died that very same year. He was 969 years old, which is the nearest any human being has come to living a thousand years insofar as history records. It must have been an occasion of great solemnity for Noah when he laid to rest the last of the Adamic patriarchs. Of all the great multitudes who now lived upon the earth, Noah and his three sons were the only ones who bore the Priesthood.

THE ARK BECOMES A SANCTUARY OF LIFE

The Ark must have taken many years to complete. Whether Noah and his sons were assisted by hired labor in building this gigantic vessel we are not told. No doubt the Ark was the object of international interest and became the major theme for sarcastic ridicule by the multitudes who flocked about on feast days and holidays to see "Noah's Monstrosity," or "Noah's Folly."

Finally, however, all was ready. Not only had Noah and his sons completed the Ark but they had gathered

[12]Genesis 6:14
[13]Clarke, *op. cit.,* Vol. I, p: 68

together large quantities of seeds and foodstuffs both for themselves and the animal life which was to be preserved in the Ark. (Genesis 6:21) The question may be raised as to what provision would be made for the carnivorous creatures who would need flesh of other animals to feed upon. The scripture does not deal with the problem directly but one passage suggests a possible answer.

To Noah the Lord said: "Of every clean beast thou shalt take to thee by *sevens* . . . and of beasts that are not clean by two, the male and the female."[14] Was the Lord favoring the ratio of clean animals over the unclean or were these extra animals of the "clean" species to be used in part for food? The fact that the uneven number of seven was designated rather than an even number (to permit mating "in pairs") would strongly suggest that some of these creatures were to be used for purposes other than mating. Certainly we are assured that Noah had in the Ark sufficient quantities of animals so that if some of them were used for food there would still be adequate numbers of each species available "to keep seed alive upon the face of all the earth."

Now on the tenth day of the second month when Noah was in his 600th year the Lord commanded Noah and his immediate family to enter into the Ark.[15] Then a miraculous thing occurred.

Members of the animal kingdom which had undoubtedly been gravitating to this spot for quite some time, began to assemble themselves on the ramp which led up to the large doorway high on the side of the Ark. Anyone who might have been watching would have found it difficult to believe his eyes. These animals quietly and peacefully assembled as though driven by a common instinct. Apparently animals of prey mingled harmlessly with those creatures which ordinarily would have been their victims.

It is clear from the scripture that these animals did not have to be herded into the Ark. They went in of their own volition.[16] They were answering the same voice as

[14]Genesis 7:2
[15]*Ibid.,* 8:7-11
[16]*Ibid.,* 7:9

that which spoke peace to the lions in the den with Daniel[17] and the same voice which instructed the ravens to take food to the prophet Elijah.[18] There is one language which the members of the animal kingdom can understand and that is the language of the Priesthood.[19] Thus we read that Noah went into the Ark and the animals came voluntarily in unto him: "There went in two and two unto Noah into the ark, the male and the female, as God had commanded Noah."[20]

As these creatures came into the Ark they were no doubt led to pens which had been appropriately prepared for each species. This was hard work for Noah and his sons, and it would appear from the scripture that it required seven days to complete the task of separating these animals and placing them in their various pens inside the Ark. The work started seven days before the Flood[21] and it reads as though they were still hard at it the "self-same day" that the Flood was scheduled to begin.[22]

How many animals could be accommodated in the Ark? Scientists and scholars have wondered how a single vessel—even as large as the Ark—could have possibly housed enough animals to account for all of the species which now exist on the earth. However, the problem is simplified somewhat as we gain a better knowledge of the laws of heredity and learn that from a single set of parents a great variety of "breeds" or types may eventually be produced.

In this connection one authority states: "The term species may be defined as a group of individuals of animals or plants which breed together freely and reproduce fertile offspring; hence all dogs, wolves, coyotes, jackals and dingoes, all of which are interfertile, needed to have only one pair to represent them in the Ark. The same applied to the cat family which includes the lions, tigers, pumas, leopards, jaguars, wild cats, ocelots and others. One pair may have represented this group in the Ark.

[17]Daniel 6:22
[18]I Kings 17:4-6
[19]Jacob 4:6; Helaman 10:5-10
[20]Genesis 7:9
[21]*Ibid.*, 7:7-10
[22]*Ibid.*, 7:11-13

All horses whether Shetland ponies, racers or heavy draft horses form one species and have all descended from a common ancestor. . . . Not every variety of this large group need to have been in the Ark. A representative was sufficient to supply the great number of varieties of forms found on the earth today."[23]

Darwin observed the fact that many different types are merely variations of a common ancestor. He cited the classical example of the pigeon. He found that if the almost endless varieties of pigeons were allowed to breed together, they went back to the rock pigeon; therefore if there were seven pigeons in the Ark as the Bible indicates there were, there would be thousands of varieties potentially preserved.

Authorities also point out that the adequacy of the Ark may be better appreciated when it is realized that the number of large species in the animal kingdom is comparatively small. It is estimated, for example, that "land mammalia above the size of a sheep at the present time number about 290 (species); those from the sheep to rats, 757, and those smaller than rats, 1,359. The average size is about that of a cat, a pair of which would require less than two square feet of space."[24]

It will be recalled that the Ark was provided with three decks. Authorities state that these three decks would have a total of 101,250 square feet of floor space. It is also reasonable to assume that the small and medium sized animals would be placed in tiers of cages, one above the other. Therefore, it is likely that much of the space between the decks was used as well as the deck floors. Authorities estimate the interior of the Ark to have been 1,500,000 cubic feet,[25] most of which would have been available for cages and the storage of feed.

When all of these possibilities are considered it will be seen that the housing of the requisite number of species in the Ark is much more plausible than many had previously supposed.

[23]Rehwinkel, A. M., *The Flood,* p. 70
[24]*Ibid.,* p. 69
[25]*Ibid.,* p. 68

The Great Flood Strikes Humanity 2,344 B.C.

It was on the seventeenth day of the second month in the year that Noah became 600 that the great Flood began. As we have previously pointed out, all of this historical information was given to Moses by direct revelation. Note the care with which the date of the Flood is chronicled.

There have been few moments in the history of humanity when the elements of drama and pathos have hung more heavily over the earth than in this hour. Millions upon millions of human beings were about to be ushered involuntarily back into the spirit world. To their Heavenly Father this was a mere transition—a change of assignment which would take them out of mortality. But for the teeming multitudes of sneering, immoral and degenerate humanity this was the hour of terrible retribution which they had refused to believe could come. It was more than a time of judgment. It was the zero hour of execution.

As Noah and his wife went into the Ark they were accompanied by none but Shem, Japheth, Ham and their three wives. These eight people watched the great door on the side of the Ark as it was slowly pulled into closed position. Suddenly they were imprisoned in the only safe place on the face of the whole earth.

On the top deck there were a number of windows[26] and no doubt they made their way to them and used these apertures for observation. There must have been mixed emotions in the breasts of these eight people as they caught their last glimpse of the antediluvian civilization. Out there in the bustling cities of the plains people were "eating and drinking, marrying and giving in marriage." They were trafficking in criminal commerce, plotting intrigue, lavishing their passions with every conceivable indulgence. These were they of whom God had said: "among all the workmanship of my hands there has not been so great wickedness."[27]

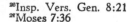
[26]Insp. Vers. Gen. 8:21
[27]Moses 7:36

But out there in the cities of the wicked were some of their own flesh and blood. Shem, Japheth and Ham all had daughters who were being left behind.[28] Perhaps there were many other close kinsmen who had also been blinded by this age of apostasy and were therefore doomed with those whom they had chosen to follow in preference to the prophets of God. The hearts of these eight people must have ached with sorrow as they saw the hour approaching when their children and former associates would face the terror of this all-consuming destruction.

When the Flood came it was not just a cloudburst from heaven. The scriptures state that the "fountains of the great deep" were "broken up," which would imply that tidal waves of churning destruction poured in upon the mainland of the continent. Water not only came pouring down from above but from all sides as well. The scriptures spare the modern student the horror of that hour. They simply say: "And the waters increased. . . . And all flesh died that moved upon the earth, both of fowl, and of cattle, and of beast, and of every creeping thing that creepeth upon the earth, and every man."[29]

It would be difficult for the modern student to imagine the feelings of Noah and his family as they saw multitudes fleeing toward the Ark, clinging to its sides and trying to save themselves in that terrible moment when they suddenly realized that Noah had prophesied truthfully and the predicted destruction was upon them.

Scriptures now available to us indicate that it required forty days to bring the water level up to a point where it lifted the Ark from its moorings and set it free on the crest of the turbulent sea.[30] From this we assume that the Ark was built on a high plateau or in a mountainous region, possibly because of the availability of materials. In any event the scripture says: "And the Flood was forty days upon the earth and the waters increased, and bare up the ark and it was lifted up above the earth."[31]

[28] Insp. Vers. Gen. 8:1-3
[29] Genesis 7:17-21
[30] Insp. Vers. Gen. 8:39
[31] *Ibid.*

This must have been a breathless moment for Noah and his sons as they waited to see whether or not the great beams they had hewn would stand the strain of the flood tide as it lifted the huge hulk of the Ark from its resting place and set it afloat on the mighty deep. No doubt there were also moments of suspense as the Ark rolled in the water and the frightened animals trumpeted their dismay as they lunged about in their cages.

Then it says the storm continued to pour down its fury for another *five months!* A passage in the modern Bible has led some to assume that the storm only lasted forty days and forty nights,[32] but this is an error. A careful reading of this passage clearly shows that it took forty days before the "ark went upon the face of the waters." The Inspired Version verifies this interpretation and states that it was *150 days* before "the fountains . . . of the deep, and the windows of heaven were stopped and the rain from heaven was restrained."[33]

This indicates that the voyage of the Ark was certainly no smooth-sailing excursion. It would appear that for five months the Ark was driven before the wind continually and the mountainous seas thundered over the hulk of this man-made vessel with great violence. The Jaredites describe what it was like when they made their voyage, and it is believed many of these elements were similar to those encountered by Noah. The scripture says:

> "And it came to pass that the Lord God caused that there should be a furious wind blow upon the face of the waters, towards the promised land; and thus they were tossed upon the waves of the sea before the wind.
>
> "And it came to pass that they were many times buried in the depths of the sea, because of the mountain waves which broke upon them, and also the great and terrible tempests which were caused by the fierceness of the wind.

[32]Genesis 8:17
[33]Insp. Vers. Gen. 8:46-48

"And it came to pass that when they were buried in the deep there was no water that could hurt them, their vessels being tight like unto a dish, and also they were *tight like unto the ark of Noah*. . . .

"And it came to pass that the wind did never cease to blow towards the promised land while they were upon the waters; and thus were they driven forth before the wind." (Ether 6:5-8)

When the Ark first began to move upon the water Noah would have been able to estimate his location by the mountain peaks which remained visible. These would also be objects of peril to the floating titanic with its precious cargo. In due time, however, the high peaks began to disappear, for the scripture says: "And the waters prevailed exceedingly upon the face of the earth, and all the high hills under the whole heaven were covered. Fifteen cubits and upward did the water prevail; and the mountains were covered."[84]

Did the Flood Cover the Entire Earth?

Many students have wondered how such a thing could be possible. Numerous explanations have been given. The important thing to keep in mind, however, is that persons living in that day witnessed the fact that it did occur. In summarizing these events for modern students the Lord Himself verifies that it did occur. The scripture could not be much plainer than to say that "all the high hills under the whole heavens were covered . . . and the mountains were covered." The scriptures indicate that it was not until the tenth month after the commencement of the Flood that the tops of the mountains were again seen![85]

Some students have assumed that this was just a local flood and have believed that the Bible is merely describing the destruction of life in a "given area." However, the scriptures clearly refute any such interpretation.

---

[84]Insp. Vers. Gen. 8:41
[85]Genesis 8:5

First, the Lord declared that this great Flood would destroy "all flesh from off the earth."[36] No local flood would have fulfilled this prediction.

Second, we know from modern scriptures that the Ark was launched from the Western Hemisphere and finally came to rest on a high peak of the Eastern Hemisphere. This would require a world-wide flood.

Third, the Lord has verified the fact that the Flood included the part of the earth which is now America. He made known to Ether that "after the waters had receded from off the face of *this land* it became a choice land above all other lands, a chosen land of the Lord."[37] Note also that after the Flood it was necessary for the Jaredites to replenish America with animal life by bringing with them "flocks and herds and whatsoever beast or animal or fowl they should carry with them." (Ether 6:4)

Fourth, the great Flood is spoken of as the "baptism" of the earth or burial of the earth in water. As Brigham Young declared: "The earth . . . has been baptized with water, and will, in the future be baptized with fire and the Holy Ghost, to be prepared to go back into the celestial presence of God."[38] The symbolism of baptism for the earth would require a universal flood. John A. Widtsoe declared: "The Latter-day Saints . . . look upon the Flood as a baptism of the earth, symbolizing a cleansing of the impurities of the past, and the beginning of a new life. This has been repeatedly taught by the leaders of the Church. The deluge was an immersion of the earth in water."[39]

As the landmarks disappeared and the fury of the waves lashed over the Ark, perhaps Noah sealed up the Ark so that it was "tight like a dish." As previously mentioned the Jaredite barges are said to have been "like unto the ark of Noah"[40] and these vessels are described as being "exceeding tight, even that they would hold water

[36]Insp. Vers. Gen. 8:17
[37]Ether 13:2
[38]*Disc. of Brigham Young,* p. 603
[39]*Evidences and Reconciliations,* Vol. I, p. 111
[40]Ether 6:7

like unto a dish; and the bottom thereof was tight like unto a dish; and the sides thereof were tight like unto a dish; and the ends thereof were peaked and the top thereof was tight like unto a dish.''[41]

About nine-and-a-half months after the commencement of the Flood Noah is described as opening a window to release a raven. This would indicate that during most of the voyage the windows had been kept sealed so as to prevent the water from swamping the great vessel during the continuous storm.

Perhaps during moments of quiet the windows were opened for air just as the Jaredites did with their barges.[42]

[41]*Ibid.*, 2:17
[42]*Ibid.*, 3:20

CHAPTER TWENTY-TWO

The Ark Lands in a New World

How long did it take the Ark to go halfway around the world?

Where did the Ark land? Do we know the date when it landed?

How long was it after the Ark grounded before Noah could see the tops of the surrounding mountains?

After waiting forty more days what did Noah do?

An exciting event took place on New Year's Day. What was it?

When Noah found that the water had receded out of sight did he leave the Ark? Why?

What was the first thing Noah did after leaving the Ark?

Was Noah justified in his fear that the children of men might try to duplicate the abominations of the pre-flood period and perhaps bring another flood upon the earth?

Does the scripture say that the rainbow now appeared in the heavens for the first time?

What is meant by a "token of covenant"?

What do you think the Lord meant by His commandment to "replenish the earth"?

Do you know of any civilized nations which use blood for food?

Is it a violation of a specific commandment of God to mistreat animals?

What did God say concerning capital punishment for the crime of murder?

From a study of the map can you tell where Noah and his family would probably go after they "descended" from the mountainous region where the Ark first landed?

THE ARK LANDS IN A NEW WORLD

For five months the Ark labored slowly across the world. As we have previously mentioned, the scripture indicates that great storms continued throughout the voyage. But after the waters had prevailed 150 days "God remembered Noah and all that were with him in the Ark. And God made a wind to pass over the earth, and the waters were assuaged. The fountains also of the great deep and the windows of heaven were stopped and the rain from heaven was restrained, and the waters returned from off the earth."[1]

It was at this time that the Ark suddenly scraped bottom on the level portion of a high mountain peak and came to rest. This mountain is designated in scripture as "the mountain of Ararat."[2] Note that the Inspired Version does not say the *mountains* of Ararat as does the King James translation.[3] It specifies the mountain. The scripture says it was "in the seventh month, on the seventeenth day of the month" that the Ark settled on Mount Ararat.[4] From the most ancient times this mountain has been identified among the people and has always been called "The place of first descent."[5]

For two-and-a-half more months Noah and his family continued to feed and tend their restless menagerie. Then they were thrilled to see from the windows of the Ark the tops of the surrounding mountains.[6] From this point on the water receded with surprising rapidity.

We are told that Noah waited forty days longer and then sent forth a raven and a dove. The raven flew about waiting for the waters to recede but the dove returned to the Ark. Seven days later Noah sent out the dove again, and she returned to the Ark bearing an olive leaf so that Noah knew the water was receding from some of the lower valleys. He waited seven more days and set forth the dove again. It never returned.

[1]Insp. Vers. Gen. 8:46-48
[2]*Ibid.*, 8:49
[3]Genesis 8:4
[4]Insp. Vers. Gen. 8:49
[5]Josephus, *Ant. of the Jews*, Book I, 3:5
[6]Genesis 8:5

On New Year's Day (which was the first day of the first month of the year that Noah became 601) the great patriarch was assisted by his sons in removing the "covering of the Ark." Then they were able to see all around them and they beheld that the "waters were dried up from off the earth."[7] Just what is meant by the "covering" of the Ark we do not know. It appears, however, that it permitted them to get their first good view of all the surrounding territory and they were pleased to see that the water had retreated out of sight.

Noah did not release the animals as yet, however. He waited on revelation. Not until God had specifically commanded him to leave the Ark did he do so. This command did not come for two more months. It was one year and three days after the Flood struck the earth that God spoke unto Noah saying: "Go forth out of the ark, thou, and thy wife, and thy sons, and thy sons' wives with thee. Bring forth with thee every living thing that is with thee, of all flesh, both of fowl, and of cattle, and of every creeping thing that creepeth upon the earth; that they may breed abundantly in the earth, and be fruitful and multiply upon the earth."[8]

The first thing Noah did was to thank God for their safe journey. There is no indication that he knew where he was but at least their lives had been preserved and he knew the Almighty would bless them as they went forth to launch the race on a fresh start. Noah built an altar and offered his sacrifice of thanksgiving to the Lord. The scripture says Noah "took of every clean beast, and of every clean fowl, and offered burnt offerings on the altar."[9]

THE RAINBOW BECOMES A TOKEN OF COVENANT

In response to Noah's sacrifice it says "the Lord spoke unto Noah and blessed him."[10] Then Noah said in his heart: "I will call on the name of the Lord that he will not again curse the ground any more for man's

[7]Genesis 8:13
[8]*Ibid.*, 8:16-17
[9]*Ibid.*, 8:20
[10]Insp. Vers. Gen. 9:5

sake, for the imagination of man's heart is evil from his youth." Noah feared lest the human race might soon repeat its abominations of the pre-flood period and he wondered if the Lord might not strike the earth again with a flood.

You will recall that it was *Noah* who had pleaded with the Lord to cleanse the earth of its degenerate humanity before the Flood.[11] In this moment, however, after he had gone through the heartaches and travail of this great experience he hoped that somehow the necessity for such a similar catastrophe could be avoided in the future. And there was good reason for Noah to fear the weaknesses of the human race. Within two or three generations Noah was to see his descendants duplicating the abominations of the pre-flood period.

In responding to Noah God said that the "bow in the cloud" would "be for a token of covenant between me and the earth. And it shall come to pass when I bring a cloud over the earth, that the bow shall be seen in the cloud and I will remember my covenant which I have made between me and you for every living creature of all flesh. And the waters shall no more become a flood to destroy all flesh."[12]

In this connection, students often ask: "Was the rainbow a new phenomenon of nature or did God just designate a familiar phenomenon as the 'token' of this covenant?" There is no statement in the scripture which states specifically that the rainbow was a new sign.

The phenomenon of the rainbow is the result of sunlight passing through raindrops. Each droplet acts as a prism to bend the light and thereby produces one of the colors of the rainbow. The amount of refraction or bending of the light determines the color which is reflected to the observer. Raindrops at different levels will receive light at different angles and therefore bend the light at varying degrees which accounts for the various colors appearing in the rainbow. All of the colors of the solar spectrum may be seen, and they always appear in this order: red, orange, yellow, green, blue, indigo and violet.

---

[11] *Ibid.*, 8:13-15
[12] *Ibid.*, 9:19-20

Probably the Lord selected this impressive phenomenon of nature which is usually associated with the end of a rainstorm as an appropriate "token" for the new covenant between Himself and Noah. It does not appear that the sign of the rainbow was new, but its use as a token between God and Noah was new.

NOAH RECEIVES FIVE SPECIAL COMMANDMENTS

On this occasion God gave Noah five special commandments which He desired to emphasize at this time:

First, He said, "be fruitful and multiply and replenish the earth."[13] He did not want men to practice selfish race suicide but provide homes, food, clothing and education for large, substantial families. He wanted them to fill up the earth, subdue it, beautify it and make it a pleasant habitation. This can only be done with large, civilized populations which are properly motivated in their pursuit of peace and prosperity. This is what the Lord had in mind when He said "multiply and replenish the earth."

Second, "Every moving thing that liveth shall be meat for you even as the green herb have I given you all things."[14] For some reason or other the Lord has had to emphasize from time to time that meat is to have its proper place in the human diet. In almost every generation certain groups arise which advocate complete abstinence from the use of meat. Paul pointed out that this type of fad partakes of an apostate spirit.[15] On occasion the Lord has warned His people against the use of certain meats (as in the case of ancient Israel) which had become "unclean" and in modern times He has warned against the *excessive* use of meat: "Yea, flesh also of beasts and of the fowls of the air, I, the Lord, have ordained for the use of man with thanksgiving; nevertheless they are to be used sparingly."[16]

---

[13]Insp. Vers. Gen. 9:8
[14]*Ibid.*, 9:9
[15]I Timothy 4:1-4
[16]D. & C. 89:12

Third, "The blood ye shall not eat."[17] The Lord has repeated this commandment many times since. He does not clearly state why blood is not to be used for food, but we can be certain there is a sound scientific reason behind it.

Fourth, "Blood (of animals) shall not be shed only for meat to save your lives; and the blood of every beast will I require at your hands."[18] God did not intend that the lives of animals should be wasted nor that they should be subjected to cruelty and abuse. The proper treatment of the animal kingdom is part of the human stewardship.

Fifth, "Whoso sheddeth man's blood, by man shall his blood be shed; for man shall not shed the blood of man. For a commandment I give that every man's brother shall preserve the life of man, for in mine own image have I made man."[19] The greatest sin of the pre-flood period was the fact that men conspired together and murdered one another that they might get gain. Sometimes it was for loot, sometimes for revenge, sometimes for political office. This was the curse of the Mahanite cult during the antediluvian civilization. In this commandment Noah was taught that the shedding of innocent blood was not to be tolerated. This crime was to be promptly punished by the execution of the guilty. In other places the Lord made provisions for those who take human life in self-defense or during an altercation.[20]

With these five commandments or special warnings, God sent Noah and his family forth to get acquainted with their new home. Although they had landed in the mountains they were not far from one of the richest agricultural basins of the east. It would appear that Noah and his family traveled quite some distance from the place of the Ark's first landing in order to find the right environment to start their new homes. From subsequent events we know that they were "east" of the Euphrates River.[21] Perhaps they first settled along the Tigris River

[17]Insp. Vers. Gen. 9:10
[18]*Ibid.*, 9:11
[19]*Ibid.*, 9:12-13
[20]Numbers 35:11-34
[21]Insp. Vers. Gen. 11:1

or even farther east in Media and Persia. In fact, the most convenient descent from the mountain region where the Ark landed would be directly into the valleys of Media.

HAVE THE REMAINS OF THE ARK BEEN FOUND?

Josephus, the Jewish historian, cites a number of ancient writers who refer to the reality of the great Flood and some of them refer to the fact that the remains of the Ark could still be seen in their day. Berosus, the Chaldean historian wrote: "It is said there is still some part of this ship in Armenia, at the mountain of the Cordyaeans; and that some people carry off pieces of the bitumen (tar), which they take away and use chiefly as amulets for the averting of mischiefs."[22]

Josephus also quotes Nicolaus of Damascus who said: "There is a great mountain in Armenia, over Minyas, called Baris, upon which it is reported . . . that one who was carried in an ark came on shore upon the top of it; and that the remains of the timber were a great while preserved." (*Ibid.*)

In referring to Mount Ararat Josephus says: "The Armenians call this place, 'The Place of Descent.' for the Ark being saved in that place, its remains are shown there by the inhabitants to this day."[23]

Footnotes in the works of Josephus indicate that explorers have thought of verifying these assertions in modern times but the task was not found to be an easy one. As one footnote says: "Mons. Tournefort had not very long since, a mind to see the place himself, but met with too great dangers and difficulties to venture through them."[24]

In recent years a great deal of discussion has centered around the claims of Vladimar Roskivitsky, a Russian pilot, who alleged that he was with a large party of Russian soldiers who located the Ark and photographed its remains just before the Russian revolution. He asserts

---

[22]Josephus, *op. cit.,* Book I, 3:6
[23]*Ibid.,* Book I, 3:5
[24]*Ibid.,* note

that the photographs and reports were immediately suppressed by the new government and that very few of those who were on the original expedition ever escaped from Russia. Thus far, Russia has not permitted explorers to enter this region to verify or refute these claims. However, the publishing house which first printed Mr. Roskivitsky's account has refused to print additional copies of his statement because they have determined that his information is not at all reliable.

Someday, perhaps, a scientific expedition will scour the battlements of Mount Ararat and determine whether or not there is any foundation for the claims that some remnants of the famous Ark are still in existence. Meanwhile, we have the statements of Noah and his contemporaries who refer to their personal knowledge of the Ark. For the time being these are the only reliable facts we have concerning this ancient historic vessel.

Chapter Twenty-three

The Descendants of Cain Seize Political Power

Whom did Ham marry? What did her name mean?

Who was Ham's heir? What did Noah predict concerning him? How was he to be distinguished from other men? Do we know whether or not a similar mark distinguished other children of Ham?

Who settled Palestine? Whose descendants were they?

Did *all* the people leave "the east" and go to Shinar to help build Babel?

Who was the political leader during the building of Babel? Did he say why they should build a city? Is there any indication of the reason why they wanted to build a great tower?

Why would the building of cities at this particular time tend to defeat the purposes of God?

Was Nimrod a mighty hunter "before the Lord"? Why was he particularly undesirable as a political leader? Would the Prophet Noah be inclined to look upon Nimrod as an apostate from the Church? Why?

Do we know the approximate date when the earth was "divided"? When was it?

Were there any righteous people in Babel who resisted the teachings of Nimrod? What was the name of the brother of Jared? Do we know how human and animal life got back to America after the Flood?

When did the Lord pour out a "multiple gift of tongues"?

In these early times was there any problem of agnosticism or atheism? What was the problem?

How the Seed of Cain Survived the Flood

The blood of Cain was perpetuated through the Flood as a result of the fact that (prior to the Flood) Ham married a woman named Egyptus who was of the forbidden race and through her the seed of Cain descended.[1] In fact, the name "Egyptus" means forbidden.[2] Ham himself was permitted to "walk with God" and possessed the Priesthood,[3] but because of his marriage to Egyptus he was never able to pass this privilege on to any of his descendants.[4]

Shortly after their arrival in the new land Noah took occasion to remind Ham that his descendants would perpetuate the curse of Cain. The occasion was a lamentable one for Noah. It occurred just after they had harvested their first crop from the vineyard. Failing in good judgment, Noah drank too much of the vintage which they had pressed from the grapes and therefore retired to his tent to sleep. While he was asleep he became uncovered and when Ham saw it he made fun of his father. Shem and Japheth, however, covered their father out of respect and love for him.

When Noah awakened he somehow learned what had happened, and it was on this occasion that Noah reminded Ham that his son, Canaan, would never have powers of presidency and Priesthood leadership but would be a "servant of servants." He also said: "A veil of darkness shall cover him, that he shall be known among all men."[5]

The descendants of this same Canaan later settled Palestine and that is how it became known as the "Land of Canaan."[6] The Philistines and other nations of Palestine who later resisted Israel were of this lineage.

It is apparent from the scriptures that not only the seed of Canaan but also Ham's other children were deprived of the Priesthood. Pharaoh, the grandson of

[1]Abraham 1:21-24
[2]*Ibid.*
[3]Insp. Vers. Gen. 8:1 plus D. C. 76:57-58
[4]Abraham 1:25-27
[5]Insp. Vers. Gen. 9:30
[6]*Ibid.,* 10:9-10

Ham through one of his daughters, is specifically mentioned as not being eligible for the Priesthood due to his lineage.[7]

Another of Ham's grandsons now came into prominence and we shall consider his biography in some detail. His name was Nimrod.

NIMROD, THE BUILDER OF BABEL

When Noah and his three sons went forth to multiply and replenish the earth, they apparently began to establish a pastoral civilization. As the population began to increase, however, there were certain factions of the people who wanted to build a city similar to the ones they had heard their fathers describe as flourishing during the pre-flood period. This group of ambitious city-builders were led by a descendant of Cain named Nimrod.

Nimrod was the grandson of Ham through Cush.[8] He is described in the King James translation as "a mighty hunter before the Lord."[9] But the Inspired Version gives him no such distinction. It says: "And Cush begat Nimrod; he began to be a mighty one in the earth. He was a mighty hunter *in the land*. Wherefore, it is said: Even as Nimrod, the mighty hunter in the land. And he began a kingdom, and the beginning of his kingdom was Babel and Erech and Accad and Calneh in the land of Shinar."[10]

From subsequent events we will see that Nimrod was a mighty hunter *against* the Lord and the Inspired Version verifies the fact that there has been a mistranslation in our modern Bible. He was a mighty hunter "in the land," not "before the Lord."

As we have already mentioned this first settlement by Noah and his sons was in the "east" and would appear to have been in Media or on the eastern side of the Mesopotamian Valley. Therefore, when Nimrod and some of the other people became restless the path of migration

[7]Abraham 1:25-27
[8]Genesis 10:8
[9]*Ibid.,* 10:9
[10]Insp. Vers. Gen. 10:5-6

was toward the west. The Inspired Version says: "And it came to pass that *many* journeyed *from the east* and as they journeyed from the east, they found a plain in the land of Shinar and dwelt there in the plain of Shinar. And they said one to another, Come, go to, let us make brick, and burn them thoroughly. And they had brick for stone, and they had slime (asphalt) for mortar. And they said, Come, go to, let us build a city, and a tower whose top will be high, nigh unto heaven; and let us make us a name lest we be scattered abroad upon the face of the whole earth."[11]

This is the city which became Babel. Three things are noteworthy about this city. First, that it was built for purposes which were in direct opposition to the commandment of God. The Lord had told them to spread abroad in the earth, but they built this city to concentrate the population. The Lord knew that city life under the wrong kind of leadership could corrupt a whole nation in one generation. You will observe that as long as patriarchal government survived it encouraged pastoral living. The "tent" of Noah and "the tents of Shem" are mentioned specifically.[12]

Before the Flood, the City of Enoch was an exception but it was set up under divine guidance and was governed in righteousness.

The second thing to observe about Babel is the fact that it was governed by the seed of Cain. Nimrod, grandson of Ham, is given specific credit for the founding of the city.[13]

Third, a brief comment might be made concerning the tower which these people determined to build. Note that it was to be high, nigh unto heaven. The purpose of this tower was to escape the vengeance of a just God if there should ever be another flood. Apparently Nimrod had no confidence in the covenant between Noah and the Lord.

This begins to give us some insight into the personality of Nimrod. He was a defiant, rebellious son of Cain.

[11]*Ibid.,* 11:1-3
[12]Genesis 9:21, 27
[13]*Ibid.,* 10:8-10

Josephus gives us the judgment of Jewish history on Nimrod:

"Now it was Nimrod who excited them (the people of Shinar) to such an affront and contempt of God (such as refusing to spread abroad in the earth). He was the grandson of Ham, the son of Noah, a bold man, and of great strength of hand. He persuaded them not to ascribe it (their prosperity) to God, as if it was through his means they were happy, but to believe that it was their own courage which procured that happiness. He also changed the government into tyranny, seeing no other way of turning man from the fear of God, but to bring them into a constant dependence on his power. He also said he would be revenged of God, if He should have a mind to drown the world again; for that he would build a tower too high for the waters to be able to reach! and that he would avenge himself on God for destroying their forefathers.

"Now the multitude were very ready to follow the determination of Nimrod, and to esteem it as a piece of cowardice to submit to God; and they built a tower, neither sparing any pains, nor being in any degree negligent about the work; and, by reason of the multitude of hands employed in it, it grew very high, sooner than anyone could expect; but the thickness of it was so great, and it was so strongly built, that thereby its great height seemed, upon the view, to be less than it really was. It was built of burnt brick, cemented together with mortar, made of bitumen, that it might not be liable to admit water."[14]

Notice that this description of Nimrod duplicates the attitude and spirit of Cain when he declared: "Who is the Lord, that I should know him?"[15] Although Nimrod may not have realized it, he was building the foundation for a great heathen culture which would be the curse of civilization for more than four thousand years.

The building and establishing of Babel undoubtedly required many years. It was probably during the con-

[14]Josephus, op. cit., Book I, Ch. 4
[15]Moses 5:16

struction of this city that a great change occurred in the geography of the earth.

IN THE DAYS OF PELEG THE EARTH WAS DIVIDED

We are able to fix the date for the division of the earth with fairly good accuracy. That is because the Lord told Moses the age of each descendant of Shem at the time his patriarchal heir was born. Thus, the scripture says that Shem begat Arphaxad two years after the Flood which would be 2,342 B.C.[16] Arphaxad was thirty-five when he begat Salah which would be 2,307 B.C.[17] Salah lived thirty years and begat Eber which would be 2,277 B.C.[18] Eber lived thirty-four years and begat Peleg which would be 2,243 B.C.[19]

This would mean that Peleg was born exactly 100 years after Noah and his family arrived in the new world. The division of the earth occurred early in the life of this patriarch, for he was given a name which meant "Division." We will therefore say for chronological convenience that the earth was divided approximately 2,240 B.C.

Now since only a century had passed since the arrival of Noah and his family in this new world, it is likely that the city of Babel was just getting a good start when the great division occurred.

We now know more about the significance of "the division" than students of the past. This is because we have a modern revelation in which the Lord describes how the division of the earth will be healed before the millennium. The Lord has declared: "He shall command the great deep, and it shall be driven back into the north countries, and the islands shall become one land; And the land of Jerusalem and the land of Zion shall be turned back into their own place, and *the earth shall be like as it was in the days before it was divided.*"[20]

---

[16]Insp. Vers. Gen. 11:7
[17]*Ibid.*, verse 8
[18]*Ibid.*, verse 9
[19]*Ibid.*, verse 10
[20]D. & C. 133:23-24

This gives us a clear indication that the dividing of the earth in the days of Peleg was the result of the sinking of the land in certain areas so that the sea could rush in from the polar regions. Apparently there was a sinking of the Pacific floor, and there may have been a sinking of the Atlantic floor although the scriptures point out that there was a "sea east" in that area even before the division.[21] Whether or not the "sea east" was as large as the Atlantic Ocean of modern times we are not certain. But in any event, we do know that when the division occurred around 2,240 B.C., America, Australia and the islands of the sea were cut off from the "one land."

This event was of world-shaking proportions, and the prophets appear to have known that this marked the "dividing" of the land. It was for the reason Peleg was given a name which meant "Division."[22]

THE DEPARTURE OF THE PEOPLE OF JARED FROM BABEL

In due process of time the city of Babel began to become a strong metropolis under the dictatorial government of Nimrod, and the tower of Babel began to attract widespread attention. In this hour the Lord pronounced judgment upon the city. Undoubtedly He revealed to His prophets His intentions, for the Lord said: "Behold, the people are the same, and they all have the same language; and this tower they begin to build, and now, nothing will be restrained from them which they have imagined, except I, the Lord, confound their language, that they may not understand one another's speech. So I, the Lord will scatter them abroad from thence, upon all the face of the land, and unto every quarter of the earth."[23]

Living in the city of Babel or its vicinity at this time was a group of righteous people who had resisted the teachings of Nimrod. One of them was Mahonri-Moriancumr and another was his brother, Jared.[24] The

---

[21]Moses 6:42; 7:14
[22]Gen. 10:25, marginal reading
[23]Insp. verse. Genesis 11:5
[24]See *Dictionary of the Book of Mormon*, "Brother of Jared"

dramatic history of these people is not in the Bible, but it is given in considerable detail in the Book of Mormon. It says:

"And the brother of Jared (Mahonri-Moriancumr) being a large and mighty man, and a man highly favored of the Lord, Jared, his brother, said unto him: Cry unto the Lord, that he will not confound us that we may not understand our words." This shows that the people had been warned of what was about to befall them. Then the record continues: "And it came to pass that the brother of Jared did cry unto the Lord, and the Lord had compassion upon Jared; therefore he did not confound the language of Jared; and Jared and his brother were not confounded.

"Then Jared said unto his brother: Cry again unto the Lord, and it may be that he will turn away his anger from them who are our friends, that he confound not their language. And it came to pass that the brother of Jared did cry unto the Lord, and the Lord had compassion upon their friends and their families also, that they were not confounded."[25]

But one other thing worried these people. Since the Lord did not want them to stay in Babel, where would He like them to go? Jared said to his brother: "Go and inquire of the Lord whether he will drive us out of the land, and if he will drive us out of the land, cry unto him whither we shall go. And who knoweth but the Lord will carry us forth into a land which is choice above all the earth? And if it so be, let us be faithful unto the Lord, that we may receive our inheritance."[26]

Mahonri-Moriancumr did plead with the Lord and finally received this revelation: "Go to and gather together thy flocks, both male and female, of every kind; and also of the seed of the earth of every kind; and thy families; and also Jared thy brother and his family; and also thy friends and their families, and the friends of Jared and their families.

"And when thou hast done this thou shalt go at the head of them down into the valley which is northward.

²⁵Ether 1:34-37
²⁰Ibid., 1:38

And there will I meet thee, and I will go before thee into a land which is choice above all the lands of the earth. . . . And there shall be none greater than the nation which I will raise up unto me of thy seed, upon all the face of the earth."[27]

Although Jared and Mahonri-Moriancumr did not know it, they were about to begin a journey which would take them halfway around the world. The Lord had in mind the repopulating of the Western Hemisphere which was now completely cut off from the "one land" to which it was formerly joined.

Note also that the nation which was to be raised up in America was to be greater than any other contemporary nation on the face of the earth. The Jaredite civilization was contemporaneous with Babylon, China, Egypt and Assyria, and according to this promise excelled them all.

Jared and his brother gathered animals, birds, and fresh-water fish. They also took the honeybee, called deseret, and gathered together the seeds for all types of domestic crops. Then they went into the valley "northward" which was called the Valley of Nimrod.

"And it came to pass that the Lord commanded them that they should go forth into the wilderness, yea, into that quarter where there never had man been. . . . And it came to pass that they did travel in the wilderness, and did build barges, in which they did cross many waters, being directed continually by the hand of the Lord."[28]

Whether the Jaredites traveled east or west we are not certain. The Flood had left large inland seas in both directions. In any event, we know that they successfully crossed these "many waters" on barges which they were taught to build and finally they came to "that great sea which divideth the lands."[29] Here they dwelt in tents for a period of four years.[30]

At the end of this time the brother of Jared was severely rebuked by the Lord. "For the space of three

[27]*Ibid.*, 1:41-43
[28]*Ibid.*, 2:5-6
[29]*Ibid.*, 2:13
[30]*Ibid.*

hours did the Lord talk with the brother of Jared, and chastened him because he remembered not to call upon the name of the Lord. And the brother of Jared repented. . . ."[81]

Then the Lord told him to build eight barges similar to the ones they had previously made to cross the inland seas. The scriptures gives us only a brief description of these barges but it says they were "tight like unto the ark of Noah" which would lead us to assume that they were similar in some respects to the Ark. However, they were much smaller.[82] They were extremely well built so that no water could get into them even when they were submerged.[83]

"And it came to pass that when they had prepared all manner of food, that thereby they might subsist upon the water, and also food for their flocks and herds, and whatsoever beast or animal or fowl that they should carry with them . . . they got aboard their vessels or barges and set forth into the sea, commending themselves unto the Lord their God."[84]

Then an epic voyage began: "And it came to pass that the Lord God caused that there should be a furious wind blow upon the face of the waters, towards the promised land; and thus they were tossed upon the waves of the sea before the wind. And it came to pass that they were many times buried in the depths of the sea, because the mountain waves which broke upon them, and also the great and terrible tempests which were caused by the fierceness of the wind."[85]

It took them 344 days to cross the ocean—nearly a year. Finally their barges slid into the coasts of their new homeland. "And when they had set their feet upon the shores of the promised land they bowed themselves down upon the face of the land, and did humble themselves before the Lord, and did shed tears of joy before

[81] Ibid., 2:14-15
[82] Ibid., 3:16
[83] Ibid., 3:17; 6:7
[84] Ibid., 6:4
[85] Ibid., 6:5-6

the Lord, because of the multitude of his tender mercies over them.''[36]

Thus the sound of human laughter returned once more to the Western Hemisphere—the cradle of the race and therefore the "old" world. Animal life soon spread across the width and breadth of the land. Cities were built and a great civilization soon came into being. The scripture says these people brought records with them so the teachings of the ancient patriarchs and the true history of the race was preserved among them.[37]

Now we can return to historical developments in Babel.

THE CONFUSION OF TONGUES

Sometime after the departure of the Jaredites from Babel a great calamity fell upon that city. By a simple psychological device known to the Lord several different systems of linguistic phonetics suddenly appeared among the people. "The confusion of tongues" was really a multiple "gift of tongues" which conferred various languages upon the people so that they now expressed themselves by different linguistic sounds from the ones they had originally learned.

The psychological principle upon which the gift of tongues is based is not known to us, but Paul assures us that of all the special dispensations of heaven this is one of the most ordinary.[38]

The scripture states that as soon as the languages were changed and men found themselves speaking differently from their friends, the original spirit of unity among them disappeared. Immediately they set out in groups to find new homes and new lands. Apparently they did this with a full knowledge that this is what God wanted them to do. They had been warned that this calamity would fall upon them if they did not disperse and spread abroad in the earth. Now the power of God had been

---

[36]*Ibid.*, 6:12
[37]*Ibid.*, 8:9
[38]I Cor. Ch. 14

manifested. No doubt many of them hurried off like punished children to follow a pattern of life which they knew they should have been following from the beginning.

Notice that there was no problem of agnosticism or atheism at this time. A man who has just been given a new language as a punishment from God isn't likely to deny His existence! Like Cain of old these people had a full knowledge of God's divinity, but they resented His commandments and resisted obedience. They had partaken of the spirit of Nimrod whose attitude was one of defiance.

Now there began to be many nations. As the people spread abroad they are described as originally settling in the following areas:

Ham's descendants settled:[39]

>   Egypt
>   Canaan (Palestine)
>   Continental Africa
>   India
>   Australia
>   Assyria (North Mesopotamia)

Japheth's descendants settled:[40]

>   Galatia (Asia Minor)
>   Macedonia
>   Armenia
>   Gaul (France)
>   Spain
>   Greece
>   Italy
>   Central Europe
>   Southern Asia
>   Media
>   Persia

---

[39]See Clarke, *Bible Commentary,* Vol. 1, pp. 83-85
[40]See *Ibid.,* p. 83

Shem's descendants settled:[41]
    Chaldea
    Syria
    Part of Armenia
    Salem (Jerusalem)
    Damascus
    Eastern Mesopotamia

It should not be assumed, however, that these tribal settlements were exclusive to the nationalities designated. We know that there was a great mixing of all peoples; for example, even though Shem's descendants occupied much of Mesopotamia, nevertheless Nimrod and other rebellious elements of the Hamitic tribe remained in that vicinity and built Babylon, Nineveh and other great cities. The above tabulations are merely the *principal* groups found in each region.

Thus the foundations of nations were laid. Most of them afterwards lost track of their origins and filled in their histories with myths or distorted versions of true history. Research has revealed that neither their genealogies nor their fictionalized histories can be trusted.

[41]See *Ibid.*, p. 85

CHAPTER TWENTY-FOUR

Ten Generations of Apostasy

How long did Noah live after the Flood? Did he live down to the days of Abraham or did he die before that prophet was born?

Do you think Noah had cause for more sorrow or more happiness during these years?

Is there any indication that Noah, Shem, Japheth or Ham ever left the "east" and joined the people of Shinar in the valley of the Euphrates?

Do we now have sufficient information to clearly show the origin of heathen religious cults?

Do you think every generation has a certain number of ego-maniacs who are power hungry and would like to be "worshiped"? Why do you think this became the cornerstone of most heathen religions?

Do you know of any countries where animal worship survives to this day?

Has astrology continued to enjoy the confidence of many people—even in modern times?

The worship of men, the worship of animals and the worship of stars destroyed some of the most important concepts God had revealed to man. Can you name some of them?

What was there about the ritual of the heathen religions which made them spread so rapidly? Why did ancient Israel turn to idolatry time after time in spite of God's warning against it?

Why do you think the ancient heathen religions are referred to as "mystery" religions? How does a study of heathen worship help us to understand why God exterminated whole nations who practiced it?

Ten Generations of Apostasy

The scripture says Noah lived 350 years after the Flood.[1] He lived to see Abraham's day—Abraham being among the tenth generation of Noah's descendants!

In many ways these must have been sad years for Noah. During those ten generations extending over 350 years Noah saw many of his descendants reestablish the wicked abominations of the pre-flood period. No doubt he labored against these degenerate trends with the last vestige of vigor left in his aging body. Perhaps that is why Nimrod and "many" of the people "journeyed from the east" and came over to the Euphrates Valley—called Shinar—where they would not have to listen to Noah and his sons preaching to them. As in all generations the wicked like nothing better than to "work in the dark" without molestation. A man whose imagination is evil continually does not enjoy the companionship of prophets. Such a one was Nimrod.

It does not appear that Noah, Shem, Japheth or Ham ever left "the east." At least none of their subsequent activities are mentioned again in the scripture. They seem to have been isolated from the Mesopotamian Valley where the Bible history now focuses its narration.

After the confusion of tongues and the dispersion of the people we find Nimrod stubbornly holding to his resolution "to be revenged on God."[2] In the Syriac he is referred to as a "warlike giant."[3] The Jewish historians say that his name comes from the Hebrew word, *marad,* meaning "he rebelled." They say: "Nimrod began to be mighty in sin, a murderer of innocent men and a rebel before the Lord."[4] In another place they say: "He was mighty in hunting (or in prey) and in sin before God, for he was a hunter of the children of men . . . and he said unto them, Depart from the religion of Shem, and cleave to the institutes of Nimrod!"[5]

---

[1]Genesis 9:28
[2]Josephus, *op. cit.,* Book 1, Ch. 4
[3]*Ibid.*
[4]Clarke, *op. cit.,* Vol. I, p. 84
[5]*Ibid.*

Some authorities consider Nimrod the "principal instrument of the idolatry that afterwards prevailed in the family of Cush."[6] We know that idolatry also found an early acceptance among the Egyptians and other branches of the Hamitic peoples. Since they could not have the true Priesthood they were quick to establish their own form of priestcraft.

What Was the Origin of the Heathen Religions?

As we have previously pointed out, Nimrod is described as having established a kingdom through rapine, murder and tyranny.[7] It says he did it because he could discover "no other way of turning men from the fear of God."[8] After he had gained political control over the people he preached his new religion saying: "Depart from the religion of Shem, and cleave to the institutes of Nimrod!"[9] What were the "institutes of Nimrod"?

First of all, Josephus states that he belittled God and tried to destroy men's confidence in God.[10] He did not deny His existence. He just said God wasn't important. He said men were their own benefactors and didn't need to thank God for the prosperity which they had worked so hard themselves to acquire.

Here is the cornerstone of heathen worship—*to place man above God.*

The next step is to worship great conquerors such as Nimrod and call *them* gods. This was exactly what Nimrod undertook to do. As the historian says: "And not all this sufficed unto Nimrod's evil desire. Not enough that he turned men away from God, he did all he could to make them pay divine honors unto himself. He set himself up as a god, and made a seat for himself in imitation of the seat of God. It was a tower built out of a round rock, and on it he placed a throne of cedar wood,

[6]*Ibid.*
[7]Josephus, *op. cit.,* Book I, Ch. 4:2
[8]*Ibid.*
[9]Clarke, *op. cit.,* Vol. I, p. 84
[10]*Ibid.*

upon which arose, one above the other, four thrones, of iron, copper, silver and gold. Crowning all, upon the golden throne, lay a precious stone, round in shape and gigantic in size. This served him as a seat, and as he sat upon it, all nations came and paid him divine homage."[11]

No doubt other conquerors imitated Nimrod. In due process of time the worship of these men completely obscured the existence of the Almighty insofar as the worshiping masses were concerned. The deifying of human beings is one of the chief characteristics of heathen religions whether in Egypt, Babylon, Greece, Rome, China or India. If Nimrod wanted to establish a heathen culture, he was following the prescribed formula.

The next thing which began to characterize heathen worship—including the institutes of Nimrod—was the elevating of animals above humanity. This philosophy reversed the divine command to man which said: "the fear of you, and the dread of you shall be upon every beast of the earth, and upon every fowl of the air, upon all that moveth upon the earth, and upon all the fishes of the sea; *into your hand are they delivered.*"[12]

Heathen religions delivered human beings over to the real or fancied whims of animals. In many cases animal life was made more sacred than human life, and humans were sacrificed to animal gods. The curse of animal worship and the false philosophy associated with it survive to this day among large segments of humanity.

Another fiction which was probably introduced into the "institutes of Nimrod" just as it was in similar man-made religions at a later date was the idea that human beings are somehow influenced in their daily actions by the sun, moon and stars. These astronomical bodies were credited with the power to bestow special gifts, tastes, tendencies and qualities of personality upon each person. If a person were born at a particular time when the sign of one of these stars or groups of stars was in the ascendancy then this person was told during his youth that throughout his life he would be influenced to follow a

[11]Ginzberg, L., *The Legends of the Jews,* Vol. I, p. 1788
[12]Insp. Version Gen. 9:8

certain course of conduct and *there was nothing he could do about it!*

This destroyed the concept of "free agency" and "will." Whatever a person did he could always excuse himself by blaming it on the stars. As Jeremiah declared in his day: "Thus saith the Lord, Learn not the way of the heathen, and be not dismayed at the signs of heaven; for the heathen are dismayed at them."[13] This form of superstitious fakery survives in modern times and is respected by many people who have been favored with both education and wealth.

Now, having destroyed the worship of the one true God, the dignity of humanity and the concept of free agency or personal responsibility for conduct, the Satan-inspired originators of heathen worship next turned to the exploitation of human passion and degenerate sadism.

WHY WERE HEATHEN RELIGIONS SO POPULAR?

The amazing popularity of heathen idolatry can never be understood unless a study is made of the ritual which was practiced. Heathen ritual was frequently devoted almost exclusively to the stimulating and satisfying of human passion. The words *adultery* and *idolatry* both come from the same derivation.[14] The heathen religions *institutionalized* immorality.[15] As one authority points out: "Sacramental fornication was a regular feature of (heathen) religious life."[16]

Some Bible students find it difficult to understand why ancient Israel would continually fall for the snare of idolatry as practiced by neighboring nations. The scripture says they would plant "groves" and set up images in spite of everything God had said against it from the beginning. But this takes on greater significance when we learn that the groves were the convenient centers for the deification of sensual practices. Sexual gratification was not only condoned but under heathen influence it was

[13]Jer. 10:2
[14]*Encyc. Britannica* (1952), Vol. 18, p. 596
[15]See Schaff-Herzog, *Enc. of Religious Knowledge,* Vol. I, pp. 312-314
[16]Oesterly, W. O. E., *Hebrew Religion,* p. 167

also given sanctified sublimation as part of the religious rites.[17] Here was the secret snare of idolatry to ancient Israel. It was not so much the worship of images that tempted Israel, for that was nothing; rather it was the temptation of riotous indulgences which were sensually alluring once they had been tried.

In addition to immoral practices, the heathen priests almost universally adopted sadistic devices to satisfy the morbid appetites of their worshipers. This included the sacrifice of human beings by burning or slaughter. It included such fiendish practices as those followed in the worship of *Moloch*. The metal image of this god had a furnace inside which heated the image to a glowing hue. When the metal was red hot the priest placed a tiny infant in the cradled arms of the image where it was instantly roasted.[18]

Other practices included the binding of a human being to an altar. The priest began his devilish chant which ended in the stroke of a razor-sharp knife which disemboweled the victim. As the thoracic cavity was opened the priest pulled the beating heart from its roots and held it up before the blood-spattered image. The countenances of these man-made statues frequently bore the carved expression of moronic delight as though they were highly pleased with the scene of ritualistic horror enacted before them.[19]

Only when the degenerate immorality and fiendish cruelty of heathen worship is properly understood can the student appreciate the extreme abhorrence with which the prophets of God have continually expressed themselves against these abominations. It must also be kept in mind that the God of Israel who later ordered some of these nations completely wiped out was the same God and Judge who for centuries had listened to the screams of sacrificial victims, who had seen parents cast their children to the flames and who had observed the wholesale corruption of the youth of each generation as they

---

[17]See *Encyc. Britannica* (1952 ed.), Vol. 18, p. 596
[18]*Encyc. Americana,* Vol. 19, p. 329 under Moloch.
[19]See *Encyc. of Religion & Ethics* by James Hastings, Vol. 6, pp. 840-865 under "Human Sacrifices"

were tutored by adults in the most impure practices of sensual perversion. In that hour when God ordered the execution of such nations it was no more than the voice of justice pronouncing a long deserved judgment for criminal conduct of the most heinous kind. And not until these nations had pushed their defiant debauchery to the lowest denominator did God permit the wrath of judgment to fall upon them. (Genesis 15:16)

You will recall that Satan had tried (in the very beginning) to capture Cain so that he could have the benefit of Cain's earthly experience and natural ingenuity in promoting the various plans which were needed to try and defeat the Lord's program for the second estate. Whether or not Cain was the source of inspiration for the heathen rituals we do not know, but it certainly appears to have been devised by a mind which had a diabolical genius for destroying the souls of human beings.

Revelation Reveals an Error in Man's Interpretation of History

You will observe that the scriptural material now available to us repudiates the interpretation of many modern historians who have tried to determine the origin of religious philosophy and religious practices. The majority have concluded that religious understanding and religious expression "evolved." They feel that heathen religions are merely a primitive means of expressing the "instinctive desire to worship." They look upon idolatry and its attendant rituals as just part of the "upward reach of man." They seek to excuse the cruelty, immorality and barbarism of heathen worship on the ground that it was the best their primitive mentalities were capable of producing. It is urged that these practices had their origin "when man's reasoning powers were of so primitive a character that it is perhaps not possible for us to get down to his mentality."[20] Such scholars even believe that after the Hebrews came in contact with these degenerate practices it gave them "the gradual beginnings of the upward

---

[20]Oesterly, *op. cit.*, p. 48

growth whereby, through slow states, the Israelites attained to a *deeper apprehension of God!*"[21]

Nothing could be much further from the truth. Because of insufficient data these scholars have erred. They have failed to discover the origin of heathen religion, and they have failed to appreciate the origin of revealed religion. It was for this very reason that God warned his modern servants against pseudo-scholarship—where men are ever learning but never coming to a knowledge of the truth. The Lord knew that whole libraries have been loaded with misinformation and therefore He said: "Hearken ye elders of my church, whom I have appointed: Ye are *not* sent forth to be taught, but to teach the children of men the things which I have put into your hands by the power of my Spirit; And ye are to be taught from on high."[22]

In other words, where God has revealed the truth concerning any particular subject why should time be wasted in studying or teaching those things which are known *not* to be true? In those areas of human knowledge where God has not yet spoken we are expected to continue exploring, but the moment He illuminates our minds with a knowledge of that field what advantage is there in continuing to gather data designed to support some opposite view?

EVALUATION OF DATA RELATING TO HEATHEN RELIGIONS

And when we are inquiring about the origin of heathen religions we are in one of those areas where God has revealed considerably more than scholars have been able to discover through research. From sources now available we are able to draw a number of conclusions concerning heathen worship:

First, heathen religions did not evolve, they were "promoted." They were not the outgrowth of man's "instinctive desire to worship" but the outgrowth of man's instinctive desire to grasp for power. Nimrod conceived

[21]*Ibid.,* p. 127
[22]D. & C. 43:15-16

of his man-made "institutes" as a tool to alienate the loyalty of mankind from their Creator and His Priesthood and attach it to himself. As Josephus points out, Nimrod promoted his system because he could discover "no other way of turning men from the fear of God."[23] Similar devices were employed by ambitious men in Egypt and other nations.[24]

Second, heathen worship is not the primitive source of true religion. Heathen "institutes" were set up to destroy true religion which had been revealed by God through direct revelation. Idolatrous practices did not come into existence until long *after* true religion had been revealed from heaven. Heathen worship was set up by defiant and rebellious men to *compete* against true religion. As Nimrod had declared: "Depart from the religion of Shem and cleave to the institutes of Nimrod!"

Third, heathen worship was not the product of primitive minds manifesting the "upward reach of man." These abominations were originally germinated in the sophisticated intellects of apostate men who lived when the gospel was on the earth, when the true history of the race was available in written documents, when the existence of God was understood and recognized and when the commandments of God for happy living were available and taught. Heathen philosophy was brewed in the dark minds of men who had apostatized from the truth and had set about to destroy the gospel and the influence of the Priesthood by any means they could think of. Their technique consisted primarily in taking concepts which the people already believed and then rationalizing and twisting them so that they might become more appealing to the common man by making allowances for vices and indulgences which true religion forbade.

Fourth, revealed religion is the original source for most of the ethical and philosophical knowledge generally attributed to the intellectual leaders of heathen nations. Studies have been made which show that all of those basic ethics and philosophical beliefs which have been

---

[23]Josephus, *op. cit.*, Book I, 4:2
[24]Abraham 1:27

found in one form or another among nearly every people of the earth have a common origin. They are actually remnants of true gospel principles which originally came from the prophets of God. (See *The Gospel Through the Ages,* by Milton R. Hunter. The entire book is devoted to this problem).

In the hands of such men as Nimrod these teachings of the prophets and patriarchs were deliberately distorted. Subsequent generations therefore received only a few crumbs of truth, and these had been camouflaged by man-made mysteries and fabricated superstitions.

When modern scholars began their study of the customs and beliefs of ancient peoples they found some of their concepts to be similar to our modern ideas of ethics, religion and philosophy. Applying the evolutionary theory to these findings, they concluded that the modern concepts of God, ethics, religion and philosophy are simply the outgrowth of these early beliefs. Inadequate data and improper evaluation of some of the evidence led to this error. Now it has been corrected. Modern revelation has confirmed the declaration of the ancient prophets that ethics, religion and the related philosophical concepts growing out of them all came by direct revelation from God in earliest times. Authoritative sources now available to us also indicate that heathen religions and heathen philosophies came later as diluted substitutes designed to satisfy people who felt disinclined to subscribe to the ideals and standards of conduct revealed from God.

Now let us turn to the program which God launched soon after the Flood to challenge these forces of apostasy and idolatry and save the human race.

CHAPTER TWENTY-FIVE

God Launches a Program to Save the Race

To combat idolatry and wickedness the Lord launched a new kind of program. What was it? How did it differ from the program which Enoch was told to follow?

Have there been a great many prophets whom the scriptures do not mention? Will we ever have their writings and histories?

Do you think students may have underestimated the importance of the leadership provided by the Priesthood in various parts of the world?

Who was the famous prophet who presided over the first colony of the Priesthood in Palestine?

How did Melchizedek succeed in establishing peace in Salem "in all his days"? Do you think the same formula would work today?

Was Melchizedek the same person as Shem?

What happened to the people of Melchizedek?

From available evidence what language did the Jaredites bring to America? Do we know what the sealed portion of the gold plates contained? Who received this revelation?

Who ordained Esaias to the Priesthood? What does this indicate? Was this the same Priesthood conferred upon Moses by Jethro?

What three things do we learn from the visit of the "wise men" to Jerusalem some time after the birth of Christ? Did they find Jesus in a stable? What significance do you gather from the fact that there were "wise men" in the east who received revelation?

During ten generations what happened to Shem's descendants at Ur in Chaldea? Does it appear that they had lost their rights to the Priesthood? Why do you think the Lord had Abraham born in this community?

How much significance did the Lord attach to the ministry of Abraham?

Setting up Priesthood Colonies around the World

As we have now seen, Noah was correct in suspecting that his descendants might indulge in wicked practices soon after the Flood. During the 350 years which Noah lived after the Flood he saw ten generations of humanity descend to a level which was almost equal to the degeneracy of the pre-flood period. Human sacrifices, heathen idolatry, imperialistic conquest, priestcraft and institutionalized immorality characterized civilization. Once again the race was corrupting its way upon the earth. It was as though the majority of humanity had become like a lethal swamp filled with decay and stagnation.

But as God had promised both Enoch and Noah, He would not send another flood to cleanse this swamp.[1] Instead, He established "islands" or communities of righteous groups who held the Priesthood, and these were placed in various parts of the earth to preserve God's ways among men. Notice that this program of the Lord reversed His usual procedure of gathering all of the Saints together in one place.

Because the scriptures only refer to a few of these missionary-prophet groups we may have underestimated the extent of their work. The Lord disclosed to Nephi that he had spoken through His servants in "all the nations of the earth" and He said these various prophets had recorded their revelations and histories just as the Jewish and Nephite prophets had done.[2] He promised that eventually these would all be revealed [3]

---

[1]Moses 7:50-51; Gen. 9:11
[2]2 Nephi 29:12
[3]*Ibid.*, 30:16-17

In most nations time erased the memory of the great work done by these enlightened leaders, but probably many of their teachings survived and were adopted by the people as their own. A case in point—and one which we will discuss later in detail—is the contribution made by Abraham when he went down into Egypt and taught from the throne of Pharaoh the revelations he had received on astronomy, mathematics and other subjects. The Egyptians later passed on much of their knowledge to the Greeks and their system of mathematics became the foundation of modern science.[4] In the passing years, however, Egypt gave no credit to the source of this knowledge and if it were not for the Book of Abraham we wouldn't know that this prophet had ever contributed to the learning of the Egyptians.

The disclosures of the Book of Mormon show us that in the early history of America's aborigines the prophets of God were the greatest single influence in their entire civilization. In fact, their greatest prosperity and progress were made under the leadership of the Priesthood and just as soon as they drove the prophets from among them they began to degenerate to a state of uncivilized savagery. Some of them devolved to the lowest levels of human survival where many of their descendants remain to this day.

It is because of examples such as these that it is felt that the colonies of prophets which God scattered across the earth were much more influential in molding history than we have previously supposed.

THE PEOPLE OF MELCHIZEDEK IN THE LAND OF SALEM

One of the most important colonies raised up by the members of the Priesthood during the lifetime of Noah was in Palestine. Most of this territory was dominated by the seed of Ham. The land was even named after Ham's oldest son, Canaan. But the seed of Seth had carved out a mountainous kingdom over toward the northern end of

---

[4]Wells, H. G., *Outline of History,* p. 377

the Dead Sea called Salem. This is the territory which surrounds the modern city of Jerusalem (Jeru-salem).[5]

We have no indication that Noah or Shem ever visited this kingdom, but its leaders apparently kept in close contact with the early patriarchs because it was from them that the blessings of the Priesthood were received.[6]

The only reason we have found historical references to Salem is due to the fact that this kingdom was governed by the prophet-king, Melchizedek, and the annals of sacred history have preserved some most interesting facts concerning his life and ministry.

> "Now Melchizedek was a man of faith, who wrought righteousness and when a child he feared God, and stopped the mouths of lions, and quenched the violence of fire. And thus, having been approved of God, he was ordained a High Priest after the order of the covenant which God made with Enoch."[7]

When Melchizedek became the king of Salem it says he "did reign under his father,"[8] which would indicate that Melchizedek was raised as a prince of royal lineage and that his forefathers were the rulers of Salem.

Since Melchizedek left such a distinguished record both as a spiritual and political leader the ancient Hebrew scholars wondered if Melchizedek might not be identical with Shem. We know that Shem was living at this time (around 2000 B.C.) because he lived 502 years after the Flood and did not die until 1,842 B.C. Nevertheless, modern revelation has made it plain that Shem and Melchizedek were two different persons. In the Doctrine and Covenants 84:14 the Lord says: "Melchizedek . . . received it (the Priesthood) through the *lineage of his fathers,* even till Noah." Obviously, Shem had no "lineage of his fathers, even till Noah" because Noah *was* his father. The fact that the word *fathers* is in the plural

---

[5]Psalm 76:2; Peloubet, *Bible Dictionary* under "Salem"
[6]D. & C. 84:14
[7]Insp. Vers. Gen. 14:26
[8]Alma 13:18

would indicate that Melchizedek was probably removed from Shem by several generations.

The scripture says Melchizedek ruled over Salem during a period of great difficulty. The spirit of apostasy had spread throughout the land so that there were scarcely any righteous people left. In fact, the record says: "His people had waxed strong in iniquity and abomination; yea, they had *all* gone astray; they were full of all manner of wickedness."[9] No doubt a spirit of war and contention was also beginning to manifest itself which would threaten the peace of the whole land. Nimrod would have had a quick answer for such troubles. He would have sent his soldiers throughout the land, slaughtering a few citizens as an example to the rest. He would have met force with force. Melchizedek, however, was no Nimrod.

The scripture pays a high tribute to the skill and courage of this prophet in dealing with the threatening crisis. It says: "But Melchizedek, having exercised mighty faith, and (having) received the office of the high priesthood according to the holy order of God, did *preach repentance unto his people*. And behold, *they did repent;* and Melchizedek did establish peace in the land *in his days;* therefore he was called the prince of peace. . . . Now, there were many before him, and also there were many afterwards, but none were greater; therefore, of him they have more particularly made mention."[10]

Melchizedek discovered and used the only perfect formula for permanent peace ever devised. It was the same formula the early patriarchs used. It has been consistently advocated by all the prophets since. Peace is one of the by-products of the gospel. It cannot be had by force, by treaties, or by licentious wickedness. Permanent peace comes only to the repentant and the righteous.

The power of the Priesthood possessed by Melchizedek was displayed on so many occasions that all the people were able to witness that he was indeed "approved

---

[9]Alma 13:17
[10]*Ibid.,* 13:18-19

of God." In process of time the members of the Church decided always to refer to the delegated authority of God as "the priesthood after the order of Melchizedek." In modern times the Lord has revealed that: "Before his (Melchizedek's) day it was called the Holy Priesthood after the Order of the Son of God. But out of respect or reverence to the name of the Supreme Being, to avoid the too frequent repetition of his name, they, the church, in ancient days, called the priesthood after Melchizedek, or the Melchizedek Priesthood."[11]

Certainly any person who had been ordained "after the order of Melchizedek" would be recognized among the people as having the true agency or power of God and not the man-made priesthood such as the Egyptians had conferred upon themselves.[12] King David even spoke of the Savior as "a priest for ever after the order of Melchizedek."[13] The Apostle Paul commented on this in his epistle to the Hebrews.[14] The Savior could also have been called a High Priest after the order of Jesus Christ, the Son of God, but this would not have carried the weight with the people that the ancient title carried. All Israelites had come to recognize the "order of Melchizedek" as the true authority or Priesthood of God. That is why this title was applied even to Jesus Christ, the author of this Priesthood.

The kingdom of Melchizedek in the land of Salem did not remain in existence for long. It was there when Abraham returned to Palestine from Egypt, but it appears to have been gone a few years afterwards. You will recall that after his battle with the kings, Abraham met Melchizedek and honored him as the local presiding authority by paying tithes to him.[15] This incident happened prior to the birth of Ishmael which occurred when Abraham was eighty-six. We know then, that Melchizedek was ruling over the kingdom of Salem up to about that time. However, by the time Abraham was nearing

---

[11]D. & C. 107:3-4
[12]Abraham 1:27
[13]Psalm 110:4
[14]Heb. 5:6, 10; 6:20; 7:1-21
[15]Insp. Vers. Gen. 14:36-39; Genesis 14:18-20

the age of 140 and needed to find a person of the proper
lineage as a wife for Isaac, there appears to have been
none of the people of Melchizedek left. In fact, Abraham
had to send all the way to Mesopotamia to get a wife for
Isaac.

On that occasion Abraham said to his eldest servant:
"I will make thee swear before the Lord, the God of heav-
en and the God of the earth, that thou shalt not take a
wife unto my son of the daughters of the Canaanites
among whom I dwell; but thou shalt go unto my country
and to *my kindred* and take a wife unto my son Isaac.[16]
Then it says the servant "arose and went to Mesopotamia."[17]

But what happened to the people of Melchizedek?
Why couldn't Abraham obtain a wife for Isaac from
among these choice people who were Abraham's not-too-
distant relatives and certainly not Canaanites? Why, at
this time, does Abraham imply that there were only
Canaanites in this land where he lived?

Originally the Bible contained the answers to these
questions, but over the centuries this information was left
out of the transcripts. Now it has been restored to us.
The inspired version indicates a reason for this situation
by explaining that Melchizedek and his people had been
allowed to enjoy the blessings of Enoch. It says: "And
men having this faith, coming up unto this order of God,
were *translated and taken up into heaven.* And now,
Melchizedek was a priest of this order; therefore he obtained peace in Salem, and was called the prince of peace.
And his people wrought righteousness and *obtained
heaven,* and *sought for the city of Enoch* which God had
before taken, separating it from the earth, having reserved it unto the latter days, or the end of the world."[18]

So here is an epic of history which had been lost from
the annals of scripture. It explains why Abraham no
longer had any kindred in the land of Canaan from among
whom Isaac could obtain a wife. In his latter days Abra-

[16]*Ibid.,* 24:2
[17]*Ibid.,* 24:10
[18]*Ibid.,* 14:32-34

ham even had to bury his dead in a tomb purchased from one of the Canaanites.[19] Apparently none of his people were left in the land.

THE COLONY OF PROPHETS WHICH CAME TO AMERICA

We have already discussed the American migration of Mahonri-Moriancumr and his brother, Jared, after the Flood. They brought with them various kinds of plant and animal life to "replenish" the Western Hemisphere. They also brought with them a language which had not been confounded and which we assume was the Adamic tongue. This assumption is based on the fact that the language of the Jaredites was obtained from Noah and his sons. Noah had been a contemporary of nearly all of the Adamic patriarchs including Enos, Cainan, Mahalaleel, Jared, Methuselah and Lamech. In all probability he was also made custodian of the "books of remembrance" which were written in a language which was "pure and undefiled."[20] It also says that the patriarchs taught their children to read and write in this language.[21] All this would seem to indicate that the Adamic tongue was preserved during the pre-flood period and that the Jaredites brought this uncorrupted language with them to America.

These prophets also carried with them the ancient scriptures which told the history of the race from the beginning.[22]

Mahonri-Moriancumr enjoyed some of the greatest revelations ever vouchsafed to man. Moroni recorded them on the gold plates and said: "Behold, I have written upon these plates the very things which the brother of Jared saw, and there never were greater things made manifest than those which were made manifest unto the brother of Jared."[23] This was the sealed portion of the plates received by Joseph Smith.[24] These writings contain

[19]Gen. 23:3-16
[20]Moses 6:5-6
[21]*Ibid.*
[22]Ether 8:9
[23]*Ibid.,* 4:4
[24]*Ibid.,* 4:5-6

a prophetic history of the world from the beginning to the end.[25]

A great civilization was established in America by the Jaredites which apparently lasted from somewhere around 2200 B.C. until it began to destroy itself in civil war around 600 B.C. The Lord then replaced this people with the Nephite civilization which was brought to America just about the time the Jaredites became extinct.

THE COLONY OF PROPHETS IN MIDIAN

During the lifetime of Abraham a group of righteous people gathered in Midian which was located south of Palestine. This land was named after one of Abraham's sons who settled in this region. These people traced their Priesthood back to a man named Esaias who lived in the days of Abraham. The Lord has declared in modern times that Esaias "received it (the Priesthood) under the hand of God."[26] This would indicate that the people in Midian were probably isolated in some way from the other prophets, otherwise it would seem that Esaias would have been ordained through the regular channels of the Priesthood. During his lifetime, however, Esaias made contact with Abraham "and was blessed by him."[27]

The people of Midian preserved the Priesthood among them throughout many centuries. This was the colony of people through whom Moses received the Priesthood about 450 years after Abraham's ministry. When Moses fled from Egypt he stopped at Midian and was befriended by Jethro, the high priest. Moses became the manager of Jethro's flocks and married his daughter. It was under the hands of Jethro that Moses received the Priesthood.[28]

Later, when Moses had been sent back to Egypt by the Lord and had rescued the people of Israel, it was Jethro who came out into the wilderness and instructed Moses in the proper method of organizing a system of

[25]*Ibid.*, 3:25-27
[26]D. & C. 84:12
[27]*Ibid.*, 84:13
[28]*Ibid.*, 84:6

judges for the camps of Israel so that Moses would not have to bear the whole burden of leadership. Jethro was shocked when he saw that Moses was trying to do all this work by himself. He said: "What is this thing that thou doest to the people? why sittest thou thyself alone, and all the people stand by thee from morning unto even?"[29]

When Moses said he was trying to settle disputes and teach the people the statutes of the Lord, Jethro told him: "The thing that thou doest is not good. Thou wilt surely wear away."[30] Then Jethro told Moses to organize the camps of Israel with "able men, such as fear God, men of truth, hating covetousness; and place such over them, to be rulers of thousands, and rulers of hundreds, rulers of fifties and rulers of tens: And let them judge the people at all seasons: and it shall be, that every great matter they shall bring unto thee, but every small matter they shall judge: so shall it be easier for thyself, and they shall bear the burden with thee."[31]

Thus Moses was tutored by his father-in-law. Jethro had enjoyed many generations of Priesthood training which Moses had not. The spirit of Jethro's counsel shows that he had a true understanding of Priesthood leadership. From what we know of Jethro it would also indicate that the colony of prophets in Midian had honored their callings and maintained a proper understanding of gospel principles from generation to generation.

THE COLONY OF PROPHETS IN "THE EAST"

Whether or not Noah and Shem continued to maintain their headquarters in "the east" where they first settled after the landing of the Ark, we are not certain. There is scriptural evidence, however, that either they or some other colony of prophets established a community of righteous people in the east. Their existence became known at the time of Christ's birth when "there came wise men from the east to Jerusalem."[32] Several interest-

[29]Exodus 18:24
[30]*Ibid.*, 18:17-18
[31]*Ibid.*, 18:21-22
[32]Matthew 2:1

ing things occurred in connection with the appearance of
of these wise men.

First, it disclosed the fact that there were people in
"the east" who knew that a great new star would appear
as a sign of Christ's birth just as the prophets in America
had been told.[33]

Second, these men appear to have been worthy and
righteous individuals who were entitled to receive revelation.[34]

Third, they seem to have come from a considerable
distance to Jerusalem to inquire of Herod about the new
king. The scripture is clear that they did not arrive on
the night of Christ's birth (Christmas pageants to the
contrary notwithstanding!) but they reached Jerusalem
long afterwards. In fact, they would not have left their
own country until the great new star appeared, and the
scripture says they saw the star a *second time* in Palestine
indicating that there had been an interval of time between
their departure from the east and their arrival in
Jerusalem.[35]

Notice that Herod "diligently" inquired of the wise
men as to the specific date when the star first appeared
in their own country.[36] The scripture does not say how
long ago it had been but observe that when Herod sent
his soldiers to Bethlehem a short time later he ordered
them to slay all children *two years* and under.[37] This age
limit would have been set in the light of the knowledge
which Herod had received from the wise men as to how
old the Christ child would be by this time.

We also know that Mary and Joseph had taken Jesus
to the temple forty-two days after his birth,[38] and it is
apparent that their flight into Egypt was not until after
this trip to the temple.

It was the arrival of the wise men in Jerusalem and
their visit with Herod which precipitated the flight of

---

[33]Helaman 14:5
[34]Matthew 2:12
[35]*Ibid.,* 2:9-10
[36]*Ibid.,* 2:7
[37]*Ibid.,* 2:16
[38]Luke 2:21-22; Lev. 12:2-26

Mary, Joseph, and Jesus into Egypt. Therefore we know the wise men did not come until *at least* six weeks after the birth of Jesus. And it may have been nearly two years later. Notice that when the wise men found Joseph, Mary and Jesus in Bethlehem they were no longer in a stable but in a "house."[39]

The fact that it required a considerable length of time for the wise men to reach Jerusalem would indicate that their home in "the east" was at least as far away as Mesopotamia and perhaps even farther. Somewhere in that distant land was hidden away a righteous colony of people.

The Colony of Prophets at Ur in Chaldea

During these early years the main line of Shem's patriarchal heirs apparently maintained their headquarters in Mesopotamia. Shem's selected heir was Arphaxad who was born two years after the Flood—2,342 B.C.[40]

Arphaxad chose Salah who was born 2,307 B.C. Salah chose Eber who was born 2,277 B.C. Eber chose Peleg who was born 2,243 B.C. Peleg chose Reu who was born 2,213 B.C. Reu chose Serug who was born 2,181 B.C. Serug chose Nahor who was born 2,151 B.C. Nahor chose Terah who was born 2,122 B.C. Terah was the father of Abraham and lived in Ur of Chaldea which was in the southern portion of Mesopotamia along the Euphrates River.

However, in the history of this particular colony of prophets there is a chapter of tragic apostasy. By the time Abraham had reached adolescence this colony had come under the influence of the most degenerate idolatrous practices and it would appear that they had lost their rights to the Priesthood. Abraham later wrote:

"My fathers (note the plural) having turned from their righteousness, and from the holy commandments which the Lord their God had given them, unto the worshiping of the gods of the heathen, utterly refused to hearken to my voice; For their hearts were set to do evil,

---

[39]Matt. 2:11
[40]See Gen. Chapter 11 for chronology of Shem's heirs

and were wholly turned to the god of Elkenah, and the god of Libnah, and the god of Mahmackrah, and the god of Korash, and the god of Pharaoh, king of Egypt."[41] This is also confirmed by a Biblical source.[42]

As we shall see later, when Abraham sought for the Priesthood he obtained it from "the fathers"[43] but they were not *his* fathers. He had to obtain the Priesthood from a different branch of Shem's descendants where the Priesthood had been maintained undefiled.[44]

It is also plain from the scripture that the Lord was making one last effort to reclaim the colony at Ur when He sent Abraham among them. This colony may not have realized it, but they had been honored with the presence of one of the greatest defenders of the faith the Lord had ever raised up. In fact, the Lord indicated that of all the missionary-prophet colonies which He had established, He was relying particularly upon Abraham and his seed to be the rallying standard for the entire human race. To him the Lord said: "In thee shall all families of the earth be blessed,"[45] and "As it was with Noah, so shall it be with thee; but through *thy ministry my name shall be known in the earth forever.*"[46]

There are few biographies more interesting to study than that of Abraham. Let us now turn to the life and ministry of this great prince of Shem.

---

[41]Abraham 1:5-6
[42]Joshua 24:2
[43]Abraham 1:3
[44]D. & C. 84:14
[45]Genesis 12:3
[46]Abraham 1:19

CHAPTER TWENTY-SIX

The Early Life of Abraham

Do we know the exact year when Abraham was born? Do we know the exact year of birth for the patriarchs who preceded him? How many generations were there from Adam to Abraham?

Where was Abraham when he "sought for the blessings of the fathers" and "became a rightful heir, a High Priest"? Who ordained him? Why wasn't Abraham ordained by his father, Terah?

Is there any evidence that Melchizedek had some influence on the early life of Abraham?

Where was Abraham when he first received the Urim and Thummim? Did he enjoy the spirit of prophecy? What had happened to the "records of the fathers" during Abraham's day? What did they contain?

Was it a very serious offense against God when Abraham's fathers joined in the rites of heathen worship? How was the priest of Pharaoh able to deceive Terah, Abraham's father? Who does Abraham say "offered up their children unto their dumb idols"?

What is the significance of the statement that three virgins were slain upon the altar "because of their virtue"?

Who was behind the plot to capture Abraham and make him the victim of a human sacrifice?

What appears to have been the meaning of the Lord when He told Abraham that He would put upon him the "Priesthood of thy father"? Why was this a special comfort to Abraham?

What caused Abraham's father to repent? How did this affect Abraham? During the famine what happened to Haran, Abraham's brother? What happened to Haran's family?

Whom did Abraham marry? Why was she his "sister"? Whom did Nehor marry? Was she Nehor's "sister"? The descendants of Abraham and Nehor later intermarried. Did this produce a weak strain?

Why do we think Abraham and Nehor were probably close to the same age?

THE EARLY LIFE OF ABRAHAM

Abraham constituted the twentieth generation after Adam and he is the first patriarch whose birthdate cannot be fixed with absolute accuracy in the scriptures. However, it can be closely approximated. For reasons which are set forth in the appendix under "The Chronological Time Table Covering the Period of the Patriarchs" we have set the birthdate of Abraham at 2,022 B.C. which would mean that he was born when his father, Terah, was 100. Abraham had two brothers, Haran and Nehor. As we shall see later, Haran was considerably older than Abraham, and Nehor was probably close to Abraham's own age.

It is apparent from Abraham's own writing that the environment into which he was born was a social and moral cesspool, but it is entirely clear that Abraham did not fall under its influence. His early training and guidance were inspired by another source.

In the writings of Abraham we find that while he was living in Chaldea and was still in his early manhood (which is evidenced by the fact that he did not marry until considerably later) he could see that it was not a desirable place to remain, therefore he determined to take a course which would provide him with "greater happiness and peace."[1] To accomplish this he says he "sought for the blessings of the fathers" and "became a rightful heir, a High Priest, holding the right belonging to the fathers."[2]

In referring to the Priesthood which he had received, Abraham says: "It was conferred upon me from the

---

[1]Abraham 1:2
[2]*Ibid.*

fathers."³ Now Abraham does not mention who the fathers were through whom he received the Priesthood, but he explains in the next few verses that *his* fathers "had turned from their righteousness,"⁴ so it is obvious that he had to go to other fathers to receive "mine appointment unto the Priesthood." Modern revelation discloses the specific identity of the person who ordained him: "Abraham received the priesthood from Melchizedek, who received it through the lineage of his fathers, even till Noah."⁵

When did Melchizedek ordain Abraham? Many students have assumed that this ordination did not take place until Abraham met Melchizedek in Palestine and paid tithes to him.⁶ By that time, however, Abraham was seventy-five years old. He had been exercising the powers of the Priesthood for many years. The problem is clarified now that we have Abraham's own explanation indicating that while "In the land of the Chaldeans, at the residence of my father . . . I became a rightful heir, a High Priest, holding the right belonging to the fathers."⁷

Nowhere in scripture do we find a recitation of the exact circumstances surrounding Abraham's ordination, but we do have sufficient evidence in the above circumstances to indicate that Abraham had contact with Melchizedek during his early manhood and was ordained by him at that time. There is also considerable evidence that the personality and achievements of Melchizedek had a strong influence upon Abraham.

You will recall that Melchizedek had succeeded in calling all of the people in his kingdom to repentance so that peace was established in Salem. Because of this accomplishment Melchizedek was given the title of "the prince of peace."⁸ Now notice what Abraham says concerning his early desires to obtain the Priesthood: "I sought for the blessings of the fathers, and the right whereunto I should be ordained to administer the same;

³*Ibid.*, 1:3
⁴*Ibid.*, 1:5
⁵D. & C. 84:14
⁶Gen. 14:19-20
⁷Abraham 1:1-2
⁸Alma 13:18

having been myself a follower of righteousness, desiring
also to be one who possessed great knowledge, and to be
a greater follower of righteousness, and to possess a
greater knowledge, and to be a father of many nations, a
prince of peace, and desiring to receive instructions, and
to keep the commandments of God."[9]

Now that we know it was Melchizedek to whom
Abraham went for his appointment in the Priesthood we
can also see the influence of that "prince of peace" in the
early life of Abraham as indicated by the above passage.

Not only does Abraham confirm that he was ordained
a High Priest before leaving Ur, but he also tells us that
while there he received the Urim and Thummim,[10] and
prophesied to the wicked citizens of Ur that if they did
not repent a great famine would descend upon them.[11] By
some means he also gained possession of the precious
"records of the fathers" which were apparently the
"Books of Remembrance" handed down through the line
of the patriarchs since the days of Adam.[12]

In spite of all these blessings, however, Abraham
soon discovered that his missionary efforts among the
people of Ur were not going to be favored with the success which Melchizedek had enjoyed among the people
of Salem. Not only did the general populace reject Abraham but he also ran into serious difficulty with his own
"fathers." We know this included Terah,[13] and one or
more of his other paternal ancestors. These men had been
led away by the heathen priests who claimed they had
the Priesthood through Ham. Abraham says this "deceived" his father. It led him to accept their abominable
rituals as being sanctioned by God.[14]

Abraham is clear that his fathers not only condoned
the heathen rituals but also took a disgraceful and murderous part in them. He says: "they turned their hearts
to the sacrifice of the heathen in *offering up their children*

---

[9]Abraham 1:2
[10]Abraham 3:1
[11]Abraham 1:29
[12]*Ibid.*, 1:31; Moses 6:5
[13]Abraham 1:30
[14]*Ibid.*, 1:27

unto their dumb idols."[15] Abraham denounced these apostate forefathers and found himself immediately enmeshed in a conspiracy designed to take his life. Instead of repenting, his fathers plotted with the priest of Elkenah to have Abraham captured and offered up as a human sacrifice!

To get some idea of the wanton baseness of the idolatry which was practiced in Chaldea, Abraham tells us that "it was the custom of the priest of Pharaoh, the king of Egypt, (who was also the priest of Elkenah) to offer up upon the altar which was built in the land of Chaldea, for the offering unto these strange gods, *men, women and children.*"[16] The altar where this priest of Pharaoh presided was apparently a very prominent heathen shrine located in Ur "by the hill called Potiphar's Hill at the head of the plain of Olishem."[17] Human sacrifices on this altar were outstanding community events.

Abraham states that the priest of Pharaoh had recently offered a small child on this altar as a thank offering to the god of Pharaoh and the god of Shagreel which was the sun.[18] Abraham says this was also the same altar where this priest had sacrificed three young virgins "at one time."

Each of these young girls was a princess. They "were the daughters of Onitah, one of the royal descent directly from the loins of Ham."[19] Abraham says they were sacrificed "because of their virtue."[20] It was a common heathen practice to require all young maidens who were to be admitted to the worship of a heathen god to submit themselves to the priests of the god and participate in the sensuous and degenerate rituals which were associated with such worship.[21] These three virgins "would not bow down to worship gods of wood or of stone" and they refused to sacrifice themselves to the profligate ritual of the sensuous priests. Therefore, Abra-

---

[15]*Ibid.,* 1:7
[16]*Ibid.,* 1:8
[17]*Ibid.,* 1:10, 20
[18]*Ibid.,* 1:9
[19]*Ibid.,* 1:11
[20]*Ibid.*
[21]See Appendix: "Immorality in Heathen Ritual"

ham says, "they were killed upon this altar, and it was done after the manner of the Egyptians."[22]

THE CONSPIRACY TO SLAY ABRAHAM

Abraham was therefore well aware of the fate which was in store for him when he suddenly found himself captured by the priests. He says: "The priests laid violence upon me, that they might slay me also, as they did those virgins."[23] Abraham had previously stated that his fathers were participants in this conspiracy and they had "endeavored to take away my life by the hand of the priest of Elkenah . . . who was also the priest of Pharaoh."[24]

So the plot had succeeded. The young prince of Ur was dragged to the foot of Potiphar's Hill at the head of the plain of Olishem. He was bound to the altar which stood before the gods of Elkenah, Libnah, Mahmackrah, Korash, "and also a god like unto that of Pharaoh, king of Egypt." This last statement might be taken to mean that the Pharaoh of that dynasty had deified himself (as many monarchs were doing in those days) and had placed a statue of himself in all the temples to be worshiped by the masses.

Abraham has left us an illustration of the altar to which he was bound.[25] It was like a bedstead with legs carved to look like those of a lion. At the top of the bedstead was a lion's head, and at the foot of the bedstead was a lion's tail. Note that the Egyptian priest is pictured in Abraham's illustration as dark-skinned. In this connection Herodotus, the Greek historian, called the Egyptians "blacks" and R. A. Rawlinson says: "The Egyptians appear to have been among the darkest races with which the Greeks of early times came into direct contact."[26]

From later developments we know that among the people of Ur there were still a few righteous people

[22]Abraham 1:11
[23]Ibid., 1:12
[24]Ibid., 1:7
[25]Ibid., plate 1
[26]Rawlinson, R. A., History of Ancient Egypt, p. 103

(Sarai and Lot, for example) but there was none sufficiently strong or influential to save Abraham. The wrath of his fathers and the politically powerful heathen priests was about to be unleashed upon him.

In that hour Abraham called upon his Father in heaven with all the faith he possessed. Abraham had been bound to the altar with strong bands and the priests were prepared to raise the sacrificial knife and slay him after "the manner of the Egyptians" which was a cruel and horrible death.

Then suddenly it happened. Abraham says: "the Lord . . . filled me with the vision of the Almighty, and the angel of his presence stood by me, and immediately unloosed my bands."[27] Then the wrath of God fell violently upon the place which "broke down the altar of Elkenah, and of the gods of the land, and utterly destroyed them."[28] Whether this was by lightning or earthquake it does not say but some great force struck the high place on which the altar was located and broke it down with all the heathen paraphernalia that was on it. Furthermore, the murderous priest of Elkenah and Pharaoh did not escape. The power of God "smote the priest that he died!"[29]

These events were interpreted as a great national calamity in Chaldea. God had smashed the shrine and principal objects of devotion in the state religious cult of Ur. And because the priest of Pharaoh had died and the image "like unto that of Pharaoh" had also fallen to destruction there were repercussions as far away as Egypt. Abraham recorded that "there was great mourning in Chaldea, and also in the court of Pharaoh."[30]

However, it does not say there was any repentance, only mourning. The mourning of the people was the sorrow of the wicked who had seen their murderous priest and his heathen images cast down before their very eyes. And they saw Abraham on whom they hoped to avenge themselves, set at liberty.

[27]Abraham 1:15
[28]Ibid., 1:20
[29]Ibid.
[30]Ibid.

Abraham states that in that moment when he was rescued from the sacrificial altar he received a revelation which served to comfort and sustain him throughout his life. The voice of the Lord said:

"Abraham, Abraham, behold, my name is Jehovah, and I have heard thee, and have come down to deliver thee, and to take thee away from thy father's house, and from all thy kins-folk, into a strange land which thou knowest not of.

"And this because they have turned their hearts away from me, to worship the God of Elkenah, and the god of Libnah, and the god of Mahmackrah, and the god of Korash, and the god of Pharaoh, king of Egypt; therefore I have come down to visit them and to destroy him who hath lifted his hand against thee, Abraham, my son, to take away thy life." (Abraham 1:16-17)

The Lord then added these words which must have carried particular significance to Abraham:

"Behold, I will lead thee by my hand, and I will take thee, to put upon thee my name, even the Priesthood of thy father, and my power shall be over thee." (*Ibid.*, 1:18)

The "Priesthood of thy father" probably had reference to the Patriarchal Priesthood which follows a particular lineage from father to son. A modern revelation refers to the special calling of a presiding patriarch and says: "The order of this priesthood was confirmed to be handed down from father to son, and rightly belongs to the literal descendants of the chosen seed, to whom the promises were made. This order was instituted in the days of Adam."[31]

Abraham was of the "chosen seed to whom the promises were made," and he was therefore entitled to the evangelical or Patriarchal Priesthood. But no doubt the apostasy of his father had made Abraham wonder how he might receive his patriarchal calling. Here the Lord appears to be assuring Abraham that the link in the

---

[31]D. & C. 107:40-41

patriarchal line will not be broken and that this special office of the Priesthood will be conferred upon him. Whether it was bestowed on Abraham by Terah after the latter's repentance or whether it was given to Abraham by the person holding the keys of that dispensation, we are not informed. We are simply assured through this passage that Abraham did eventually receive the Patriarchal Priesthood of his father.

THE FAMINE IN CHALDEA

The wrath of the Lord not only struck the heathen altar and "smote the priest . . . that he died" but a devastating famine fell upon the land so that the whole populace was afflicted. Abraham says this "came in fulfilment of those things which were said unto me concerning the land of Chaldea, that there should be a famine in the land."[32]

When Abraham was first told this by the Lord we do not know. Perhaps it was during the time he was preaching to his people before his capture when they "utterly refused to hearken to my voice."[33]

In any event, this prophecy concerning a coming famine was literally fulfilled, and the people of Chaldea suffered bitterly. Even Abraham's own brother died from it.

The distress of Abraham in these terrible days must have been acute. Even with suffering and death on every hand Terah appears to have continued for some time in his antagonism against Abraham. Only when the intensity of the famine had reached that point where his father was "sorely tormented" did the spirit of repentance finally reach him and then his fickle religious convictions of the several previous years of apostasy collapsed in a shambles. Abraham says: "he repented of the evil which he had determined against me, to take away my life."[34]

Here are chapters of drama which Abraham did not record in detail. How did he protect himself during this period of bitter persecution? Where did he go after he

[32]Abraham 1:29
[33]Ibid., 1:5
[34]Ibid., 1:30

escaped from the heathen altar of Elkenah? The student cannot help but wonder how he managed to survive during the early days of the famine. And even after his father had repented and Abraham returned home there must have been days of deep sorrow and physical suffering that have gone unrecorded.

At this point Abraham suddenly interrupts the narrative to say: "But the records of the fathers, even the patriarchs . . . the Lord my God preserved in my own hands."[35] This would indicate that the protection of these precious historical documents was one of Abraham's greatest concerns. And there is no reason for mentioning the records at this point unless they had been in danger during this period of persecution. He rejoiced that through it all they had been preserved.

Abraham explains that these invaluable records not only contained "a knowledge of the beginning of the creation," and a chronology running back from Abraham to the beginning, but they contained a great amount of scientific information—facts concerning the "planets, and of the stars, as they were made known unto the fathers."[36] The ancient patriarchs were better informed on these subjects than historians have thought.

ABRAHAM'S MARRIAGE

Continuing his account, Abraham says: "Now the Lord God caused the famine to wax sore in the land of Ur, insomuch that Haran, my brother, died; but Terah, my father, yet lived in the land of Ur, of the Chaldees."[37]

It is apparent that Haran was considerably older than Abraham. He had a daughter who was only ten years younger than Abraham.[38] When Haran died he left three grown children—two daughters, Sarai and Milcah, and one son named Lot. These three were taken into the household of their grandfather, Terah, and the record implies that Terah legally adopted them. Therefore they were elevated from the status of grandchildren to the status of Terah's own children.

[35]Ibid., 1:31
[36]Ibid., 1:28, 31
[37]Ibid., 2:1
[38]Genesis 17:17

This is made clear by Abraham when he explained at a later date that Sarai was his sister. Said he: "Indeed she is my sister; she is the daughter of my father, but not the daughter of my mother."[39] Some authorities mistook this passage to mean that Sarai was the daughter of Terah by another wife, but now that we have the book of Abraham it is confirmed that Sarai was really Terah's granddaughter but Terah became her "father" when he absorbed Haran's family into his own household following Haran's death.

As we shall see later, Abraham not only referred to Sarai as his sister on a number of occasions but also referred to Lot as his brother.[40] The Lord also referred to Lot as Abraham's brother.[41]

Sarai was a remarkable young princess of the royal lineage of Shem. She was so beautiful that the life of Abraham was placed in jeopardy twice because of it. Like Abraham, she was born at a time when moral decay and social degeneracy had swept across the land but she remained true to the principles of the gospel throughout her life and on many occasions exhibited faith of the highest order.

After the death of Haran, Abraham says: "And it came to pass that I, Abraham, took Sarai to wife, and Nehor, my brother, took Milcah to wife."[42]

It would appear that since neither Abraham nor Nehor had married prior to this time they were probably close to the same age. As we have previously observed, marriage to close relatives was not an uncommon practice in this early day when inherited weaknesses had not yet corrupted many family strains. History has shown that the marriage of Abraham and Nehor to their nieces, Sarai and Milcah, produced strength, not weakness. From them came the mighty multitudes of Israel as well as the prophets and patriarchs of all subsequent dispensations.

[39]*Ibid.*, 20:12
[40]*Ibid.*, 13:8
[41]Insp. Vers. Gen. 19:35
[42]Abraham 2:2

CHAPTER TWENTY-SEVEN

Abraham Migrates from Chaldea to Canaan

Why did Abraham leave Ur? Whom did he take with him? What happened to Abraham's father?

What great river did Abraham follow when he left Ur? In which direction did this take him?

Why did Abraham stop before he reached Canaan? What did he call this settlement? Did it become a permanent community?

Did Abraham's father want to proceed to Canaan? What did he do?

Who joined Abraham in praying for continued guidance? Was he with Abraham when the Lord appeared to answer these prayers? Was this the first time Abraham had seen the Lord in person?

Can you name the eight promises which the Lord made to Abraham? Are there many descendants of Abraham in the world today? From the scripture does it appear whether Abraham was a poor nomad or a wealthy prince?

Approximately what percentage of the earth's population honors the name of Abraham today?

Was Jesus a descendant of Abraham? Was Lehi? Was Joseph Smith? Are you?

How old was Abraham when he left Haran? Whom did he take with him? Would his caravan be large or small? Why?

En route Abraham stopped at Jershon to make a special petition of the Lord. What was the reason for his concern?

Do the available facts raise some question as to the fidelity of Abraham's brother, Nehor? Is it significant that Abraham did not take Nehor with him when he left Ur?

Is there any explanation for the fact that ancient peoples sometimes openly acknowledged the divinity of Jehovah even though they were practicing idolatry?

Why did Abraham offer a special sacrifice as he entered the borders of Canaan? Was there a good reason for his concern? Why didn't Abraham stay in Canaan?

ABRAHAM LEAVES UR

Shortly after Abraham's marriage he received a commandment from the Lord saying: "Abraham, get thee out of thy country, and from thy kindred, and from thy father's house, unto a land that I will show thee."[1]

It seems that Abraham was told where this new land would be because he says that when he left the land of Ur it was "to go into the land of Canaan."[2] En route he stopped at Haran but Abraham seems to have known that Haran was only a temporary resting place.

It is clear that the Lord wanted Abraham to make a clean break with the past. Abraham no doubt had a deep affection and concern for all of his kindred who were suffering from the famine as much as he was. He could not help but worry about the welfare of the people among whom he had grown up and who were also members of his father's household. But the Lord told Abraham to tear up his roots and transplant himself to a new land. He was to cut himself free from Ur, and from his kinsmen and from his father's house.

Abraham therefore says: "And I took Lot, my brother's son, and his wife, and Sarai, my wife."[3]

Then a strange twist of circumstances occurred. Abraham says: "And also my father followed after me."[4]

[1] Abraham 2:3
[2] *Ibid.,* 2:4
[3] *Ibid.,* 2:4
[4] *Ibid.,* 2:4

This dissolute father who had been "sorely tormented by the famine" could not stand the prospect of seeing his son leave for a new land where there might be food and flocks. Since Terah had partially repented of his disgraceful conduct of the past he no doubt recognized with some reluctance that the power of revelation was in Abraham and that he was a chosen servant of the Lord. When the spirit of revelation led Abraham out of Chaldea, nothing would do but that Terah should attach himself to the party. Notice that Abraham says he "took" Lot and his wife but that "my father followed after me."

From subsequent events it would appear that Abraham did not leave Ur as a poor itinerant nomad but as a rather wealthy prince of Chaldea. His original name, Abram, meant a "high father"[5] and there is a subsequent reference to his "silver and gold."[6]

The route from Chaldea to Canaan would be up the Euphrates River and then across the bridge of settlements in Syria which connected the Mesopotamian Valley with the cultures of the Mediterranean coast in Canaan. This would mean that Abraham and his party would travel up the Euphrates in a northwesterly direction until they reached the headwaters of that river in Assyria. When Abraham reached this area he ordered his party to stop. They named this settlement Haran in honor of Abraham's dead brother.

Apparently Abraham maintained residence at Haran for several years. Here he found that the famine had "abated" and therefore it would be only natural to stop long enough to replenish the flocks which the famine must have practically wiped out.

Later scripture indicates that Haran was built into a permanent community and attracted a number of people to it. Abraham mentions those whom he succeeded in converting while in Haran.[7] He also says "there were many flocks in Haran," which would indicate that it became a prosperous community.[8]

[5]Irwin, *Bible Commentary on Genesis* 17:5
[6]Genesis 13:2
[7]Abraham 3:15
[8]*Ibid.*, 2:5

Abraham observed that the prosperous circumstances in Haran pleased his father mightily and Terah promptly sank his roots in Haran with the intention of permanently remaining there even though he knew the Lord eventually intended to lead Abraham to Canaan. Now that Terah could feed once again on the fat of the land his repentance and humility fell away like a cheap mantle and Abraham says "my father turned again unto his idolatry."[9]

ABRAHAM ENTERS CANAAN

This must have come as a great disappointment to Abraham. Haran could no longer be a pleasant habitation for him, therefore he felt the necessity of leaving his father and all others who indulged in the immorality of heathen ritual and make his way toward Canaan. He wrote: "I, Abraham, and Lot, my brother's son, prayed unto the Lord."[10] It is significant that Lot remained loyal to Abraham in these early tribulations. In response to these prayers Abraham says: "The Lord appeared unto me, and said unto me: Arise, and take Lot with thee; for I have purposed to take thee away out of Haran, and to make of thee a minister to bear my name in a strange land which I will give unto thy seed after thee for an everlasting possession, when they hearken to my voice."[11]

Then the Lord identified Himself to Abraham with these words: "My name is Jehovah, and I know the end from the beginning; therefore my hand shall be over thee." Then Jehovah made Abraham eight wonderful promises:

First, "I will make of thee a great nation."[12] Today the descendants of Abraham total hundreds of millions. Modern patriarchal blessings reveal that the seed of Abraham is in almost every corner of the globe. Genealogical research reveals that the principal populations of Europe, North, Central and South America, the islands of the Pacific and certain portions of Eurasia can all trace some branch of their lineage back to Abraham.

[9]*Ibid.,* 2:5
[10]*Ibid.,* 2:6
[11]*Idem* (When the reference is exactly the same, the word *idem* is used.)
[12]*Ibid.,* 2:8-9

Researchers in this field find that this first promise to Abraham has been fulfilled to an extent which is well-nigh miraculous.

Second, "I will bless thee above measure."[13] This included material blessings as well as spiritual. During Abraham's lifetime it was said of him: "And Abraham was very rich in cattle, in silver and gold."[14]

Third, "I will . . . make thy name great among all nations."[15] Today Abraham is honored by 609,414,000 Christians scattered across the world.[16] He is equally honored as a prophet and patriarch by 175,000,000 Mohammedans who are the dominant religious groups in Turkey, Syria, Palestine, Arabia, Persia, Asia Minor, Afghanistan, Baluchistan, Turkestan and the Malay Peninsula. This figure also includes 57,000,000 Mohammedans in India and 25,000,000 Mohammedans in China.[17] Then, of course, Abraham is one of the most honored prophets among the millions of Jews who have survived as a national entity and are scattered around the world. Altogether, about one-half of the earth's population honors the name of Abraham. In time the rest will honor him also.

Fourth, "Thy seed . . . shall bear this ministry and Priesthood unto all nations."[18] In every dispensation since that time it has been the seed of Abraham who have been commissioned by divine revelation to carry the ministry and Priesthood of God to the nations of the world. The Savior was a descendant of Abraham. So were all of his Apostles. The ancient American prophets were his descendants. So was Joseph Smith. The custodians of the Priesthood in modern times have been the descendants of Abraham.

Fifth, "As many as receive the Gospel shall be . . . accounted thy seed."[19] Paul made it very clear that Abraham was "the father of all them that believe, *though they*

---

[13]*Ibid.*
[14]Genesis 13:2
[15]Abraham 2:9
[16]*Encyc. Americana,* Vol. 6, p. 607
[17]*Ibid.,* Vol. 19, p. 302
[18]Abraham 2:9
[19]*Ibid.,* 2:10

be not circumcised."[20] Joseph Smith explained that those who are not the blood descendants of Abraham but accept the gospel are adopted and become his "seed" and are entitled to all the blessings of his literal descendants.[21]

Sixth, "I will bless them that bless thee, and curse them that curse thee."[22] The Lord has always promised to bless those who aid his servants. As Jesus said: "He that receiveth you, receiveth me."[23] And concerning those cities in which the prophets and Apostles were persecuted and rejected, Jesus said: "Verily, I say unto you, it shall be more tolerable for the land of Sodom and Gomorrah in the day of judgment than for that city."[24] As we pursue the history of Abraham we shall see that those who befriended him were blessed while his enemies were confounded.

Seventh, "I give unto thee a promise that this right (of the Priesthood) shall continue in thee."[25] This was a great comfort to Abraham. He had seen his fathers who were patriarchs of the royal lineage apostatize and lose their Priesthood. Here the Lord who knows "the end from the beginning," assures Abraham that the right of the Priesthood shall continue in him.

Eighth, "In thy seed after thee (that is to say, the literal seed of thy body) shall all the families of the earth be blessed, even with the blessings of the Gospel."[26] No more joyful promise could come to a parent than to know that his children would be the harbingers of the gospel down through the ages. There is a vacuum in the happiness of a parent who has lived a righteous life but finds that his children refuse to perpetuate the same pattern. Here Abraham is promised that his seed will be of lasting benefit to humanity by bringing them "the blessings of the Gospel, which are the blessings of salvation, even of life eternal."[27]

---

[20]Romans 4:11
[21]*Teachings of Joseph Smith,* pp. 149-150
[22]Abraham 2:11
[23]Matt. 10:40
[24]*Ibid.,* 10:15
[25]Abraham 2:11
[26]*Ibid.,* 2:11
[27]*Idem*

When this revelation was completed Abraham could not help but exclaim: "Thy servant has sought thee earnestly; now I have found thee!" This statement reflects the joy which Abraham felt in being able to see the personage of Jehovah for the first time. Previously he had seen an angel.[28] Now, after these many years of prayer and faithfulness, he had been privileged to behold the Lord in person. He could not help but feel the triumph of that moment: "Now I have found thee!"

In the Biblical text it states that Abraham left Haran when he was seventy-five.[29] This is an error. Abraham says: "I, Abraham, was sixty and two years old when I departed out of Haran."[30] As we shall see later he was seventy-five when he came into Canaan to make it his permanent home—but that was after he had sojourned in Egypt for some time. Some ancient scribe apparently allowed an error to creep into the Biblical text during transcription.

Abraham's account continues: "And I took Sarai, whom I took to wife when I was in Ur, in Chaldea, and Lot, my brother's son, and all our substance that we had gathered."[31]

In the huge caravan which departed out of Haran there were also others besides the families of Abraham and Lot. Abraham says his party included "the souls that we had won in Haran."[32] This shows that Abraham had continued his missionary efforts after his departure from Ur. In that wicked city he had been rejected but in Haran he had apparently met with some success.

After leaving Haran Abraham says his party "came forth in the way to the land of Canaan, and dwelt in tents on our way."[33] En route to Canaan Abraham stopped in Jershon where he built an altar and made an offering unto the Lord. Abraham was worried. He had a special petition to make of the Lord. Abraham says he "prayed that

---

[28] *Ibid.,* 1:15
[29] Genesis 12:4
[30] Abraham 2:14
[31] *Ibid.,* 2:15
[32] *Idem*
[33] *Idem*

the famine might be turned away from my father's house, that they might not perish."[34]

This could not mean his father's house in Haran for there were many flocks there and the famine had "abated." It obviously means his father's house in Ur where Abraham's brother had died and where there yet remained many of his immediate family and relatives. Among these would be Abraham's brother, Nehor, and Sarai's sister, Milcah, who married Nehor. If Nehor had been a valiant supporter of the gospel no doubt Abraham would have taken him away from Ur as he did Lot. The fact that he left Nehor and Milcah behind is significant. But even so, the magnanimous heart of Abraham could not resist a feeling of anxiety for their safety and welfare. At Jershon he therefore offered up a special sacrifice in their behalf that the members of his father's household might not perish from the famine which continued in Ur.

We find later that Nehor and his family came up and settled near Haran in a place called Padan-aram. This community became known as "the city of Nahor"— Nahor being the Biblical spelling for Nehor, brother of Abraham.[35] From this we deduct that Nehor and Milcah must have received word that much more favorable conditions existed in the land of Haran and therefore they left Ur and went to the area which Abraham had pioneered.

After Abraham's departure from Haran, however, the people of that community adopted a strange mixture of idolatry and truth. For example, Nehor's grandson kept images of heathen gods in his house (Genesis 31:19, 30) yet at the same time openly acknowledged that Jehovah was the divine personality to whom loyal obedience rightly belonged.[36]

It is helpful to understand that in these early times heathen ritual was not necessarily an outright substitution for the worship of Jehovah. Instead, it was a kind of supplemental worship which introduced "other institutes"

---

[34]*Ibid.,* 2:17
[35]Genesis 24:10; 25:5, 10; 29:4-5
[36]*Ibid.,* 24:50; 31:51-53

and provided an excuse for licentious practices. The people often passively acknowledged the divinity of Jehovah and yet, like the children of Israel centuries later, also insisted upon having a golden calf or some other heathen diversion which gave them a ritual involving sensuous indulgences. Thus Nehor's grandson, who apparently had been taught the gospel, did not think it particularly inconsistent to have heathen images in his house even though he likewise gave casual recognition to Jehovah as the one true God.

This circumstance verifies the taint of idolatry in the household of Nehor and lends further credence to the conclusion that this is why Abraham must have left Nehor and his family behind when he departed from Ur.

So, having prayed for his father's household, Abraham now continued on his journey. As he came down into the borders of the land of the Canaanites he says: "I offered sacrifice there in the plains of Moreh, and called on the Lord devoutly, because we had already come into the land of this idolatrous nation."[37] It was no small thing for a devout member of the Priesthood to venture into the land of these people who followed the popular practice of sacrificing human beings when they refused to bow down to their heathen deities. Abraham had gone through a terrifying experience with their murderous priests in Chaldea. Unless the Lord were continuously with him he could very well become the victim of a similar conspiracy in Canaan. Therefore Abraham "called on the Lord devoutly" for protection as he made his way through the land of these treacherous Canaanites.

In answer to his petition, Abraham was permitted once more to see the personage of Jehovah. The Lord comforted Abraham and said: "Unto thy seed will I give this land."[38] Not only would Abraham be protected but through the providence of heaven his children would one day inherit this land even though it was now overrun with heathen-worshiping sons of Cain.

[37]Abraham 2:18
[38]*Ibid.*, 2:19

Abraham states that his next stop was near Bethel where he built another altar. Then he continued through southern Palestine and found that in every place the famine was like a plague. He says it became "very grievous" and therefore "I, Abraham, concluded to go down into Egypt, to sojourn there."[39] The lack of rain not only made it impossible to grow crops but the grass and forage for the sheep and cattle was likewise scarce. Abraham therefore considered it expedient to temporarily leave this land of his inheritance until the famine had abated.

---

[37]*Ibid.*, 2:21

CHAPTER TWENTY-EIGHT

Abraham's Mission To The Egyptians

Is it possible for God to reveal "scientific" knowledge?

Name three principles of astronomy which God revealed to Abraham. Did the ancient Nephites have a basic knowledge of astronomy? (See Helaman 12:15) In the light of such knowledge in ancient times, how do you account for the fact that during the dark ages men believed the earth was flat and that the sun traveled around the earth?

Was Abraham given any mathematical data concerning the universe? Did he record it?

What is intelligence? Did God create it? With respect to intelligence, are all men born equal? Why are there different grades of intelligence?

Did Abraham know about the pre-existence? Is Jehovah of the Old Testament the same person as Jesus Christ in the New Testament?

Were we tested in the First Estate? What is the purpose of the Second Estate?

Can you name seven distinct facts recorded by Abraham concerning the origin of the Egyptians? Is this information an important contribution to man's knowledge or did scientists already know it?

Why was Abraham's life in danger as he went into Egypt? How did Sarai happen to be the "sister" of Abraham as well as his wife?

Why was Abraham permitted to deliver his message from the throne of Pharaoh? What did he teach the Egyptians? Do the writings of Josephus corroborate the Book of Abraham?

What was the reaction of Pharaoh when he discovered that Sarai was Abraham's wife? What did he do to show his good will toward Abraham?

How old was Abraham when he came up out of Egypt to dwell in the land of Canaan?

ABRAHAM RECEIVES A REVELATION ON ASTRONOMY

Just before Abraham went down into Egypt the Lord shared with him many secrets of the universe. Abraham received a revelation which projected his personal knowledge over into the field of science. First, he was shown a revelation on astronomy and then he was told how the earth was planned for human habitation. In the midst of the revelation the Lord made a most significant statement. Said He:

"Abraham, I show these things unto thee before ye go into Egypt, *that ye may declare all these words.*" (Abraham 3:15)

The great truths shown to Abraham were not for him alone. He was to declare "all these words" to the Egyptians. The Lord knew that some of the learning of the Egyptians would be passed on to the Greeks and that the Greeks in turn would teach the Romans. He also knew that through Rome this knowledge would spread to other parts of the world as a blessing to humanity.

During these transitions many precious truths were lost but some of them survived and became the foundation for modern science. In certain phases of modern research we have spent fortunes trying to recapture some of the lost knowledge which the Lord gave to the race in earlier times by open revelation.

In this revelation Abraham was not merely told about the cosmic universe, but he was *shown* the inter-relation between many of the heavenly bodies. The Lord said: "Behold, thine eyes see it; it is given unto thee to know the *times of reckoning* and the *set time*" of the earth, the sun, the moon, "and it is given unto thee to know the set time of all the stars which are set to give light until thou come near unto the throne of God."[1]

If this information were available today, universities, governments and research institutes would pay millions of dollars to possess it. Abraham was being tutored by the very personality who organized these vast bodies of matter. He says: "I, Abraham, talked with the Lord, face to face, as one man talketh with another; and he told me of the works which his hands had made."[2] This indicates that much of this information was received in open revelation and may not have required the aid of the Urim and Thummim which Abraham had previously mentioned.[3]

Abraham continues: "And he said unto me: My son, my son (and his hand was stretched out), behold I will show you all these. And he put his hand upon mine eyes, and I saw those things which his hands had made, which were many; and they multiplied before mine eyes, and I could not see the end thereof. And he said unto me: This is Shinehah, which is the sun, and he said unto me: Kokob, which is star. And he said unto me: Olea, which is the moon. And he said unto me: Kokaubeam, which signifies stars, or all the great lights, which are in the firmament of heaven. And it was in the night time when the Lord spake these words unto me."[4]

In a previous statement the Lord declared that the things which he was being shown were the great astronomical bodies "which belong to the same order as that upon which thou standest."[5] This would indicate that this vision was directed primarily toward our own galaxy. It is particularly significant that the Lord told Abraham that "it is given unto thee to know the set time of *all the stars.*" A previous statement indicates that this constituted the "reckoning of the time of one planet above another, until thou come nigh unto Kolob, which Kolob . . . is set nigh unto the throne of God, to govern all those planets which belong to the same order as that upon which thou standest."[6] So Abraham was apparently

---

[1]Abzaham 3:6-10
[2]*Ibid.,* 3:11
[3]*Ibid.,* 3:1

[4]*Ibid.,* 3:12-14
[5]*Ibid.,* 3:3
[6]*Ibid.,* 3:9

given the time of reckoning of "all the stars" in our own system which lie between the sun and Kolob. Or, as the Lord described it: "the reckoning of one planet above another until thou come unto Kolob."

Joseph Smith pointed out that when the papyrus scroll written by Abraham was found in Egypt, it was also discovered that "two or three other small pieces of papyrus, with *astronomical calculations,* epitaphs, etc., were found with others of the mummies."[7] In other words, Abraham not only received astronomical data from the Lord but he recorded it.

It is quite obvious that if this highly technical information were given to Abraham so that he could "declare all these words" to the Egyptians, he would undoubtedly make a detailed written record of the information revealed to him. Particularly would this be true of mathematical data which would be impossible to remember with any degree of accuracy unless these "astronomical calculations" were recorded as the above statement indicates that they were.

The information given to Abraham regarding astronomical principles is only referred to briefly in the book of Abraham. Nevertheless, it is sufficient to reveal to us that the ancient patriarchs had a knowledge of astronomical science far over and beyond anything which we have yet been able to discover through our giant telescopes and sensitive photographic plates. Elder Milton R. Hunter has made a most interesting comparison between the revelation to Abraham on astronomy and the findings of modern astronomers. This comparison is contained in the *Pearl of Great Price Commentary* and by permission of Elder Hunter it is set forth in the appendix of this book for the convenience of the reader.

ABRAHAM RECEIVES A REVELATION ON PRE-EARTH LIFE

In this same revelation the Lord explained that just as one astronomical body is above another even unto

---

[7]*Doc. History of the Church,* Vol. II, p. 349

Kolob so also intelligences vary in their capacity one above another until one comes unto God who is "more intelligent than they all."[8] The Lord taught Abraham that the great variety of intelligences found in God's spirit creations of the pre-earth life are eternal entities. They "have no beginning"; the Lord said, "they existed before (they were spirits), they shall have no end . . . they are gnolaum, or eternal."[9]

This doctrine is confirmed by a modern revelation wherein the Lord says: "Intelligence, or the light of truth, was not created or made, neither indeed can be."[10]

This revelation carries another important implication. Since all spirits are an embodiment of some type of intelligence then would not the spirit creations of the plant and animal kingdoms also be the tabernacles for lower levels of intelligent entities? Brigham Young went even further than this by declaring that the principle of intelligence or life is "in all matter throughout the vast extent of all the eternities; it is in the rock, the sand, the dust, in water, air, the gases, and in short, in every description and organization of matter, whether it be solid, liquid or gaseous, particle operating with particle."[11]

If there are organized bodies of intelligent entities in all of God's creations then this would account for a number of scriptures indicating that when God speaks the elements "obey."[12] The power to obey implies the capacity to hear, to understand and to initiate action. In short, the powers of intelligence.

Through this revelation Abraham had received a penetrating insight into God's organizing power in the universe.

Abraham was also shown the chief intelligences which were to comprise the members of the human family. As we know from other scriptures all these had been given spirit tabernacles in the image of God, and were, in fact, begotten unto God.[13] Abraham says:

[8]Abraham 3:19
[9]*Ibid.*, 3:18
[10]D. & C. 93:29
[11]*Brigham Young's Disc.*, p. 566
[12]Abraham 4:12, 18, 21
[13]D. & C. 76:24

"And among all these there were many of the noble and great ones; And God saw these souls that they were good, and he stood in the midst of them, and he said: These I will make my rulers; for he stood among those that were spirits, and he saw that they were good; and he said unto me: Abraham, thou art one of them; thou wast chosen before thou wast born." (Abraham 3:22-23)

Abraham was also shown the grand council in heaven when the plan for earth life was presented to this vast body of spirit children begotten of God. He says:

"And there stood one among them that was like unto God, and he said unto those who were with him: We will go down, for there is space there, and we will take of these materials, and we will make an earth whereon these may dwell; And we will prove them herewith, to see if they will do all things whatsoever the Lord their God shall command them; And they who keep their first estate shall be added upon; and they who keep not their first estate shall not have glory in the same kingdom with those who keep their first estate; and they who keep their second estate shall have glory added upon their heads for ever and ever."[14]

Then Abraham was shown that a great controversy raged among the spirit children of the father. We have previously discussed the problem that was raised. Jehovah or Jesus Christ, expressed a willingness to follow the Father's plan for the Second Estate. Lucifer, a son of the morning and one of the brilliant leaders of the preexistence, concocted a plan which would violate the principle of free agency but would eliminate the element of risk during mortal probation. He was so proud of his brain child that he boasted before the Father saying: "I will redeem all mankind, that one soul shall not be lost, and surely *I will do it;* wherefore *give me thine honor.*"[15]

Abraham saw that the Father declared: "I will send the first." Then Abraham saw that Lucifer "was angry

[14]Abraham 3:24-26
[15]Moses 4:1

and kept not his first estate; and at that day, many followed after him."[16] From other scriptures we know that one third of the Father's spirit children were casualties during the "war in heaven" and had to be exiled from the celestial home they had enjoyed so long.[17]

Abraham was then told about the preparation of this temporal earth and the engineering principles which were carefully employed. He learned about the Garden of Eden period when Adam and Eve first came to inhabit this planet. He was told that prior to the Fall, Adam's time on this earth "was after the Lord's time, which was after the time of Kolob, for as yet the Gods had not appointed unto Adam his reckoning."[18] What was the Lord's time or the time of Kolob? Earlier Abraham had been shown that one revolution or day "after the time of Kolob" was equal to one thousand years of the earth's present time of reckoning.[19] To know that the earth once had a much different cosmic environment than at present should carry deep significance to the student of earth-science. It gave Abraham a keener appreciation of the status of the earth during its period of preparation prior to the Fall.

We have briefly summarized the revelations given to Abraham so that it might be possible to appreciate the scope of Abraham's understanding and also his credentials as a teacher when he went down into Egypt.

In addition to the above information we also know that Abraham shared with the Egyptians his knowledge of the gospel. In his excellent treatise on the book of Abraham, James R. Clark points out that: "In the Egyptian Alphabet compiled by Joseph Smith at the time he translated the Book of Abraham we are given the added information that Abraham was called as a missionary of Christ to go into Egypt and preach the Gospel of Jesus Christ to the Egyptians."[20]

---

[16]Abraham 3:27-28
[17]D. & C. 29:36
[18]Abraham 5:13
[19]Ibid., 3:4
[20]Clark, James R., Before Ye Go Into Egypt, Mimeographed ed. Vol. 2, p. 2

That these teachings concerning the coming Messiah and the plan of salvation left their impact in Egypt seems apparent from the number of gospel principles which may be found scattered among the religious concepts of the Egyptians.

What Was the Origin of the Egyptians?

While recording the experiences of his life, Abraham inserts a statement which is a precious contribution to modern ethnology. He gives us the only authoritative statement in existence on the origin of the Egyptians. Modern students have been baffled by the conflicting evidence and frankly admit: "The origin of the Egyptians is unknown."[21] But their origin was not unknown to Abraham. He tells us seven things about their origin.

1. The land of Egypt was discovered soon after the Flood by a woman named Egyptus. (Abraham 1:23)

2. This woman was the daughter of Ham. Prior to the great Flood Ham had married a woman whose name was also Egyptus—meaning "forbidden." Because this daughter born to them carried the same lineal restriction she was likewise given the same name as her mother. (*Ibid.*)

3. When Egyptus first came to this land it was under water. When the water receded she settled her family and followers upon it. (Verse 24)

4. Her eldest son became the first ruler. His name was Pharaoh. (Verse 25)

5. The first Pharaoh was a righteous man and set up a patriarchal government. (Verse 26)

6. Pharaoh received a blessing from Noah "who blessed him with the blessings of the earth, and with the blessings of wisdom, but cursed him as pertaining to the Priesthood." (Verse 26) Abraham explains that this was because he was "a partaker of the blood of the Canaanites by birth" (Verse 21)

---

[21]*Encyc. Americana*, 1946 ed., Vol. 10, p. 3

and was therefore "of that lineage by which he could not have the right of Priesthood." (Verse 27)

7. Subsequent Pharaohs falsely claimed that they had the Priesthood from Noah through Ham and thereby led away many people who thought they had the true authority. (Verse 27)

Once the Egyptian kings or Pharaohs had launched into a program of deception based on their illegal claims to the Priesthood, their ambitions knew no bounds. They set up all manner of "institutes" similar to Nimrod who was also of Hamitic descent, and it was not long before the Egyptian priests were setting up idols and slaughtering human sacrifices upon their altars.

Now it will be recalled that it was one of the priests of Pharaoh in Chaldea who had tried to slay Abraham by offering him up as a human sacrifice. However, the power of God "smote the priest that he died" and there was great mourning—even in the court of Pharaoh, clear down in Egypt. Undoubtedly the princes of Pharaoh had received a complete report of that catastrophe. Therefore, how would they receive Abraham now? Would these heathen princes in the court of Pharaoh remember him? Would they associate him with the calamity in Chaldea? Undoubtedly Abraham contemplated the potential risk of incurring their wrath and vengeance as he came down among them.

ABRAHAM GOES DOWN INTO EGYPT

But when Abraham drew near to the land of Egypt the Lord revealed to him that his life was in danger for an entirely different reason. The Lord said the Egyptians would plot against his life because of the beauty of his wife, Sarai!

"And it came to pass when I was come near to enter into Egypt, the Lord said unto me: Behold, Sarai, thy wife, is a very fair woman to look upon; therefore it shall come to pass when the Egyptians shall see her, they will say—She is his wife; and

they will kill you, but they will save her alive."
(Abraham 2:22-23)

The Lord was trying to confer a great blessing upon the Egyptians by having Abraham teach them. Nevertheless, it involved great personal danger to both Abraham and Sarai because of the lustful sensuality which characterized the Egyptians. Therefore, the Lord said to Abraham: "See that ye do on this wise: Let her say unto the Egyptians, she is thy sister, and thy soul shall live."[22]

As we have previously seen, Sarai was his foster-sister and the Lord knew that if this relationship were emphasized when they went down into Egypt it would give Abraham the opportunity of fulfilling his mission without endangering his life. No doubt Sarai also appreciated this warning for her own protection. Abraham was not the only one in danger. Nothing could have been more abhorrent to this princess of Shem than the prospect of captivity by the Egyptians. She heartily agreed when Abraham said to her: "Say unto them, I pray thee, thou art my sister, that it may be well with me for thy sake, and my soul shall live because of thee."[23]

When Abraham led his extensive caravan into Egypt he found that Sarai's beauty opened the gates of cities and the doors of palaces. She was admired by all who saw her. The scripture says: "The Egyptians beheld the woman, that she was very fair. The princes also of Pharaoh saw her, and *commanded* her to be brought before Pharaoh; and the woman was taken in Pharaoh's house."[24]

What must have been the feelings of Sarai as she was escorted into the precincts of this monarch's palace! The intentions of the Pharaoh were most obvious. He desired to gain the confidence of Sarai and make her his wife.[25] And "for her sake" he also tried to show the utmost consideration and solicitude for Abraham. It is

---

[22]Abraham 2:23-24
[23]*Ibid.,* 2:25
[24]Insp. Version, Gen. 12:10-11
[25]*Ibid.,* 12:14

apparent that it was no small matter to entertain Abraham and his entourage for he had vast numbers of oxen, sheep, camels, donkeys, men servants and maid servants.[26] Nevertheless, it appears that Abraham's party and all his flocks received every consideration and attention.

The friendly attitude of the Pharaoh also permitted Abraham to commence his mission among the Egyptians. Abraham gives us an illustration in his writings depicting himself seated upon the throne of Pharaoh. He explains that this was through "the courtesy of the king."[27] From this singular position of authority he was permitted to explain the principles of the gospel.

The words of Abraham concerning this exciting adventure are corroborated by Josephus. He states that in his day (75-100 A.D.) there were available writings by a number of ancient historians who referred to the great knowledge possessed by Abraham and the contribution which he made in "celestial science." Josephus states that the Pharaoh gave Abraham permission "to enter into conversation with the most learned among the Egyptians; from which conversation his virtue and his reputation became more conspicuous than they had been before. For whereas the Egyptians were formerly addicted to different customs, and despised one another's sacred and accustomed rites . . . Abraham conferred with each of them, and, confuting the reasonings they made use of, every one for their own practices, demonstrated that such reasonings were vain and void of truth.

"Whereupon he was admired by them in those conferences as a very wise man, and one of great sagacity, when he discoursed on any subject he undertook; and this not only in understanding it, but in persuading other men also to assent to him. He communicated to them *arithmetic*, and delivered to them the science of *astronomy; for before Abram came into Egypt they were unacquainted with those parts of learning;* for that science came from

---

[26]*Ibid.*, 12:12
[27]See facsimile number 3, Pearl of Great Price, p. 42

the Chaldeans (by Abraham)* into Egypt, and from thence to the Greeks also."[28]

We do not know exactly how long Abraham remained in Egypt, but it may have been longer than some scholars have supposed. We know that he was 62 when he came down from Haran into Canaan[29] and because of the famine he apparently did not remain in Canaan long but went down almost immediately into Egypt. He was 75 when he returned to Canaan from Egypt.[30] This indicates that thirteen years elapsed between the time Abraham left Haran and the time when he came up out of Egypt.

Josephus states that after Sarai had been in the palace of the Pharaoh for quite a period of time the Pharaoh discovered that she was not only the "sister" of Abraham but also his wife. The Jewish historian says the Pharaoh was extremely embarrassed by this turn of events. He promptly "excused himself to Abram" and gave him "a large present of money."[31] But by this time Abraham's mission to Egypt had been successfully completed. Because of Sarai's prestige he had been granted time and attention by the royal court of Pharaoh. He had taught them astronomy, mathematics and the gospel. Through it all the wisdom of God had not only protected the lives of Abraham and Sarai but it had also permitted Abraham to render a great service to the Egyptian people. Nevertheless, the Pharaoh now desired that Abraham should depart from Egypt. Perhaps the presence of Abraham and Sarai gave cause for embarrassment in view of the king's past attentions to Sarai. In any event the scripture closes this incident by saying: "Pharaoh commanded men concerning him (Abraham); and they sent him away, and his wife, and all that he had."[32]

Thus concluded another epic in the fast-moving events of Abraham's life.

---

*Author's parenthesis
[28]Josephus, *op. cit.*, Chapter 8:1-2
[29]Abraham 3:14
[30]Compare Gen. 16:3 and 16:16
[31]Josephus, *op. cit.*
[32]Insp. Version, Gen. 12:15

CHAPTER TWENTY-NINE

Abraham Becomes a Person of Power and Influence in Canaan

When Abraham came up out of Egypt was he merely a poor, wandering shepherd?

Where did he first settle? How far was this from Salem, residence of Melchizedek?

Why did Abraham and Lot now come to a parting of the ways? Did Lot's actions show that he was "cleaving unto righteousness" or flirting with sin and disaster?

Did Abraham ever gain a legal inheritance in Canaan during his lifetime?

After dividing the land with Lot, where did Abraham take up residence? Did he build a house and set up an estate there? How far was this new home from Salem?

What were the events leading up to the capture of Lot by King Chedorlaomer?

Did Abraham rescue Lot with just his own servants or did he have strong allies to assist him? Is there any account of Abraham having had previous military experience? In his battle with the kings was Abraham acting in the role of a peace officer or an army officer?

Who were the two distinguished personalities who came out to meet Abraham when he returned? What was Abraham's conversation with the first one? What did he receive from the second?

How did Abraham show his respect for Melchizedek's keys of authority over that region? Is there evidence that Abraham had met Melchizedek prior to this time?

Following his military triumph why did Abraham feel discouraged? Did the Lord's revelation give Abraham understanding or simply an assurance?

What qualities of character do you feel were manifested by Sarai when she asked Abraham to accept Hagar and bear a son by her? Did she ask Abraham to take Hagar into full marriage status as a "wife"?

How old was Abraham when Ishmael was born?

ABRAHAM RETURNS TO CANAAN

When Abraham returned to Canaan the famine had apparently ended, for no further mention is made of it. The scripture says: "And Abram went up out of Egypt, he, and his wife, and all that he had, and Lot with him, into the south. And Abram was very rich in cattle, in silver, and in gold."[1]

This large party made its way to Bethel which is believed to have been located about twelve miles north of Jerusalem—a city which in those days was called Salem. Although the scriptures do not mention it, the circumstances would indicate that Abraham was probably in communication with the people of Salem and also with the High Priest, Melchizedek, to whom he later paid tithes. Throughout most of the remainder of his days, Abraham lived within a comparatively short distance of Salem.

THE DIVISION OF THE LAND

It was at Bethel that Abraham and Lot came to a parting of the ways.

"And the land was not able to bear them, that they might dwell together: for their substance was great, so that they could not dwell together. And there was a strife between the herdmen of Abram's cattle and the herdmen of Lot's cattle." (Gen. 13:6-7)

Now, most of the land was already occupied by the Canaanite and Perizzite peoples,[2] and therefore Abraham was no doubt anxious to maintain unity between himself and Lot so that any advantage which was gained in ac-

[1] Genesis 13:1-2
[2] *Ibid.*, 13:7

quiring a foothold in this land would not be endangered by conflict or misunderstanding between them. Abraham's generous nature is reflected in this statement to Lot: "Let there be no strife, I pray thee, between me and thee, and between my herdmen and thy herdmen; *for we are brethren*. Is not the whole land before thee? separate thyself, I pray thee, from me; if thou wilt take the left hand, then I will go to the right; or if thou depart to the right hand, then I will go to the left."[3]

Then the scripture says: "Lot lifted up his eyes, and beheld all the plain of Jordan, that it was well watered every where. . . . Then Lot chose him all the plain of Jordan; and Lot journeyed east: and they separated themselves the one from the other." Lot was attracted to the city life of Sodom which was a wicked and notorious city located in this area. At first he just "pitched his tent toward Sodom" but later he acquired a house in the city.[4]

After Lot had departed the Lord said to Abraham: "Lift up now thine eyes, and look from the place where thou art northward, and southward, and eastward, and westward: For all the land which thou seest, to thee will I give it, and to thy seed for ever."[5]

Even though he had given Lot the choicest portion of this inheritance the Lord assured Abraham that in the final outcome of events it would all belong to Abraham and his descendants.

Abraham immediately took all his flocks and servants and departed to the plain or valley of Mamre which is in Hebron—about twenty miles south of modern Jerusalem. There he entered into a peaceful federation with three princes who were brothers and who controlled that area.[6]

It is interesting to note that while the Lord promised the land of Canaan to Abraham he did not permit him to enjoy a true legal inheritance in it during his lifetime. Abraham had to take the Lord's promise on faith. Throughout his life he had to rely upon the hospitality of the various princes in whose domain he took up resi-

---

[3]*Ibid.*, 13:8-9
[4]*Ibid.*, 3:10-12
[5]*Ibid.*, 13:14-15
[6]*Ibid.*, 14:13

dence. Stephen, the New Testament martyr, comments on Abraham's faith wherein he trusted in the Lord even though "he gave him none inheritance in it (the land of Canaan), no, not so much as to set his foot on: yet he promised that he would give it to him for a possession, and to his seed after him, when as yet he had no child."[7]

Although Abraham was wealthy he nevertheless lived in tents throughout his days. When he needed a burial place for his loved ones he had to buy a place from the legal landowners, for he had no permanent place of residence or an estate which he could call his own.[8]

The Battle of the Kings

Scattered along the east side of the Jordan Valley and probably extending down to the Dead Sea were four famous cities of antiquity. They were Sodom, Gomorrah, Admah and Bela or Zoar. As we have seen, these cities were in an area which Lot had chosen as an inheritance because it was well watered everywhere.[9] These cities had become very prosperous and several years earlier they had attracted the greedy appetites of five eastern kings who conquered them during a raiding expedition. The leader of these conquering kings was Chedorlaomer, and he extracted tribute from Sodom and the other Jordan cities for twelve years. But in the thirteenth year the king of Sodom led a revolt against Chedorlaomer.

Immediately Chedorlaomer and his four confederate kings made preparation to come down and subdue the cities of the Jordan plain. On the way Chedorlaomer conquered the Rephaims in Ashteroth, the Susims in Ham and the Emims in Shaveh.[10] These were kingdoms which authorities believe were located on the high plateaus east of the Jordan Valley. Then these kings swept down into the plains of Jordan and attacked Sodom, Gomorrah, Admah and Zoar. Their intent was to loot these cities because of their refusal to pay the tribute levied against them.

---

[7]Acts 7:5
[8]Gen. 24:67; 23:4
[9]*Ibid.*, 13:10
[10]*Ibid.*, 14:5

As the invading hosts drew near, the kings of Sodom
and Gomorrah retreated southward along the Dead Sea
until they were trapped in the tar pits (translated slimepits in the Bible) which abounded there. A few escaped
and fled to the mountains but the main armies were destroyed. King Chedorlaomer and his raiding confeder-
ates were then free to return to the cities of the Jordan
Valley and systematically sack them. They took many
captives (for slavery, no doubt), and these included the
women of these cities. "And they took all the goods
of Sodom and Gomorrah, and all their victuals, and went
their way."[11]

A rich prize in the city of Sodom was the wealthy
Shemite, Lot. "And they took Lot, Abram's brother's
son, who dwelt in Sodom, and his goods, and departed."[12]
But one of the citizens of Sodom escaped and fled around
the Dead Sea and into the plains of Mamre where Abraham lived at Hebron. He recounted to Abraham the
tragic news. "And when Abram heard that his brother
was taken captive, he armed his trained servants, born in
his own house, three hundred and eighteen, and pursued
them unto Dan."[13] We later learn that Abraham and his
servants were not alone in this venture to rescue Lot but
were accompanied by the armies of Mamre, Eshcol and
Aner—the three Amorite princes who were rulers in this
land.

The direction of pursuit was northward "unto Dan."
We do not know just where Dan was located, but it
should not be confused with the inheritance given to the
tribe of Dan in west Canaan several hundred years later.

It was at Dan that Abraham and his Amorite allies
came by night upon the sleeping camps of the five conquering kings. The scripture says: "And he divided himself against them, he and his servants, by night, and smote
them."[14] Then the armies of King Chedorlaomer and the
other kings fled in terror while Abraham and his armies
followed in close pursuit. Abraham made second contact

---

[11]*Ibid.,* 14:11
[12]*Ibid.,* 14:12
[13]*Ibid.,* 14:14
[14]*Ibid.,* 14:15

with his enemy at Hobah "on the left hand of Damascus" and there "the slaughter of Chedorlaomer and of the kings that were with him" took place. Abraham succeeded in rescuing Lot and all of the loot which had been taken from Sodom, Gomorrah and the other conquered cities. The scripture says: "And he brought back all the goods, and also brought again his brother Lot, and his goods, and the women also, and the people."[15]

Abraham was hailed as a great hero when he came back to southern Palestine. It says: "the king of Sodom went out to meet him." If this was King Bera who had been trapped in the tar pits during the earlier battle then we must assume that somehow he escaped. Some authorities have suggested that it must have been a new king of Sodom who had been appointed to take the place of Bera since it says that Bera "fell" in the vale of Siddim which "was full of slimepits."[16]

In any event, when this "king of Sodom" came forth to meet Abraham he found another royal host also awaiting the return of Abraham. It was none other than Melchizedek, king of Salem, who "brought forth bread and wine. . . . And he blessed him (Abraham) and said: Blessed be Abram of the most high God, possessor of heaven and earth: And blessed be the most high God, which hath delivered thine enemies into thy hand."[17]

Because this is the first passage which mentions Melchizedek, many have assumed that this was the first time Melchizedek and Abraham had met. However, we have seen that it was this same High Priest who had given Abraham his Priesthood[18] and we know from Abraham's own writings that he received the Priesthood while he was living in Ur.[19] So the paths of Abraham and Melchizedek must have crossed before. In fact, since Abraham had been living in this vicinity for a considerable period of time it is likely that these two patriarchal leaders had been in frequent association and counsel.

[15]*Ibid.*, 14:16
[16]*Ibid.*, 14:10
[17]*Ibid.*, 14:18-20
[18]D. & C. 84:14
[19]Abraham 1:1-3

At this time Abraham expressed through his actions a fitting respect for Melchizedek's authority in this region. He paid tithes to him of all the property which had come into his possession as a result of the battle at Hobah. It is interesting to note, however, that he did not count as his own any of the loot which had been taken originally from the cities of Sodom and Gomorrah. The king of Sodom said to Abraham: "Give me the persons (who were captured at Sodom by Chedorlaomer), and take the goods to thyself."[20] But Abraham would have none of it. He said to the king of Sodom: "I will not take from a thread even a shoelatchet ... I will not take any thing that is thine, let thou shouldest say, I have made Abram rich."[21] Then Abraham said the Amorite kings who had helped him could take their portion if they desired, but as for Abraham he intended to return all of the goods belonging to Sodom "save only that which the young men have eaten" (while serving as soldiers in Abraham's army).

It is obvious that Abraham did not intend to have any kind of traffic with the king of Sodom. In spite of the afflictions which had befallen them the king and the citizens of Sodom had no repentance in them. Abraham knew that they had become notorious for their degenerate offenses against children and adults alike, and Abraham held only the deepest contempt for any overtures of friendship from such a tainted source. Abraham put the king on notice that he wanted nothing from Sodom.

Lot, however, had not learned his lesson. While he had remained faithful to his own religious teachings he could not resist the infatuating attraction of city life in Sodom. He therefore returned to his home in Sodom, and Abraham returned to his tent in Hebron.

Abraham Is Encouraged by the Lord

Abraham had just passed through a thrilling experience. He had been blessed with victory in the first military venture of his life—so far as the scripture tells.

---

[20]Genesis 14:21
[21]Ibid., 14:23

Abraham was not a man of war, but a prophet of peace and good will. Nevertheless, in the hour of need when predatory forces trod upon his rights and his loved ones, Abraham rose up in the wrath of righteous indignation and struck with strength for what he knew was right. Having attained total victory, Abraham had then been blessed by Melchizedek and honored by the kings of the region for his valor. Now, however, he was back in his tent at Hebron where there was peace and quiet and time to think. But Abraham was not at peace. His thoughts were all questions. It is plain from the scripture that in this hour Abraham was filled with anxiety. How and when would the Lord make Canaan his inheritance? And who would be his heir? Sarai, his wife, was fast approaching the age when the time for child bearing would be past. How then would the Lord fulfil his promise? At this moment Abraham was in need of encouragement and the Lord stood ready to provide it.

"The word of the Lord came to Abraham in vision, saying, Fear not, Abram; I am thy shield, and thy exceeding great reward."[22] Abraham found this an opportunity to give vent to his anxiety. Said he: "Lord, God, what wilt thou give me, seeing I go childless, and the steward of my house is this Eliezer of Damascus? . . . Behold, to me thou hast given no seed: and lo, one born in mine house is mine heir."[23]

This would indicate that it was the custom for persons of wealth who had no heir to make a principal servant or steward the heir. But Abraham knew this would not fulfil the previous promise of the Lord. In response to his inquiry the Lord said: "This shall not be thine heir; but he that shall come forth out of thine own bowels shall be thine heir."[24] Then Abraham was asked to look into the starry heavens, and the Lord said: "Look now toward heaven, and tell the stars, if thou be able to number them: and he said unto him, So shall thy seed be."[25]

---

[22]*Ibid.,* 15:1
[23]*Ibid.,* 15:2-3
[24]*Ibid.,* 15:4
[25]*Ibid.,* 15:5

The scripture then states that Abraham was comforted: "And he believed in the Lord; and he counted
it to him for righteousness." (Abraham 15:6)

Notice that Abraham still didn't know how the promise would be fulfilled. The simple assurance by the Lord
that it would be, however, so renewed his faith that the
Lord "counted it to him for righteousness."

And the Lord said to Abraham: "I am the Lord that
brought thee out of Ur of the Chaldees, to give thee this
land to inherit."[26] This gave Abraham a chance to inquire
about the manner in which this promise would be fulfilled.
Said he: "Whereby shall I know that I shall inherit it?"
The Lord did not reply immediately but told him to offer
a sacrifice.

"And when the sun was going down, a deep sleep
fell upon Abram; and lo, an horror of great darkness
fell upon him. And he (the Lord) said unto Abram,
Know of a surety that thy seed shall be a stranger
in a land that is not their's, and shall serve them; and
they shall be afflicted four hundred years;

"And also that nation, whom they shall serve,
will I judge: and afterward shall they come out with
great substance." (Gen. 15:12-14)

So that was the way it would be! Abraham's descendants would become slaves in some land which would not
be theirs. Four hundred years of bondage and affliction
would transpire before they regained their freedom and
came forth "with great substance." The name of the
strange land where Abraham's descendants would live is
not given in this prophecy, but Abraham knew it would
be outside of Canaan. The Lord said "In the fourth generation they shall come hither (to Canaan) again."[27]
Then the Lord added a statement of the deepest significance: "for the iniquity of the Amorites is not yet full."[28]

This statement had reference to the fact that when the
hosts of Israel came up out of Egypt about 1,450 B.C.
the inheritance of the Amorites would be declared for-

---

[26]*Ibid.*, 15:7
[27]*Ibid.*, 15:16
[28]*Ibid.*

feited because of wickedness, and the Israelites would be commanded to take over the land by force of arms.[29]

Having disclosed to Abraham that the Lord's promises to him would be fulfilled in the future centuries, the Lord then comforted Abraham and said: "Thou shalt go to thy fathers in peace; thou shalt be buried in a good old age."[30]

"And in the same day the Lord made a covenant with Abram, saying, Unto thy seed have I given this land, from the river of Egypt unto the great river, the river Euphrates." (Gen. 15:18)

This extended Abraham's inheritance even farther than before. Now he knew enough about this promised inheritance to stop worrying about it.

The Birth of Ishmael

After Abraham had been living in Canaan for ten years,[31] Sarai became discouraged and feared that she would never have children herself. She therefore determined to take the following course:

"Sarai said unto Abraham, Behold now, the Lord hath restrained me from bearing: I pray thee, go in unto my maid; it may be that I may obtain children by her. And Abram hearkened to the voice of Sarai. And Sarai Abram's wife took Hagar her maid the Egyptian . . . and gave her to her husband Abram *to be his wife*." (*Ibid.*, 16:2-3)

This was looked upon as a personal triumph by Hagar and when she had conceived she "despised" Sarai because she had been blessed above her mistress. This was a great trial to Sarai, and the situation finally created such family tension that Sarai said to Abraham: "My wrong is upon thee."[32] She felt that something had to be done to clarify this unexpected difficulty. Abraham said: "Behold, thy maid is in thy hand; do to her as it pleaseth thee."[33] Sarai therefore reprimanded Hagar for her con-

[29]*See* Deut. 1:7-8
[30]Gen. 15:15
[31]Gen. 16:3
[32]Insp. Version, Gen. 16:5
[33]Gen. 16:6

duct, and when the issue was pressed with Hagar, she fled into the wilderness.

"And the angel of the Lord found her by a fountain of water in the wilderness, by the fountain in the way to Shur. And he said, Hagar, Sarai's maid, whence camest thou? and whither wilt thou go? And she said, I flee from the face of my mistress, Sarai.

"And the angel of the Lord said unto her, Return to thy mistress, and submit thyself under her hands." (Gen. 16:7-9)

Hagar had been wrong. Instead of being a comfort to Sarai and sharing with her the joy of welcoming into the house of Abraham this first child she had flagrantly violated the confidence of Sarai and treated her with impudence and disrespect. Now the angel told her to return and humble herself. Before departing the angel made this prediction concerning the son who would be born to Hagar:

"Behold, thou art with child, and shalt bear a son, and shalt call his name Ishmael; because the Lord hath heard thy affliction. And he will be a wild man; his hand will be against every man, and every man's hand against him; and he shall dwell in the presence of all his brethren." (*Ibid.,* 16:11-12)

Then the angel said: "Knowest thou that God seest thee? And she said, I know that God seest me."[34]

If all humanity could remember this fact it would undoubtedly restrain many from their evil ways. Sometimes men forget that God sees them, knows their every secret and records even the hidden things done in darkness.

So Hagar returned to Sarai. Then the scripture says: "And Hagar bare Abram a son: and Abram called his son's name, which Hagar bare, Ishmael. And Abram was fourscore and six (eight-six) years old, when Hagar bare Ishmael to Abram."[35]

---

[34]Insp. Vers. Gen. 16:15-16
[35]Genesis 16:15-16

CHAPTER THIRTY

A Year of Exciting Events

Why did the Lord initiate the ordinance of circumcision? How was this related to the ordinance of baptism? Was circumcision to replace baptism?

What does the name "Abram" mean? What does "Abraham" mean? What does the name "Sarai" mean? What does "Sarah" mean?

Is there an indication in the scripture that Abraham had a deep affection for Ishmael? Was he placed under the covenant of circumcision?

Could translated beings be accurately described as "angels which were holy men"? Can a translated being or a resurrected being appear without revealing his glory? Can a ministering spirit appear except in glory? (See *Teachings of Joseph Smith*, p. 325.)

Did Abraham seem to recognize the three angels who came to visit him? Why did Sarah laugh when she heard the angel promise Abraham that she would bear a son? How old was Sarah at this time?

Why did Abraham accompany the three angels as they continued their journey toward Sodom? What great secret did they share with him on the way? Is there any indication that God does his work beyond the veil through the Priesthood just as he does here?

What special favor did Abraham now seek from the Lord? Does it seem strange to you that among all the men and women of Sodom there were not ten persons whose righteousness could save the city?

Do you think from the description of events in this chapter that Lot should have known better than to continue living in Sodom?

Was Lot reluctant to leave Sodom? Where did he flee? What great tragedy occurred en route?

Where did Lot finally go? Who went with him? Who was the father of the Moabites? Who was the father of the Ammonites?

THE BEGINNING OF THE ORDINANCE OF CIRCUMCISION

Thirteen years after the birth of Ishmael, when Abraham was ninety-nine, the Lord appeared to Abraham and said, "I, the Almighty God, give unto thee a commandment that thou shalt walk uprightly before me, and be perfect."[1]

Then the Lord said something which has been lost from our modern Bible but was restored by a revelation to Joseph Smith. The Lord said: "My people have gone astray from my precepts, and have not kept mine ordinances which I gave unto their fathers; and they have not observed mine anointing, and the burial *or baptism* wherewith I commanded them; but have turned from the commandment, and taken unto themselves the washing of children, and the blood of sprinkling."[2]

Here the Lord clearly teaches that baptism and the related ordinances are not to be neglected in any age. It is clear that the Lord's people had felt the apostate influence of heathen nations and heathen ways. The practices of "washing of children" and "the blood of sprinkling" indicate the possibility of a kind of infant baptism and the heathen practice of sprinkling infants with blood as an indication that their sins were forgiven through the shedding of the blood of atonement. Then the Lord indicates that the people had even confused the real significance of the future atoning sacrifice of Jesus Christ. The people "have said that the blood of righteous Abel was shed for sins, and have not known wherein they are accountable before me."[3]

To correct these evils and impress upon parents their responsibility toward their children the Lord said He

[1] Insp. Vers. Gen. 17:1
[2] *Ibid.*, 17:4-6
[3] *Ibid.*, 17:7

would make a new covenant with Abraham which would thereafter identify the descendants of Abraham among all nations. "And this shall be my covenant which ye shall keep between me and thee and thy seed after thee; every man child among you shall be circumcised . . . and it shall be a token of the covenant betwixt me and you."[4] The Lord said the circumcision should take place when the child was *eight days old*. Then He revealed the reason for initiating this new ordinance which placed a mark in the flesh of all male children.

He said it was so that all the descendants of Abraham would remember that *"Children are not accountable before me until they are eight years old."*[5] There was not to be any washing of children or sprinkling of infants with blood after the manner of the heathens. Male children were to be circumcised at eight days of age to help parents remember that their accountability does not begin until they are eight years of age. Then they should be baptized.

The Lord assured Abraham that circumcision was not to take the place of baptism and all the other holy ordinances which were revealed to the fathers from the beginning. He said: "And thou shalt observe to keep *all* my covenants wherein I covenanted with thy fathers; and thou shalt keep the commandments which I have given thee with mine own mouth, and I will be a God unto thee and thy seed after thee."[6]

On this occasion the Lord gave Abraham his new name. Prior to this time he had been called Abram which is said to have meant "exalted father."[7] The name was slightly changed by the Lord to give it added significance: "Thy name shall be called Abraham; for a father *of many nations* have I made thee."[8]

Now the Lord was ready to tell Abraham something which was a reward for his long years of faithful waiting. Said He: "As for Sarai thy wife, thou shalt not call her name Sarai, but Sarah shall her name be. And I will

---

[4]*Ibid.,* 17:15-16
[5]*Ibid.,* 16:11
[6]*Ibid.,* 16:12
[7]Clarke, *op. cit.,* Vol. I, p. 111
[8]Genesis 17:5

bless her, and give thee a son also of her: yea, I will bless her, and she shall be a mother of nations; kings of people shall be of her."[9] The name "Sarai" is said to mean "my princess" whereas "Sarah" is said to mean a "princess of nations."[10]

Abraham's reaction to this exciting news was prompt and emphatic. "Then Abraham fell on his face and rejoiced, and said in his heart, There shall a child be born unto him that is an hundred years old, and Sarah that is ninety years old shall bear."[11] Notice that the translation of this verse as given to Joseph Smith provides an entirely different connotation than the erroneous translation in our modern Bible.[12]

With the prospect of having a son through Sarah, Abraham immediately thought of Ishmael whom he also loved. Ishmael was now thirteen years of age.[13] "And Abraham said unto God, "Oh that Ishmael might live uprightly before thee." To this the Lord answered: "As for Ishmael, I have heard thee: Behold, I have blessed him, and will make him fruitful, and will multiply him exceedingly; twelve princes shall he beget, and I will make him a great nation."[14]

However, the Lord made it clear that the patriarchal covenant was not for Ishmael. He said: "But my covenant will I establish with Isaac, which Sarah shall bear unto thee at this set time in the next year."[15]

"And he left off talking wtih him, and God went up from Abraham. And Abraham took Ishmael his son, and all that were born in his house, and all that were bought with his money, every male among the men of Abraham's house and circumcised the flesh of their foreskin in the selfsame day, as God had said unto him." (Gen. 17:22-23)

[9]*Ibid.*, 17:15-16
[10]Peloubet, *op. cit.*, under "Sarah"
[11]Insp. Vers. Gen. 17:23
[12]Gen. 17:17
[13]*Ibid.*, 17:25
[14]*Ibid.*, 17:20
[15]*Ibid.*, 17:21

ABRAHAM IS VISITED BY THREE MESSENGERS FROM GOD

The next important event to take place after the inauguration of the covenant of circumcision was the arrival of three unusual persons at Abraham's residence. The translation by Joseph Smith is more complete in describing these visitors and so we turn to that source for a description of what happened.

These three visitors are sometimes referred to as "angels"[16] and sometimes they are called "men."[17] Perhaps a better explanation is found in the verse which says they were "angels which were holy men."[18] These messengers were in direct communication with God and were instructed to "go down" and judge Sodom and Gomorrah.[19] This would seem to imply that they had come from another planet or distant place of residence to fulfil their mission. It is highly possible that they may have been members of the Priesthood from the community of Enoch. Joseph Smith was told that the righteous people in the translated city of Enoch are "held in reserve to be ministering angels unto many planets, and who as yet have not entered into so great a fulness as those who are resurrected from the dead."[20] Joseph Smith also had this to say concerning Enoch, himself: "He is a ministering angel, to minister to those who shall be heirs of salvation, and appeared unto Jude. . . ."[21]

It might also be kept in mind that this was about the time that Melchizedek and his people "wrought righteousness and obtained heaven, and sought for the city of Enoch which God had before taken."[22] The scripture says that Melchizedek and his people were of that order which made it possible for righteous men and women to be "translated and taken into heaven."[23]

---

[16]Insp. Vers. Gen. 18:16
[17]*Ibid.,* 18:2
[18]*Ibid.,* 18:23
[19]*Ibid.,* 18:19-20
[20]*Teachings of Joseph Smith,* p. 170
[21]*Ibid.*
[22]Insp. Vers. Gen. 14:30-34
[23]*Ibid.*

Could these three messengers have been Melchizedek and two of his companions after their translation? In a later passage the leader of these three angels says that he *knew Abraham*[24] and it appears from the text that Abraham also knew them. Lot also appears to have recognized these men when they came to Sodom. If these angels were Melchizedek and two of his associates they would be well known to both Abraham and Lot. Nevertheless, for the present, we cannot say for certain who these messengers were. We simply mention these various possibilities for the student's consideration.

The scripture says that these three angels "who were holy men" were first seen by Abraham as he sat in his tent door in the heat of the day. Immediately he seemed to recognize them as very special visitors. He "ran to meet them from his tent door, and bowed himself toward the ground, and said, My brethren, if now I have found favor in your sight, pass not away I pray you from thy servant. Let a little water I pray you be fetched and wash your feet, and rest yourselves under the tree, and I will fetch a morsel of bread and comfort ye your hearts; after that you shall pass on; for therefore are ye come to your servant. And they said, So do, as thou hast said."[25]

Notice that these "angels" did not come in glory but as common men who were travel-stained and willing to accept an invitation to dine with Abraham. Because both translated beings and resurrected beings can serve as ministering angels without revealing their glory,[26] Paul warned the Saints of his day: "Be not forgetful to entertain strangers: for thereby some have entertained angels unawares."[27]

The events of this chapter would clearly indicate that Abraham was aware that he was entertaining angels or special emissaries of God. One of the three seems to have been the presiding authority and is consistantly referred to as "the angel of the Lord."

[24]*Ibid.*, 18:18
[25]*Ibid.*, 18:2-4
[26]*Teachings of Joseph Smith*, p. 325
[27]Hebrews 13:2

After these three had eaten they said to Abraham, "Where is Sarah thy wife? And he said, Behold, in the tent."[28]

"And one of them blessed Abraham, and he said, I will certainly return unto thee from my journey, and lo, according to the time of life, Sarah thy wife shall have a son. And Sarah heard him in the tent door. And now Abraham and Sarah being old, and stricken in age, therefore it had ceased to be with Sarah after the manner of women." (Insp. Vers. Gen. 18:9-11)

Sarah had completely given up hope that she would ever have children. She was coming on to her ninetieth year and it had "ceased to be with Sarah after the manner of women." Therefore she "laughed within herself" when she heard the promise that she yet would have a son. From this it would appear that Abraham had not told Sarah the identity of these visitors and she therefore assumed they were common men merely expressing hope for her. She had no sooner "laughed within herself" than the angel of the Lord demanded of Abraham, "Wherefore did Sarah laugh, saying, Shall I of a surety bear a child, which am old?" Then the angel shot out this challenge which was obviously intended for Sarah, "Is anything too hard for the Lord?"[29]

"And the angels rose up from thence, and looked toward Sodom; and Abraham went with them to bring them on the way." (*Ibid.*, 18:16)

As they were traveling along, the angel of the Lord wondered if he might not share with Abraham the purpose of this journey to Sodom. According to the scripture he reasoned within himself, saying: "Shall I hide from Abraham that thing which the Lord will do for him; seeing that Abraham shall surely become a great and mighty nation, and all the nations of the earth shall be blessed in him? For *I know him*, that he will command his children, and his household after him, and they shall

---

[28]Insp. Vers. Gen. 18:8
[29]*Ibid.*, 18:13

keep the way of the Lord, to do justice and judgment, that the Lord may bring upon Abraham that which he has spoken of him."[30]

After such reflections the angel of the Lord apparently felt that he could share the secret of their mission with Abraham and therefore he said:

"The Lord said unto us, Because the cry of Sodom and Gomorrah is great, and because their sin is very grievous, I will destroy them. And I will send you, and *ye shall go down* and see that their iniquities are rewarded unto them. . . . And if ye do it not, it shall be upon your heads; for I will destroy them, and you shall know that I will do it, for it shall be before your eyes." (*Ibid.*, 18:19-22)

It is clear from this that the Lord had already judged these wicked cities and determined to destroy them. Nevertheless, He put it into the hands of these three "angels which were holy men, and were sent forth after the order of God,"[31] to judge the people and exercise their powers of Priesthood in destroying these cities. The Lord had previously said concerning His Priesthood: "that every one being ordained after this order and calling should have power, by faith, to break mountains, to divide the seas, to dry up waters, to turn them out of their course; to put at defiance the armies of nations, to divide the earth, to break every band, to stand in the presence of God; to do all things *according to his will, according to his command,* subdue principalities and powers; and this by the will of the Son of God which was from before the foundation of the earth."[32]

These three holy men were "after the order of God," and they had heard the will of God expressed as He pronounced judgment on Sodom and Gomorrah. Therefore, they had been commanded to go down and see that the iniquities of these people which had been in defiance of God for so many decades should be "rewarded unto them."

[30]*Ibid.*, 18:17-18
[31]*Ibid.*, 18:23
[32]*Ibid.*, 14:30-31

This indicates, as do many other scriptural references, that God does most of His work beyond the veil through the instrumentality of the Priesthood just as He does it here. Wherever possible He accomplishes His work through authorized representatives. Note, however, that He warned these "holy men" that if they became weak-hearted and failed to go all the way in pronouncing a just punishment, then the Lord would take the initiative away from them and do it Himself.

Then it says that "the angels which were holy men, and were sent forth after the order of God, turned their faces from thence and went toward Sodom."[33]

As soon as Abraham learned of the pending destruction of these wicked cities he immediately thought of Lot and his family.

> "And Abraham drew near to Sodom, and said unto the Lord, calling upon his name, saying, Wilt thou destroy the righteous with the wicked? Wilt thou not spare them? Peradventure there may be fifty righteous within the city, wilt thou also destroy and not spare the place for the fifty righteous that may be therein?" (*Ibid.*, 18:25-26)

In reply the Lord said: "If thou findest in Sodom, fifty righteous within the city, then I will spare all the place for their sakes."[34]

As Abraham reflected on this reply he wondered if he should have placed the number so high. He knew Sodom was so completely corrupt that it might be diffi-cult to find fifty righteous persons. He therefore reasoned with the Lord: "Will the Lord spare them peradventure there lack five of the fifty righteous?" And the Lord replied, "I will not destroy, but spare them." Abraham took greater courage and asked the Lord what He would do if only forty righteous were found. The Lord re-plied: "I will not destroy it for forty's sake." Then Abraham said: "O let not the Lord be angry. Then speak: Peradventure there shall thirty be found there?"

---

[33]*Ibid.*, 18:23
[34]*Ibid.*, 18:29

Once again the Lord consented. Abraham knew that he had already pressed himself further than he would ordinarily have dared, but his fear for Lot induced him to ask the Lord to spare the city for twenty. Again the Lord consented.

"And Abraham said unto the Lord, O let not the Lord be angry and I will speak yet but this once, peradventure *ten* shall be found there? And the Lord said, I will not destroy them for ten's sake. And the Lord ceased speaking with Abraham. And as soon as he had left communing with the Lord, Abraham went his way. And it came to pass that Abraham returned unto his tent." (*Ibid.*, 18:39-42)

Now the Lord knew that there were not ten righteous persons in Sodom and the three "holy men" who had been sent to judge these people soon found it out also.

THE DESTRUCTION OF SODOM AND GOMORRAH

When the three* ambassadors from the Lord arrived at Sodom they were seen by Lot as he sat "in the door of his house."**

"And Lot, seeing the angels, rose up to meet them; and he bowed himself with his face toward the ground; And he said, behold now, my lords, turn in, I pray you, into your servant's house, and tarry all night, and wash your feet, and ye shall rise up early, and go on your ways. And they said, Nay; but we will abide in the street all night. And he (Lot) pressed upon them greatly and they turned in unto him and entered into his house; and he made them a feast, and did bake unleavened bread, and they did eat." (Insp. Vers. Gen. 19:2-5)

Note that Lot seemed to recognize the three messengers as persons to whom he owed a special duty of hospitality. And knowing the people of Sodom as he did,

*The Bible says two. This must have been the error of some ancient copyist. Joseph Smith corrected it.

**Note the difference between this account and that found in the Bible. (Gen. 19:1)

Lot had a most urgent reason for insisting that these three visitors accept the protection of his home that night. The account continues:

> "But before they lay down to rest, the men of the city of Sodom compassed the house round, even men which were both old and young, even the people from every quarter.

> "And they called unto Lot, and said unto him, Where are the men which came in unto thee this night? Bring them out unto us that we may know them." (*Ibid.*, 19:6-7)

Lot was panic-stricken. He was one man against a mob from every quarter of the city. He was entirely familiar with the violent extremities to which these Sodomites would go to please themselves.

> "And Lot went out of the door, unto them, and shut the door after him, and said, I pray you, brethren, do not so wickedly.

> "And they said unto him, Stand back. And they were angry with him. And they said among themselves, This one man came in to sojourn among us, and he will needs now make himself to be a judge; now we will deal worse with him than with them.

> "Wherefore, they said unto the man (Lot), We will have the men and thy daughters also; and we will do with them as seemeth us good." (*Ibid.*, 19:8-11)

Then the scripture adds the comment: "Now this was after the wickedness of Sodom."

Lot pleaded with these degenerate creatures who swarmed about him but to no avail.

> "They were angry with Lot and came near to break the door, but the angels of God which were holy men put forth their hand and pulled Lot into the house unto them, and shut the door. And they smote the men with blindness, both small and great, that they could not come at the door. And they were

angry, so that they wearied themselves to find the door, and could not find it." (*Ibid.*, 19:15-16)

When the riot had quieted down the three men of God said to Lot, "Hast thou any here besides thy sons-in-law, and thy son's sons and thy daughters? And they commanded Lot, saying, Whatsoever thou hast in the city, thou shalt bring out of this place, for we will destroy this place; because the cry of them is waxen great, and their abominations have come up before the face of the Lord; and the Lord hath sent us to destroy it."[35]

Lot immediately crept out into the darkness of the night and sought the homes of his sons-in-law who had married his daughters, and said, "Up, get ye out of this place for the Lord will destroy the city." But his sons-in-law paid no attention to Lot.

"And when the morning came, the angels hastened Lot, saying, Arise, take thy wife, and thy two daughters which are here, lest thou be consumed in the iniquity of the city." (*Ibid.*, 19:23)

Lot began to contemplate the fact that his house, his friends and his own daughters who had married citizens of Sodom would fall in the destruction of this city. He therefore failed to respond promptly to the instructions of the three angels. The scripture says he lingered so long that "the angels laid hold upon his hand, and upon the hand of his wife, and upon the hand of his two daughters."[36] Almost by force they were dragged toward the gates of Sodom. As soon as they were safely out of the city the angels said to them: "Escape for your lives; look not behind you, neither stay you in all the plain; escape to the mountains lest you be consumed." Then Lot said: "Oh, not so my Lord! Behold now, thy servant hast found grace in thy sight, and thou hast magnified thy mercy which thou hast showed unto me in saving my life; and I cannot escape to the mountain, lest some evil overtake me and I die; Behold, now, here is another city, and this is near to flee unto, and it is a little one; oh, let me

---

[35]Insp. Vers. Gen. 19:18-20
[36]*Ibid.*, 19:24

escape thither, and may the Lord not destroy it, and my soul shall live."[37]

In response the angel said: "I have accepted thee concerning this thing also, that I will not overthrow this city (to which Lot was about to flee) for the which thou hast spoken; haste thee, escape thither, for I cannot do anything until thou come thither."[38] The scripture says the name of this "little" city was called Zoar and "the sun was risen upon the earth when Lot entered into Zoar."

On the way, however, a tragedy occurred. Lot's wife disobeyed the commandment of the angels and looked back toward the city of Sodom. For many years Lot and his family had strained the patience of heaven with their actions. While it appears that Lot had remained true to some of the fundamentals of his earlier religious teachings, nevertheless, he continually flirted with disaster by living as close to the fringe of iniquity as he could even though he never quite slipped over the brink. He had permitted his daughters to marry Sodomites. He had made himself a citizen of their city even though they counted him a "stranger" among them. Now the Lord had a lesson for Lot and his family. As his wife disregarded the specific instruction of the angel and looked back toward the city, her soul was required of her. She not only died but the remains of her mortal tabernacle underwent a transformation into a pillar of salt.[39] In great haste Lot continued with his two daughters into Zoar.

"And then, when Lot had entered into Zoar, the Lord rained upon Sodom, and upon Gomorrah; for the angels called upon the name of the Lord for brimstone and fire from the Lord out of heaven. And thus they overthrew those cities and all the plain, and all the inhabitants of the cities, and that which grew upon the ground." (*Ibid.*, 19:31-32)

Now, early that same morning Abraham had gone up to the sacred spot where he usually went to commune with the Lord "and he looked toward Sodom and Gomorrah

[37]*Ibid.*, 19:26-27
[38]*Ibid.*, 19:28
[39]*Ibid.*, 19:33

and toward all the land of the plain, and behold, lo, the smoke of the country went up as the smoke of a furnace." But the Lord comforted Abraham and said: "I have remembered Lot, and sent him out of the midst of the overthrow, that thy brother might not be destroyed, when I overthrew the city in which thy brother Lot dwelt."[40]

This communication must have come as a great relief to Abraham. The Lord had promised Abraham that He would not destroy Sodom if there were ten righteous people in the city. When Abraham saw the smoke rising from the plain he knew that apparently there had not been even ten righteous persons for whom the city could be saved. But what of Lot? Abraham must have felt the greatest anxiety for him until the Lord gave this word of comfort assuring Abraham that he was safe.

The scripture says that after the catastrophe of destruction had spent itself, Lot decided that he would not remain in the city of refuge to which he had fled. For some reason he "feared to dwell in Zoar." Therefore Lot went up to live in the mountains. "And he dwelt in a cave, he and his two daughters."[41]

One cannot help but wonder why Lot did not flee to the residence of Abraham. Surely he must have known he would be welcome there. Perhaps his pride would not permit him to come to Abraham and admit that his judgment had been wrong. In any event, some strong personal feeling persuaded Lot to hide in the mountains rather than further impose upon Abraham.

After Lot had established himself in the mountains the scriptures continue:

"And the first-born (of Lot's daughters) dealt wickedly, and said unto the younger, Our father has become old, and we have not a man on the earth to come in unto us, to live with us after the manner of all that live on the earth;

"Therefore come, let us make our father drink wine, and we will lie with him, that we may preserve

[40]*Ibid.,* 19:35
[41]*Ibid.,* 19:36

seed of our father. And they did wickedly, and made their father drink wine that night. . . .

"Thus were both the daughters of Lot with child by their father. And the first born bare a son, and called his name Moab; the father of the Moabites, the same which are unto this day. And the younger, she also bare a son, and called his name Ben-ammi; the father of the children which are Ammonites; the same which are unto this day." (*Ibid.*, 19:37-44)

With this incident, Lot disappears from the pages of history.

CHAPTER THIRTY-ONE

Abraham's Greatest Trial

After the destruction of Sodom and Gomorrah where did Abraham make his new home? Of what nationality were the Philistines? (See Gen. 10:29)

When Abraham came into this new land what made him afraid? What did he do to protect himself and Sarah? Were Abraham's fears well-founded?

How old was Abraham when Isaac was born? How old was Sarah? When Isaac was weaned Abraham prepared a great feast. What event marred the festivities?

Do you think Sarah was justified in her attitude toward Hagar? Approximately how much older was Ishmael than Isaac? Do you think there might have been serious difficulty if they had continued to live together in the same household?

What nationality was Hagar? Where did she go to get a wife for Ishmael?

Name three reasons why the Lord's command to sacrifice Isaac was incomprehensible to Abraham.

Where was the sacrifice of Isaac to take place? What famous temple was afterwards built on the same spot? What famous people had once occupied this area? Do we have any information which would account for the fact that this area was now uninhabited?

Should men obey God even when His commandments seem unreasonable or incomprehensible? Have any such commandments been received in modern times?

Abraham now changed his residence again. Where did he go?

How old was Sarah when she died? What was the attitude of the local landowners when Abraham tried to purchase a place of burial?

Who was buried in the cave of Machpelah besides Sarah?

ABRAHAM MOVES TO GERAR

For some reason not mentioned in the scriptures Abraham found it necessary or desirable to leave Hebron almost immediately after the destruction of Sodom and Gomorrah. He took his possessions and moved to Gerar. This was over toward the Mediterranean Sea in the land of the Philistines.

But here Abraham sensed pending trouble. As he observed the dark-skinned inhabitants of this land he said to himself: "The fear of God is not in this place; and they will slay me for my wife's sake."[1] Abraham concluded to follow the same procedure as that which the Lord had suggested to him when he went into Egypt. Therefore, as they became acquainted with the Philistines, Sarah was introduced and described to them as Abraham's sister.

As it turned out, the fears of Abraham were well-founded. The king of the Philistines was Abimelech, and soon after Abraham had settled in the country Abimelech "sent and took Sarah."[2]

Since any woman who attracted the attention of the king was supposed to be honored by his interest, Abraham did not openly resist the servants of the king who were sent to bring Sarah to his palace. Just as in Egypt Abraham trusted that through the blessings of the Lord no harm would befall her. And of course any other attitude might have cost Abraham his life and Sarah her freedom. They were living in a most perilous situation.

It is remarkable too that the beauty of Sarah should have survived until this time. She was now approaching her ninetieth year and even though physical degeneration was slower in this era of human history, nevertheless, it

[1]Gen. 20:11
[2]*Ibid.*, 20:2

is astonishing that Sarah should have retained her beauty so as to attract the attention of King Abimelech just as she had the Egyptian Pharaoh three or four decades earlier.

After Sarah had been brought to the palace a period of time passed during which no children were born in the house of Abimelech. This was looked upon as a great affliction which could not be understood.

"But God came to Abimelech in a dream by night, and said unto him, Behold, thou hast taken a woman which is not thine own, for she is Abraham's wife. And the Lord said unto him, Thou shalt return her unto Abraham, for if thou do it not thou shalt die....

"And he said, Lord, wilt thou slay me, and also a righteous nation? Behold, said he not unto me, She is my sister? And she, even she herself said, He is my brother; and in the integrity of my heart and innocency of my hands have I done this.

"And God said unto him in a dream, Yea, I know that thou didst do this in the integrity of thy heart; for I also withheld thee from sinning against me; therefore suffered I not thee to touch her. Now, therefore, restore the man's wife to him, for he is a prophet, and he shall pray for thee and thou shalt live; and if thou restore her not to him thou shalt surely die; thou and all that are thine." (Insp. Vers. Gen. 20:3-8)

The following morning Abimelech told his servants all that had occurred and they "were sore afraid." Then Abimelech called Abraham and said: "What hast thou done unto us? And what have I offended thee, that thou hast brought on me and on my kingdom a great sin?" Abimelech also wondered what advantage Abraham would have gained by this strange procedure. Therefore he said: "What sawest thou, that thou hast done this thing?" In reply, Abraham was very frank with Abimelech. Said he:

"Because I thought, Surely the fear of God is not in this place; and they will slay me for my wife's sake. (Then he quickly explained to Abimelech that when he said Sarah was his sister it was not a falsehood.) And yet indeed she is my sister; she is the daughter of my father, but not the daughter of my mother; and she became my wife." (Gen. 20:11-12)

When Abimelech realized that the offenses of himself and his people had caused Abraham to fear for his life and that the king himself had offended Abraham by his conduct he immediately made great overtures of friendship and reparation. Abimelech gave Abraham oxen, sheep and servants. He also gave him a thousand pieces of silver and said: "Behold, my land is before thee: dwell where it pleaseth thee."[3]

Abraham accepted these gifts and Abimelech's offer of hospitality knowing that it was the king's way of showing his sincerity and sorrow for what had happened. "And Abraham prayed unto God and God healed Abimelech and his wife and his maid servants and they bare children."[4]

THE BIRTH OF ISAAC

It was this same year that Sarah received the great blessing for which she had waited throughout her married life. Even though she had now passed her natural time of child-bearing she nevertheless conceived and on the anniversary of the visit of the three angels at Hebron she gave birth to a son.[5] It is not difficult to imagine the joy and celebration which brightened the scene in Abraham's community when this marvelous son was born to him out of season. Abraham was now 100 years of age and Sarah was 90.[6]

Sarah made no attempt to conceal her great happiness. Said she: "God has made me to rejoice; and also all that know me will rejoice with me."[7]

The child was given the name of Isaac for that was the name which the Lord had previously called him, even

---

[3]Gen. 20:15
[4]*Ibid.,* 20:17
[5]*Ibid.,* 16:12; 21:2
[6]*Ibid.,* 17:17; 21:5
[7]*Ibid.,* 21:4

before he was born,[8] and when he was eight days old he was circumcised as the Lord had commanded.[9]

We do not know exactly how long it was before Isaac was weaned, but the scripture says that Abraham made it the occasion for a great feast.[10] For Sarah, however, this became a day of sorrow. During the feasting Sarah observed that Hagar was mocking and making a great ridicule of what was being done in honor of Isaac. Sarah had been patient with Hagar for many years. Even when Hagar had violated her confidence and trust a few years before, Sarah had forgiven her and taken her back into the household. No doubt there had been strained relations, however, because of Hagar's ugly disposition to show jealousy and pretended superiority toward her mistress. Now, on the occasion of this feast in honor of Isaac, Sarah saw in Hagar a spirit of hateful antagonism which portended serious consequences for the future. Sarah knew that Isaac would be declared the heir of Abraham and that Hagar would be forever resentful because of her jealousy for Ishmael who was approximately fifteen years older than Isaac. Sarah therefore said to Abraham: "Cast out this bondwoman and her son; for the son of this bondwoman shall not be heir with my son, Isaac."[11]

Now this request came as a great trial to Abraham. "It was very grievous in Abraham's sight because of his son."[12] Abraham had probably been fully aware of the problem Hagar represented in his household and that is why he had told Sarah before that she was to "do to her as it pleaseth thee."[13] But now that Sarah insisted that both Hagar and Ishmael no longer remain in their household Abraham found such a decision difficult because of the love he bore Ishmael.

However, Abraham's perplexity was completely resolved when he received a revelation from the Lord:

---

[8]Gen. 17:19
[9]*Ibid.*, 21:4
[10]*Ibid.*, 21:8
[11]Insp. Version, Gen. 21:8
[12]Gen. 21:11
[13]*Ibid.*, 16:6

"God said unto Abraham, Let it not be grievous in thy sight because of the lad, and because of thy bondwoman; in all that Sarah hath said unto thee, hearken unto her voice; for in Isaac shall thy seed be called. And also of the son of the bondwoman will I make a nation, because he is thy seed."[14] This gave Abraham the necessary confidence to let them go.

The following day Abraham provided food and water for Hagar and Ishmael and sent them on their way. Since Ishmael was fourteen[15] when Isaac was born and this incident occurred the day after Isaac was weaned it is likely that Ishmael was around fifteen at this time. He and his mother did not stay on the main roads but wandered in the wilderness which was southeast of Gerar. In the process they became lost and ran out of water. The heat of this desert country soon left them both exhausted. Ishmael was the first to collapse, and Hagar placed him under the scanty shade of a bush. Then she went "a good way off, as it were a bowshot: for she said, Let me not see the death of the child. And she . . . lift up her voice, and wept."[16]

"And God heard the voice of the lad; and the angel of God called to Hagar out of heaven, and said unto her, What aileth thee, Hagar? fear not; for God hath heard the voice of the lad where he is. Arise, lift up the lad, and hold him in thine hand; for I will make him a great nation.

"And God opened her eyes, and she saw a well of water; and she went, and filled the bottle with water, and gave the lad drink.

"And God was with the lad; and he grew, and dwelt in the wilderness, and became an archer.

"And he dwelt in the wilderness of Paran; And his mother took him a wife out of the land of Egypt." Gen. 21:17-21)

Now this area where Hagar and Ishmael were wandering when they nearly lost their lives, was afterwards

---

[14]*Ibid.,* 21:12-13
[15]*Ibid.,* 16:16; 21:5
[16]*Ibid.,* 21:16

called Beer-sheba because Abraham came there with
Abimelech, and the two made a covenant together:

> "And it came to pass at that time, that Abimelech
> and Phicol the chief captain of his host spake unto
> Abraham, saying, God is with thee in all that thou
> doest: Now therefore swear unto me here by God
> that thou wilt not deal falsely with me, nor with my
> son, nor with my son's son: but according to the
> kindness that I have done unto thee, thou shalt do
> unto me, and to the land wherein thou hast so-
> journed. And Abraham said, I will swear." (*Ibid.*,
> 21:22-24)

Then Abraham thought it would be an appropriate
time to tell Abimelech about "a well of water, which
Abimelech's servant's had violently taken away. And
Abimelech said, I wot not who hath done this thing:
neither didst thou tell me, neither yet heard I of it, but
today."[17]

So the two of them made a covenant together and
Abraham gave presents to Abimelech "as a witness unto
me, that I have digged this well."[18] Therefore Abraham
named the place Beer-sheba which means "the well of
the oath."

> "Then Abimelech, and Phicol, the chief captain
> of his hosts, rose up and planted a grove in Beer-
> sheba, and called there on the name of the Lord; and
> they returned unto the land of the Philistines. And
> Abraham worshipped the everlasting God, and so-
> journed in the land of the Philistines many days."
> (Insp. Vers. Gen. 21:31-32)

ABRAHAM RECEIVES THE GREATEST TRIAL OF HIS LIFE

In the past whenever Abraham had received a revelation it had always come as a source of comfort and inspiration. One day, however, after Isaac had grown to

[17]*Ibid.*, 21:25-26
[18]*Ibid.*, 21:30

be "a lad," Abraham received a revelation which was absolutely incomprehensible:

"And the Lord said, Take now thy son, thine only Isaac, whom thou lovest, and get thee into the land of Moriah; and offer him there for a burnt offering upon one of the mountains which I will show thee." (*Ibid.*, 22:2)

What manner of commandment was this? For nearly a hundred years Abraham had preached with the greatest vehemence against human sacrifice. He had denounced his own patriarchal ancestors for this sin. Nowhere in the scriptural history of the race during the previous two thousand years was there the slightest suggestion that God would countenance human sacrifice under any circumstances. And yet, here was God commanding Abraham to sacrifice Isaac. Everything about this commandment violated reason, the teachings of the patriarchs, the previous commandments of God and the natural inclination of Abraham.

And what about Isaac? Abraham loved him with the starved affection of a father who had waited a century for this precious son. Furthermore, if Isaac were sacrificed how would the Lord's promises to Abraham be fulfilled? God had said: "In Isaac shall thy seed be called."[19]

But to all these questions there were no answers. If ever Abraham was required to show the trust of a little child in his Heavenly Father this was the time. He had exhibited faith before in leaving Ur, in leaving Haran, in going into Egypt. But all of these commandments had obvious purpose behind them. Now Abraham had received a commandment for which he could see no purpose. It seemed to destroy the very promises which God had previously made to him.

Nevertheless, Abraham arose early in the morning and saddled his donkey and took two young men and Isaac with him. He took with him the necessary pro-

---

[19]Gen. 21:12

visions and chopped a quantity of dry wood "for the burnt offering."

Three days of continuous travel finally brought the party in sight of the place which was called Moriah. And Abraham told the two young men to stay at that place with the donkey while he and Isaac went ahead to worship.

> "And Abraham took the wood of the burnt offering and laid it upon his back; and he took the fire in his hand, and a knife, and Isaac his son; and they went both of them together.
>
> "And Isaac spake unto Abraham his father, and said, My father! and he said, Here am I, my son. And he said, Behold the fire and the wood; but where is the lamb for a burnt offering?
>
> "And Abraham said, My son, God will provide himself a lamb for a burnt offering." (Insp. Vers. Gen. 22:7-10)

All of the authorities concur that the land of Moriah was the area now occupied by Jerusalem and that the altar which Abraham built was on one of its hills. In fact, the scripture later identifies "Mount Moriah" as the place where Solomon was commanded by the Lord to build the temple.[20]

In the earlier days of Abraham this site was occupied by Salem and was ruled over by Melchizedek. Now the land was vacant and uninhabited. Where had the people of Salem gone? Joseph Smith was told that Melchizedek and his people "wrought righteousness, and obtained heaven."[21] Apparently this thrilling event had taken place just previously. In this very locality made sacred by the righteousness of Melchizedek and his people Abraham was now commanded to offer his son as a sacrifice!

> "And they came to the place which God had told him of; and Abraham built an altar there, and laid the wood in order, and bound Isaac his son, and laid him on the altar upon the wood." (Gen. 22:9)

[20]2 Chronicles 3:1
[21]Insp. Vers. Gen. 15:32-34

There is no indication of any resistance by Isaac. Surely some explanation must have passed between Abraham and Isaac in this desperate hour. Paul says Abraham came to this terrible ordeal determined to offer up Isaac but "Accounting that God was able to raise him up, even from the dead."[22] Josephus attributes these words to Abraham as the moment of sacrifice drew near:

"Oh, son, I poured out a vast number of prayers that I might have thee for my son; when thou wast come into the world, there was nothing that could contribute to thy support for which I was not greatly solicitous, nor anything wherein I thought myself happier than to see thee grown up to man's estate, and that I might leave thee at my death the successor to my dominion; but since it was by God's will that I became thy father, and it is now his will that I relinquish thee, bear this consecration to God with a generous mind; for I resign thee up to God who has thought fit now to require this testimony of honour to Himself, on account of the favours He hath conferred on me, in being to me a supporter and defender. Accordingly thou, my son, wilt now die, not in any common way of going out of the world, but sent to God, the Father of all men, beforehand, by thy own father, in the nature of a sacrifice. I suppose He thinks thee worthy to get clear of this world neither by disease, neither by war, nor by any other severe way, by which death usually comes upon men, but so that He will receive thy soul with prayers and holy offices of religion, and will place thee near to Himself, and thou wilt there be to me a successor and supporter in my old age; on which account I principally brought thee up, and thou wilt thereby procure me God for my comforter instead of thyself."[23]

"And Abraham stretched forth his hand, and took the knife to slay his son." (Gen. 22:10)

This was the final gesture of absolute obedience. Beyond the veil the angel of the Lord watched this tense scene. At that very moment when Abraham raised the knife to slay his son, the voice of the angel cried out:

[22]Hebrews 11:17-19
[23]Josephus, *op. cit.*, Book I, Chap. 13:3

"Abraham! Abraham!" The aged patriarch replied:
"Here am I." And the angel said: "Lay not thine hand
upon the lad, neither do thou anything unto him: for now
I know that thou fearest God, seeing thou hast not
withheld thy son, thine only son, from me."[24]

> "And Abraham lifted up his eyes, and looked,
> and behold behind him a ram caught in a thicket by
> his horns: And Abraham went and took the ram, and
> offered him up for a burnt offering in the stead of his
> son." (*Ibid.* 22:13)

Abraham had just passed through one of the greatest
dramas in human history. From generation to generation
it would be proclaimed as one of the most outstanding
examples of righteous faith ever exhibited by a member
of the Priesthood. It would help others who followed
Abraham to trust in the Lord, particularly when his commandments were strange and incomprehensible. In
earth life as in the eternities before we learn that obedience to God is for our good. Sometimes He will ask
us to do that which may seem paradoxical and strange,
but with the faith of Abraham a man will obey God
whether he understands the reason or not.

When Abraham had completed the sacrificial ordinance at the altar he took Isaac and departed. Surely
there was no more grateful man on the face of the earth
than Abraham as he joyfully led Isaac back down to
the place where his two servants waited. Having packed
their belongings the four of them departed for home.

THE DEATH OF SARAH

It would appear that about this time Abraham decided to move to the oasis of Beer-sheba which was the
well where he and Abimelech had made their covenant
together,[25] and where a grove had been planted that it
might be a pleasant habitation.

The next important event recorded in scripture occurred a number of years later when Sarah reached the

[24]Gen. 22:12
[25]*Ibid.*, 21:31-34; 22:19

age of one hundred and twenty-seven. For some reason that is not stated Sarah had gone to Hebron, Abraham's original dwelling place in Canaan. There the long life of this princess of Shem came to a close.[26] She is the only woman in the Bible whose age, death and burial are distinctly noted.

Then the record says that "Abraham came to mourn for Sarah, and to weep for her."[27] This would indicate that perhaps they were separated at the time of Sarah's death and that Abraham had to come from Beer-sheba to Hebron when the tragic news was brought to him. It is said to be about twenty-four miles from Beer-sheba to Hebron.[28]

In this hour of sorrow Abraham was grieved by the additional fact that he had no inheritance or place he could permanently call his own where Sarah might be laid to rest with the assurance that her tomb would not be desecrated. In desperation Abraham went to the sons of Heth who had great holdings of land in this region and said: "I am a stranger and a sojourner with you: give me a possession of buryingplace with you, that I may bury my dead."[29]

The respect and affection which these Canaanite princes held for Abraham is reflected in their reply. Said they: "Hear us, my lord: thou art a mighty prince among us: in the choice of our sepulchres bury thy dead; none of us shall withhold from thee his sepulchre, but that thou mayest bury thy dead."[30] This overture of generosity must have touched Abraham deeply. He accepted this offer and said: ". . . intreat for me to Ephron the son of Zohar, That he may give me the cave of Machpelah, which he hath, which is in the end of his field; for as much money as it is worth he shall give it me for a possession of a buryingplace amongst you."[31]

[26]Ibid., 23:1-2
[27]Ibid.
[28]Clarke, op. cit., Vol. I, p. 14
[29]Genesis 23:4
[30]Ibid., 23:6
[31]Ibid., 23:8-9

But Ephron needed no entreating. Though he was a Hittite he was as generous as the sons of Heth among whom he dwelt. Said he to Abraham: "Nay, my lord, hear me: the field give I thee, and the cave that is therein, I give it thee; in the presence of the sons of my people give I it thee: bury thy dead."[32]

Abraham, however, insisted on paying the price of the field and so Ephron finally accepted four hundred shekels of silver.

"And the field of Ephron, which was in Machpelah, which was before Mamre, the field, and the cave which was therein, and all the trees that were in the field, that were in all the borders round about, were made sure unto Abraham for a possession in the presence of the children of Heth, before all that went in at the gate of his city.

"And after this, Abraham buried Sarah his wife in the cave of the field of Machpelah before Mamre; the same is Hebron in the land of Canaan." (Gen. 23:17-19)

This sepulchre became more famous than almost any ancient place of burial. It was the final resting place not only for Sarah, but also for Abraham,[33] Isaac, Rebekah,[34] Leah, and Jacob.[35] The traditional site is now covered by a large Mohammedan mosque.

---

[32]*Ibid.,* 23:11
[33]*Ibid.,* 25:9
[34]*Ibid.,* 40:30-31
[35]*Ibid.,* 50:13

CHAPTER THIRTY-TWO

The Closing Days of Abraham

Why did the servant of Abraham hesitate to take the oath which Abraham required of him?

Why did Abraham insist that Isaac should not be taken back to Mesopotamia to find himself a wife?

Where did the servant of Abraham go to find a wife for Isaac? Was Abraham accurate in describing this place as "my country" and the land of "my kindred?"

What relation was Rebekah to Isaac? (See Gen. 24:15)

Recite the circumstances which made it possible for Abraham's servant to carry out his master's instructions? What evidence was there that the angel of the Lord did go before him to prepare the way?

Was Rebekah homely or beautiful? Was there a mutual affinity between Isaac and Rebekah when they met for the first time? How old was Isaac when he married Rebekah?

How long did Abraham live after Sarah's death. What was the name of Abraham's third wife? How many sons did she bare? How many sons did Abraham have altogether?

Was Abraham wise to divide his estate among his sons while he was still alive?

How old was Abraham when he died?

Where was he buried?

How many generations were there from Adam to Abraham?

What is the greatest lesson to be learned from the history of the first two thousand years?

ABRAHAM SEEKS A WIFE FOR ISAAC

Sarah was ninety years of age when Isaac was born and 127 when she died. This would mean that Isaac was thirty-seven at the time of her death. Isaac had not married prior to this time for the very good reason that in Canaan there was no suitable person of his own race to whom he could have been married. After Sarah's death Abraham set about to remedy this defect.

He called in his eldest servant "that ruled over all that he had," and said: "Swear by the Lord, the God of heaven, and the God of the earth, that thou shalt not take a wife unto my son of the daughters of the Canaanites, among whom I dwell."[1]

Since the Canaanites were of the Hamitic tribes who could not enjoy the Priesthood Abraham was greatly concerned about the marriage of Isaac to a young woman of the proper lineage so that the promise of the Lord concerning the Priesthood could be perpetuated through him. To marry a Canaanite would cut the promise off because the children of such a union could not receive the Priesthood. Abraham therefore instructed his servant as follows: "Thou shalt go unto my country, and to my kindred, and take a wife unto my son Isaac."[2]

Abraham's eldest servant hesitated to take an oath which he might find difficult to fulfil. Said he: "Peradventure the woman will not be willing to follow me unto this land . . . from whence thou camest?" The servant thought that if his own efforts to get a wife for Isaac failed it might help if he took Isaac back with him so the young woman and her family could approve of him for themselves. But Abraham saw great danger in this: "And Abraham said unto him, Beware thou, that thou bring not my son thither again. The Lord God of heaven, which took me from my father's house, and from the land of my kindred . . . sware unto me saying, Unto thy seed will I give this land."[3] Abraham knew his son must not be tempted by the prosperity of Mesopotamia, but must

[1]Genesis 24:3
[2]*Ibid.,* 24:4
[3]*Ibid.,* 24:7

be determined to remain in Canaan where the Lord had promised an inheritance to Abraham and his descendants forever. Abraham therefore promised his servant that the Lord "shall send his angel before thee, and thou shalt take a wife unto my son from thence. And if the woman will not be willing to follow thee, then thou shalt be clear from this my oath: *only bring not my son thither again.*"[4] Abraham was most emphatic that Isaac was not to return to Mesopotamia.

With this explanation the servant felt satisfied and took an oath to perform this service. He therefore set out with a large caravan of ten camels and a number of men and "went to Mesopotamia, unto the city of Nahor."[5]

Now the city of Nahor (belonging to the brother of Abraham) was located along the headwaters of the Euphrates River where Abraham had originally established Haran. The city where Nahor and his children dwelt was called Padan-aram, but it is clear that Padan-aram was either identical with Haran or in the district of Haran.[6] In sending his servant to the city of Nahor Abraham could accurately describe it as "my country" and "my kindred."[7]

It was very significant that Abraham should have declared that there were only "daughters of the Canaanites among whom I dwell." As we have previously noted, the righteous people of Melchizedek had been residing at Salem some fifty years prior to this time but now they appear to have gone. Until the Lord gave Joseph Smith a number of verses which had been taken from the Biblical text we had no way of knowing why Abraham could not have found a daughter for Isaac among the righteous people of Melchizedek who originally lived only two or three days' journey from Hebron. In the Inspired Version we learn that:

"Melchizedek was a man of faith . . . and thus, having been approved of God, he was ordained an

[4]*Ibid.,* 24:7-8
[5]*Ibid.,* 24:10, 32
[6]*Ibid.,* 28:5, 10; 29:4-5
[7]*Ibid.,* 24:4

high priest after the order of the covenant which God made with Enoch. . . . And men having this faith, coming up unto this order of God, were *translated and taken up into heaven.*

"And now Melchizedek was a priest of *this order;* therefore he obtained peace in Salem, and was called the Prince of peace.

"And his people wrought righteousness and *obtained heaven,* and sought for the city of Enoch which God had before taken, separating it from the earth, having reserved it unto the latter days, or the end of the world." (Insp. Vers. Gen. 14:26-34)

Just as the original translation of the City of Enoch left certain ones behind to continue the work of the Lord, so the translation of the people of Melchizedek did not include Abraham because he had a different mission. For the first time we have a clear explanation of the reason why Abraham had to send his servant all the way back to Mesopotamia to obtain a wife for Isaac because there were "only the daughters of the Canaanites, among whom I dwell."

The Servant of Abraham Finds Rebekah

When the servant of Abraham had arrived at the City of Nahor he made his camels kneel beside the well from which the people of the community obtained their water. Then he prayed to the Lord, saying:

"O Lord God of my master Abraham, I pray thee, send me good speed this day, and shew kindness unto my master Abraham.

"Behold, I stand here by the well of water; and the daughters of the men of the city come out to draw water: And let it come to pass that the damsel to whom I shall say, Let down thy pitcher I pray thee, that I may drink; and she shall say, Drink, and I will give thy camels drink also: let the same be she that thou hast appointed for thy servant Isaac; and thereby shall I know that thou hast shewed kindness unto my master." (Gen. 24:12-14)

Even before he had stopped speaking his prayer was answered: "Behold, Rebekah came out, who was born to Bethuel, son of Milcah, the wife of Nahor, Abraham's brother, with her pitcher upon her shoulder."[8]

The servant of Abraham noted that she was "very fair to look upon."[9] After Rebekah had filled her pitcher he asked her for a drink. The maiden was very gracious in complying. Though the man was a stranger she did not seem to fear him. When the servant of Abraham had finished drinking he heard the girl say: "I will draw water for thy camels also until they have done drinking." This was the sign which the servant had asked from the Lord. Nevertheless, he could not help wondering if it might not be a coincidence.[10] He therefore watched the girl as she "emptied her pitcher into the trough, and ran again unto the well to draw water." She did not stop until the camels had all been satisfied. To water ten camels was an arduous task. To perform this task without complaining or receiving assistance was a strong test. Still the servant of Abraham wondered. "Whose daughter art thou? tell me, I pray thee: is there room in thy father's house for us to lodge in?"

Her answer drove all doubt from the man's mind. Said she: "I am the daughter of Bethuel, the son of Milcah, which she bare unto Nahor." Then she added: "We have both straw and provender enough, and room to lodge in."[11]

When the servant of Abraham heard this he reached forth and placed two gold bracelets on her arms and gave her jeweled earrings to wear. He was so relieved that the scripture says he "bowed his head" and publicly worshiped the Lord. He lifted his voice to heaven and said: "Blessed be the Lord God of my master Abraham, who hath not left destitute my master of his mercy and his truth; I being in the way, the Lord led me to the house of my master's brethren!"[12]

---

[8]*Ibid.,* 24:15
[9]*Ibid.,* 24:16
[10]*Ibid.,* 24:21
[11]*Ibid.,* 24:23-25
[12]*Ibid.,* 24:27

These words told Rebekah for the first time who this stranger was. When she heard that he was the servant of none other than Abraham, her famous great-uncle, she ran and told the people at her home.

"And Rebekah had a brother, and his name was Laban . . . and it came to pass, when he saw the earring and bracelets upon his sister's hands, and when he heard the words of Rebekah his sister . . . he came unto the man, and, and, behold, he stood by the camels at the well.

"And he said: Come in, thou blessed of the Lord; wherefore standest thou without? for I have prepared the house, and room for the camels.

"And the man came into the house: and he ungirded his camels, and gave straw and provender for the camels and water to wash his feet, and the men's feet that were with him." (Gen. 24:29-32)

Laban wanted the servant of Abraham to eat but he said: "I will not eat, until I have told mine errand." Then he related the whole account from the beginning. He recited Abraham's instructions to him and the oath that Abraham had required of him. He told how he had asked the Lord for a sign and said that Rebekah had satisfied that sign in every particular. He told them that the purpose of his mission was to bring a wife back to Isaac and that in delivering this message he had fulfilled his promise to Abraham. He concluded by saying: "And now if ye will deal kindly and truly with my master, tell me: and if not, tell me; that I may turn to the right hand, or the left."[13]

No doubt this request came as a shock to the household of Rebekah. The prospect of her leaving her native home and traveling all the way to Canaan to marry a second cousin might have caused deep resentment in Laban, her brother and Bethuel, her father. But the scripture says: "Laban and Bethuel answered and said: The thing proceedeth from the Lord: we cannot speak unto thee bad or good."[14] In other words the matter was not

---

[13]*Ibid.,* 24:49
[14]*Ibid.,* 24:50

for them to decide. The hand of Providence had been so strongly manifested that the decision was already made. So they said: "Behold, Rebekah is before thee, take her, and go, and let her be thy master's son's wife, as the Lord hath spoken."[15] When the servant of Abraham heard this he once more publicly worshiped the Lord, "bowing himself to the earth."

Then he took silver and gold and fine raiment and gave them to Rebekah, "He gave also to her brother and to her mother precious things."

"And they did eat and drink, he and the men that were with him, and tarried all night; and they rose up in the morning, and he said, Send me away unto my master.

"And her brother and her mother said, Let the damsel abide with us a few days, at the least ten; after that she shall go.

"And he said unto them, Hinder me not, seeing the Lord hath prospered my way; send me away that I may go to my master.

"And they said we will call the damsel, and enquire at her mouth.

"And they called Rebekah, and said unto her, Wilt thou go with this man? And she said, I will go. (*Ibid.* 24:54-58)

This entire series of incidents reflects a quality of character and spiritual stamina in Rebekah which were becoming to a princess of Shem. She was a beautiful and noble girl—one of the choicest women on the face of the earth in her day and generation.

"And they blessed Rebekah, and said unto her: Thou art our sister, be thou the mother of thousands of millions, and let thy seed possess the gate of those which hate them." (*Ibid.*, 24:60)

These words seem to show that this family was entirely familiar with the great promises which had been

---

[15]*Ibid.,* 24:51

made through the patriarchs and particularly to Abraham in this generation. In marrying Isaac, Rebekah was destined to become a "mother of nations."

"And Rebekah arose, and her damsels, and they rode upon the camels, and followed the man: and the servant took Rebekah, and went his way." (*Ibid.*, 24;61)

No romance had a more remarkable beginning than this one. There must have been anxious days for Rebekah as the caravan made its way slowly across Syria and down into the rich valleys of Canaan.

But apparently Rebekah was not the only party to this transaction who felt the anxiety of these days. We read that Isaac was near the well called Lahai-roi which had saved the life of Hagar and Ishmael, and at eventide he went out in the field to meditate. Then he saw the caravan returning from Mesopotamia and hastened forward to meet it. As Isaac approached, Rebekah quickly inquired of Abraham's servant: "What man is this that walketh in the field to meet us?" and the servant replied: "It is my master!"

Immediately Rebekah alighted from the camel and covered her face with a veil to be prepared for the proper offices of introduction after the manner of those times.

The servant of Abraham related to Isaac all that had transpired—how the hand of the Lord had led him to Rebekah and how she had accepted the many manifestations of divine approbation and was prepared to become his wife even though she had never met him.

Then there came that thrilling moment when these two important personalities met for the first time in earth life. There was a natural affinity between them. Their union was blessed of the Lord. Isaac took her to Abraham, and there must have been great joy as this aging patriarch joined them in marriage after the pattern of the Holy Priesthood which is for time and all eternity.

Then the scriptures say: "And Isaac brought her into his mother Sarah's tent, and took Rebekah, and she became his wife; and he loved her."

Isaac was forty years of age when this marriage occurred.[16] The scripture says that the companionship of
Rebekah helped to fill the void which resulted from the
death of Isaac's mother; "And Isaac was comforted after
his mother's death."[17]

THE CLOSING DAYS OF ABRAHAM

The marriage of Isaac occurred three years after
Sarah's death. Abraham continued to live another thirty-
five years. Concerning this closing period of his life, the
records state:

> "Then again Abraham took a wife, and her name
> was Keturah. And she bare him Zimran, and Jok-
> shan, and Medan, and Midian, and Ishbak, and
> Shuah." (*Gen.* 25:1-2)

Altogether Abraham now had eight sons. Being well
acquainted with the weaknesses of human nature he fore-
saw the possibility that these sons might quarrel over the
estate after he was gone. He therefore divided his inheritance among his children while he was still living.
He gave gifts to the children of Keturah and Hagar "and
sent them away from Isaac his son, while he yet lived,
eastward, unto the east country."[18] The main inheritance
was reserved for Isaac. In later years this inheritance
was so great that Abimelech, king of the Philistines, said
to Isaac: "Go from us, for thou art much mightier than
we."[19]

We see from this that while Abraham was merely "a
tenant at will" among his heathen hosts in Canaan, he
nevertheless surrounded himself with an estate of great
wealth, and when he passed this on to Isaac it gave this
new prince of Shem a position of influence and prestige
in the land.

Finally, when Abraham had reached 175, the scriptures say he was "in a good old age, an old man, and full

[16]*Ibid.,* 25:20
[17]*Idem*
[18]*Ibid.,* 25:6
[19]*Ibid.,* 26:16

of years."[20] All the Lord had said concerning the life of
Abraham had now been fulfilled. It was the end of a
great epic. At the proper moment the call went forth
from the high heavens, and Abraham was "gathered to
his people." It must have been an occasion of great
solemnity as the news swept across the land: "Abraham
is dead!"

The passing of this great patriarch was of great significance to all the people of the south country. To the
sons and friends of Abraham it was a time of deep sorrow. For the politically ambitious Philistines it was considered the opportune time to invade the inheritance of
Isaac and stop up the wells so that his great flocks would
be driven from the land.[21] But Isaac would have his day
and his blessings just as the Lord had fulfilled great promises to Abraham. Meanwhile, Isaac joined with his
older brother Ishmael to do the final honors to their de-
ceased father.[22] They took the remains of this honored
patriarch into the cave of Machpelah near Hebron and
laid them beside the resting place of his wife, Sarah.[23]

It is interesting to learn that Ishmael took part in these
final burial rites. Ishmael was greatly loved by Abraham
and because he lived just south of the area occupied by
Abraham it is highly probable that there had been occasional communication between them. Ishmael was a
hunter—"a wild man" of the desert. But in this time of
sorrow his heart was as tender as any other son's as he
did honor to his father. It was appropriate that Ishmael
should be with Isaac when the time came to lay their
illustrious father to rest.

With this closing chapter in the life of Abraham we
come to the conclusion of the first two thousand years of
human history recorded in holy writ. It constitutes
twenty generations—from Adam to Abraham—twenty
generations of humanity who were very much like ourselves; the same joys, the same sorrows, the same

---

[20]*Ibid.,* 25:7-8
[21]*Ibid.,* 26:18
[22]*Ibid.,* 25:9
[23]*Ibid.,* 25:9-10

frontiers to conquer, the same passions to control. The fulness of the gospel given to them is identical with the fulness of the gospel given to us. The God who blessed them is the same Heavenly Father who blesses us. He is the same yesterday, today and forever. This is the greatest lesson to be learned from human history during the first two thousand years.

Appendix

EXPLANATORY NOTES ON THE CHRONO-LOGICAL TIME TABLE COVERING THE PERIOD OF THE PATRIARCHS

WHEN DID HUMAN CHRONOLOGY BE-GIN? The well-known Irish archbishop, James Usher (or Ussher) who was born in Dublin in 1581 and died in 1656, devoted a great deal of his life attempting to cor-relate existing chronological data so that the events de-scribed in ancient times could be fixed with comparative accuracy. This work was complicated by the fact that genealogical tables, which he considered to be the most scientific method of fixing dates, were sometimes inac-curately recorded, and very often historians were not in agreement as to the date when a particular event of im-portance occurred As a result, the archbishop found it necessary on occasion arbitrarily to choose the date which he personally felt was most likely to be correct.

As Archbishop Usher projected his chronology back into the patriarchal period, he found his dates adding up to 4,004 B.C. for the genesis of Adam. This has since become widely accepted as the beginning of the chron-ology of the Old Testament. Just why Archbishop Usher added four years to the previously accepted date of 4,000 B.C. is not entirely clear from his writings. There are so many places where arbitrary factors entered into his compilation that the extra four years which he finally had as a surplus could have been easily accounted for in a number of places so as to leave the "beginning" date at the more logical period of 4,000 B.C.

The student of ancient and modern scriptures cannot help being impressed with the importance which God has always attached to time. The engineering precision which has characterized the unfolding of human history upon the earth would lead one to conclude that the earth's divine architect is a great respecter of mathematical accuracy and carefully predetermined the exact dates when all the important events connected with his program would occur. Thus, Abraham was told that the duration of the suffering of the Children of Israel in Egypt would be "four hundred years," (Genesis 15:13) and Lehi was told that the birth of Christ would be "six hundred years" from the time he left Jerusalem (1 Nephi 10:4). It is apparent from these and similar examples that God knew previously when each step in his program would occur.

It further appears from a study of the scriptures that God designed his program in connection with human history "a thousand years" at a time. John the Revelator saw that human history was divided into seven periods of a thousand years each (Revelations 5:1-3; D. & C. 77:6-7). This is further verified in modern revelation where the Lord declares that the great judgment at the beginning of the millennium will be accompanied by a revelation of what occurred in "the first thousand years," "the second thousand years" and so forth. (See D. & C. Section 88) These scriptures illustrate the inclination of the Lord to do things in thousand year periods and to divide his work accordingly. Therefore, with all due respect to the good work of Archbishop Usher, it is believed that the actual date for the beginning of human chronology was at the commencement of a thousand year period, i.e. 4,000 B.C., and that the birth of Christ was precisely four millenniums later.

SYNOPSIS OF DATA UTILIZED IN FIGURING CHRONOLOGY FROM NOAH TO ABRAHAM. Noah was born 1,056 years after the beginning of mortality for Adam or 2,944 B.C. He was 450 when his first son, Japheth, was born (Moses 8:12), 492 when Shem was born (*Ibid.*), and 500 years old when Ham was born (*Ibid.*). Noah was exactly 600 years of age when the Great Flood occurred (Genesis 7:11), and he lived after the Flood 350 years (Genesis 9:29). This made Noah 950 years old when he died in 1,994 B.C. or 2,006 years after Adam.

SHEM was born when Noah was 492 years old (Moses 8:12). This should have made him 108 when the Great Flood occurred because Noah was then 600 (Genesis 7:11). But according to Genesis 11:10, Shem was 98 at the time of the Flood. How did this ten year discrepancy occur? Authorities believe that Genesis 11:10 which makes Shem 98 at the time of the Flood instead of 108 was an error which was made in some ancient manuscript of Genesis, and the error was afterwards perpetuated. Any question on the matter is definitely resolved by reference to Moses 8:12 where the age of Noah at the time of Shem's birth is specifically stated as being 492. We may safely assume, therefore, that Shem was 108 when the Great Flood occurred and was 110 when Arphaxad was born two years after the Flood (Genesis 11:10). Shem lived after the birth of Arphaxad 500 years, making him 610 years old when he died in 1,842 B.C.

ARPHAXAD was born to Shem two years after the Flood (Genesis 11:10) which would be 1,658 from the time of Adam or 2,342 B.C. It is possible he was not Shem's oldest child (see genealogical listing in Genesis 10:22) but he carried the patriarchal lineage of Shem (1 Chronicles 1:24). Arphaxad was 35 when he begat Salah (Genesis 11:12) and died 403 years later (Genesis 11:13), which would make him 438 when he died in 1,904 B.C. Note that he died before his father, Shem.

SALAH was born when Arphaxad was 35 (Genesis 11:12) which was 1,693 years after the mortality of Adam or 2,307 B.C. He was 30 years old when Eber was born and lived 403 years longer. He therefore died at the age of 433 in 1,874 B.C. Note that he died before his grandfather, Shem.

EBER was born when Salah was 30 (Genesis 11:14) or 2,277 B.C. He lived 34 years before he begat Peleg and lived 430 more years before he died. This made him 464 at the time of his death in 1,843 B.C.

PELEG was born when Eber was 34 years old (Genesis 11:16) which was 1,757 from the genesis of Adam or 2,243 B.C. Peleg begat Reu when he was 30 (Genesis 11:18) and lived another 209 years (Genesis 11:19), making him 239 when he died in 2,004 B.C. Note that he died before Noah and also before his great-great-grandfather, Shem, his great-grandfather, Arphaxad, his grandfather, Selah, and his father, Eber.

REU was born when Peleg was 30 (Genesis 11:18) which was 1,787 years after Adam or 2,213 B.C. He lived 32 years and begat Serug (Genesis 11:20). He lived 207 years longer, dying when he was 239 or 1,974 B.C. Note that Reu outlived his father by only a few years and died while all his ancestors back to Shem were still alive.

SERUG was born when Reu was 32 (Genesis 11:20). This was 1,819 years after the genesis of Adam or 2,181 B.C. Serug then lived until he was 30 and begat Nahor. After Nahor's birth he lived 200 more years (Genesis 11:23), dying when he was 230 or 1,951 B.C. Note that Serug outlived his father and grandfather but died while all of his other ancestors back to Shem were still alive.

NAHOR was born when Serug was 30 which would be 1,849 years after the genesis of Adam or 2,151 B.C. He was 29 when he begat Terah (Genesis 11:24) and lived 119 years after that (Genesis 11:25), making him 148 when he died in 2,003 B.C. Note that he died one year after his great-grandfather, Peleg, and while his seven other ancestors back to and including Noah were still alive.

TERAH was born when Nahor was 29, (Genesis 11:24). This was 2,122 B.C. or 1,878 years after the genesis of Adam. He was 205 years old when he died which was 1,917 B.C.

ABRAHAM was born in Ur of Chaldees, but the exact date has never been definitely determined. Two methods have been used to fix the date, and both are now known to be erroneous. The first is based on Genesis 11:26 where it says: "And Terah lived seventy years

and begat Abram, Nahor and Haran." It was assumed
that Abram was the eldest of the three, and therefore he
was born when his father, Terah, was seventy, Nahor
and Haran being born some time later. A careful reading
of later passages, however, reveals that Haran was the
eldest. In fact, he had a daughter just ten years younger
than Abraham (Abraham 2:2; Genesis 17:17) which
means that Haran was in all probability at least twenty
to thirty years older than Abraham. We must therefore
assume that the passage in Genesis quoted above was
designed merely to point out that when Terah reached
seventy he began having the three sons whose names are
given. Adam Clark states: "Haran was certainly the
eldest son of Terah, and he appears to have been born
when Terah was about seventy years of age, and his
birth was followed in successive periods with those of
Nahor his second, and Abraham his *youngest* son. Many
have been greatly puzzled with the account here, sup-
posing because Abram is mentioned first, that therefore
he was the eldest son of Terah; but he is only put first
by way of *dignity*. An instance of this we have already
seen in Genesis 5:32, where Noah is represented as having Shem, Ham and Japheth in this order of succession;
whereas it is evident from other scriptures that Shem was
the youngest son, who for dignity is named first, as
Abram is here." (Clarke, *Commentary* under Genesis
11:26) It was probably Haran, therefore, who was born
when Terah was 70, and Abraham was born at some subsequent date which is not mentioned.

The second method of fixing Abraham's age is based
on the following passages: "And the days of Terah were
two hundred and five years: and Terah died in Haran.
Now the Lord said unto Abram, Get thee out of thy country . . . and Abram was seventy and five years old when
he departed out of Haran." (Genesis 11:32; 12:1, 4)
If Terah was 205 when he died and Abraham was
seventy-five at the same time then obviously he would
have been born when his father was 130. Many authorities have accepted this as conclusive. The restored book
of Abraham, however, eliminates the possibility of this

conclusion being correct. In the first place it points out that Abraham did not wait until his father's death (when he was 205) to leave Haran and go to Egypt. Abraham says: "And the famine abated; and my father tarried in Haran and dwelt there, as there were many flocks in Haran; and my father turned again unto his idolatry, therefore he *continued* in Haran. But I, Abraham, and Lot, my brother's son, prayed unto the Lord, and the Lord appeared unto me, and said unto me: Arise, and take Lot with thee." (Abraham 2:5-6) Then Abraham adds a postscript which shows that the text in Genesis has been tampered with. In his own account he says: "So I, Abraham, departed as the Lord had said unto me, and Lot with me; and I, Abraham, was *sixty and two years old when I departed out of Haran.*" (*Ibid.,* 2:14) From this it appears that Abraham took Lot and left for Egypt when he was 62 rather than when he was 75 and furthermore, that he departed while his father, Terah, *continued* at Haran. This explodes any possibility of using the dates in Genesis as a means of fixing the time when Abraham was born. Only an estimate can be made. This might be based on the following:

Abraham is described as having married a daughter of Haran who was ten years younger than himself and since Haran had another daughter and son who were also adults by the time Abraham was old enough to marry (Genesis 11:29, 31; Abraham 2:2) it would appear that Haran was probably twenty to thirty years older than Abraham. If Haran was the one born when Terah was 70 (Genesis 11:26) then Abraham was probably born when Terah, his father, was from ninety to a hundred years old. To assist in setting up a chronology, the latter date of one hundred has been arbitrarily selected. This would mean that Abraham was born 2,022 B.C. and died 175 years later (Genesis 25:7) or 1,847 B.C.

Why Was the Atonement Necessary?

Probably no subject in scripture has aroused more questions or provoked more wonderment than the atonement. In every dispensation the Lord has declared that it is the keystone to the entire plan of salvation. During four millenniums mankind looked forward to it, and, in obedience to God's commandments, sacrificed the first-born of their choicest flocks to remind themselves of its importance. After it occurred, the Lord instructed that the sacrament be instituted to memorialize the great event and that the emblems be given "in remembrance of his suffering" and served to the members of the Church whenever they met together. From Adam until now, the atonement has been the principal subject of all sacred scripture and true church ritual.

It is appropriate, therefore, that we study this awe-inspiring event which occupies such a prominent place in the plan of salvation.

It was just twelve hours before the occasion of His crucifixion that Jesus of Nazareth retired to the seclusion of His favorite place of prayerful meditation on the slopes of Mount Olivet. The scriptures say He walked off a little way from His disciples and suddenly threw Himself prone upon the ground. It was nighttime and quiet. From the arboreal labyrinth of Gethsemane His Apostles heard the heart stirring pleas of the very Son of God as He trembled in mortal anguish before the brink of destiny for which He was ordained and born. "O my Father," He said, "if it be possible, let this cup pass from me!"[1] And, according to Mark, He implored fervently, "Abba, Father, *all things are possible unto thee;* take away this cup from me: nevertheless, not what I will, but what thou wilt."[2]

---

[1]Matt. 26:39
[2]Mark 14:36

How did Elohim respond to this plea? We now know this was a bitter hour not only for Jesus but also for His Father. Probably the desperate grief of Abraham when he raised the sacrificial knife to slay his beloved son, Isaac, could only compare in a finite degree with the incomprehensible grief which the Eternal Father must have felt on this dark night as He beheld His own beloved Son face the ordeal of torture and death. An ordeal which could have been prevented, of course, but only at the risk of wiping out the whole plan of salvation for the human race.

Down through the corridors of nineteen hundred years there comes the echo of those pleading words: "O my Father, *if it be possible*, let this cup pass from me...."

The student cannot help asking, "Why wasn't it possible?"

Inability of God to Save Man Directly

The apparent necessity for the atonement demands an explanation. Some may say that the atoning sacrifice of Jesus Christ was to satisfy "justice." But whose justice? Justice does not exist except as a concept in the mind. Whose sense of justice had been violated? Many students will say the atonement was necessary to satisfy God's sense of justice. But let us think that through. If the Father *wanted* us to have this experience of the Fall as a means of making us eligible for exaltation and eternal life, why would it violate *His* sense of justice to take us back into His presence afterwards when the school of mortality is completed?

Why would the Father demand a vicarious atonement to redeem us from a Fall which was *His* idea in the first place?[3] The scripture plainly teaches that man's coming to earth was part of the Father's plan.[4] He wanted Adam to fall in order to partake of the experiences of mortality and provide physical tabernacles for the great family of spirit children which He had prepared for this earth. Why, then, could not the Father take us

[3]Moses 4:2
[4]2 Nephi 2:22-25

back? Why did Jesus have to "purchase" us through
suffering and act as mediator to get us back? Doesn't the
Father love us as much as the Son?

From the scriptures it is obvious that the Father was
somehow subject to an impelling circumstance which
made it impossible for Him to bring us back into His presence by acting directly or through His own initiative.[5]
As Peter declared, "There is *none other name* under
heaven given among men, whereby we must be saved."[6]
That name is Jesus Christ. No one else has the power to
take us back: Not even Elohim, our Father. The scriptures point to the reason why.

OMNIPOTENCE OF GOD CIRCUMSCRIBED BY LAW

We speak of our Heavenly Father as being omnipotent—all-powerful. But this does not mean that He is free
to do anything capricious or arbitrary. God is omnipotent, but only within the circumscribed boundaries of law,
truth, and justice. He cannot violate these or He would
cease to be God. As Mormon and Alma plainly taught:

> "And behold, I say unto you he changeth not;
> if so he would cease to be God...." (Mormon 9:19)

> "... the work of justice could not be destroyed;
> if so, God would cease to be God." (Alma 42:13,
> 22)

> "What, do ye suppose that mercy can rob
> justice? I say unto you, Nay; not one whit. If so,
> God would cease to be God." (*Ibid.*, 42:25)

In other words, if eternal principles were violated,
God could cease to be God!

But who is it that occupies a position great enough in
the universe to require of the exalted Elohim his Godhood in case He should violate any of the principles of
truth and justice? That there is such a power to which
the Father is subject would appear obvious from the
above scriptures.

----
[5] Alma 11:37
[6] Acts 4:12

The Source of God's Power

Through modern revelation we learn that the universe is filled with vast numbers of intelligences, and we further learn that Elohim is God simply because all of these intelligences honor and sustain Him as such. In other words, as God extended His power and influence throughout His great kingdom, He did so by obtaining the voluntary cooperation and support of vast concourses of intelligences.

In Section 93 of the Doctrine and Covenants, the Lord states that all of these intelligences act freely and independently in their respective spheres. They obey God because they *want* to; not because they *have* to.[7] Therefore, the Father is actually dependent upon their sustaining influence or honor to accomplish His purposes.

Here is the clue to the source of God's power.

The Lord refers to it specifically in another section of the Doctrine and Covenants. He is speaking of the great council in heaven, and He says that on that occasion Lucifer "rebelled against me, saying, Give me thine honor, *which is my power.* . . ."[8] God's "power" is derived from the honor and support of the intelligences over whom He rules. This is what Lucifer coveted.

It is apparent from these and other scriptures that the present exalted position of our Heavenly Father was gradually built up. His glory and power is something which He slowly acquired until today "all things bow in humble reverence."[9] But since God "acquired" the honor and sustaining influence of "all things" it follows as a correlary that if He should ever do anything to violate the confidence or "sense of justice" of these intelligences, they would promptly withdraw their support, and the "power" of God would disintegrate. This is what Mormon and Alma meant when they specifically stated that if God should change or act contrary to truth and justice "He would cease to be God." Our Heavenly Father can

[7]D. & C. 93:30
[8]*Ibid.,* 29:36
[9]*Ibid.,* 76:93

do only those things which the intelligences under Him
are voluntarily willing to support Him in accomplishing.

The Nature and Extent of Organized Intelligences Throughout the Universe

To appreciate better the interdependent relationship
existing between God and the intelligences over whom
He rules, it is desirable to examine the function of these
intelligences in the kingdom of God.

In the Doctrine and Covenants, "intelligence" or that
eternal, self-knowing "will" within each of us is called
by several different names. Sometimes it is called "the
light of truth," sometimes "the light of Christ," and in
one place it is identified with the phenomenon of "life."

An example of the first use is in Section 93:29: "Intelligence, or *the light of truth,* was not created or made,
neither indeed can be." An example of the second use is
in Section 88:6-7. There the scripture explains that
Christ has extended His personal influence until it comprehends all things. His will has become the accepted
criteria of all the intelligences in the universe. He has
so completely allied Himself with the "light of truth"
that this vast sea of obedient intelligences might well be
called "the light of Christ."[10] A few verses later this is
described as being the essence or force which is ordinarily referred to as "life."[11]

From the above it will be seen that "the light of truth"
and "the light of Christ" simply appear to be collective
terms to designate the masses of organized intelligences
in God's kingdom. And what are these intelligences
capable of doing?

According to the scripture, these organized intelligences which are variously referred to as "the light of
truth" and "the light of Christ" constitute the very substance "which is in all things, which is the law by which
all things are governed, *even the power of God.*"[12]

---

[10]See Joseph Fielding Smith, *The Way to Perfection,* pp. 227-229
[11]D. & C. 88:13
[12]*Idem*

The fact that the universe is literally saturated with carefully organized intelligences makes it possible for God to give "a law unto all things, by which they move in their times and their seasons."[13] It is the medium by which God extends His will into the organizing and controlling of the sun, the moon and all other heavenly bodies.[14] It explains why God could organize the earth by commanding the very elements to obey.[15] It explains the testimony of such prophets as Jacob who said: " . . . we truly can command in the name of Jesus and the very trees obey us, or the mountains, or the waves of the sea."[16]

Every creation of God is filled with the requisite order of intelligences necessary to organize it into whatever pattern the Lord has designed. And these intelligences which occupy each creation recognize the voice of the Priesthood and obey it when properly exercised.

By introspection it is a simple matter to appreciate how the human intelligence is responsible for the phenomenon of "life" in a human being, but it may be a new concept to some that this same pattern is followed in placing intelligences of life in "all things"—even in those things which are ordinarily referred to as "inorganic."

Brigham Young said: "There is life in all matter throughout the vast extent of all the eternities; it is in the rock, the sand, in water, air, the gases, and in short, in every description and organization of matter whether it be solid, liquid or gaseous, particle operating with particle."[17]

Every atom of matter is therefore an intricate compound of "element" combined with intelligence or life. When we see the so-called laws of physics, chemistry, biology or "nature" in action, we are simply observing organized intelligences operating in matter—intelligences who are honoring their supreme organizer just as they have faithfully honored Him throughout the bygone aeons of eternity.

[13]*Ibid.*, 88:42
[14]*Ibid.*, 88:7-10; 42-43
[15]Abraham 4:18
[16]Jacob 4:6; Mormon 8:24
[17]*Disc. of Brigham Young*, 1925 Ed., p. 566

The Intelligences Are Graded

In a revelation to Abraham, God taught him that there is a wide and variable range among the intelligences of the universe.[18] Some have been slow to develop. Others have forged ahead, zealously anxious to follow closely behind the greatest intelligence of them all, which is Elohim.[19]

The Lord further informs us through this same revelation that the most valiant of all the intelligences (called "the noble and great ones") were organized and set apart for training in positions of presidency in the government of heaven.[20] It was intended that those who responded to the training should eventually become like unto God, Himself.[21] These superior intelligences were honored with spirit bodies which were "begotten" of God. He thereby became our Heavenly Father in a complete and literal sense just as Paul has said, ". . . be in subjection unto the Father of spirits, and live?"[22] And again: ". . . we are the offspring of God."[23]

Obviously, the number of intelligences honored with spirit bodies in the very image of God was an infinitesimal minority among the great sea of intelligences which existed within the confines of God's kingdom. These others who had developed more slowly would necessarily have to be satisfied with much lesser blessings. And it must also be kept in mind that anything which the Father did for those of us who were being schooled for Godhood would have to be done in a way which would be acceptable to those less advanced intelligences who constituted the vast majority of the intelligences in the universe.

The Problem of the Fall

Now we who were being schooled for Godhood had to be put through a Second Estate.[24]

---

[18]Abraham 3:16-19
[19]*Ibid.,* 3:19
[20]*Ibid.,* 3:25-26
[21]D. & C. 132:19-20
[22]Hebrews 12:9
[23]Acts 17:28-29
[24]Abraham 3:23-26

From God's point of view this experience was most necessary for us and from our point of view it was the greatest blessing that could come to us. But the problem confronting the Father was the fact that a Second Estate here in mortality would necessarily involve a Fall or descent from our exalted position in the family circle of God. And once this had taken place and we had entered into this world of sin, error and rebellion it would thereafter be impossible for God to take us back into his presence on His own initiative. If He did so, it would mean that we who had deliberately fallen or sinned would be taken back into His presence as though we had not sinned. This would violate the principles of equity, justice and law which prevail in the celestial kingdom.

The scripture records the position of God as the supreme arbiter of heaven: "For I the Lord cannot look upon sin with the least degree of allowance."[25] Or if He did, He would cease to be God. The intelligences of the universe would lose confidence in Him. They would look upon His actions as discriminatory and as showing partiality to a small group of intelligences which could not be allowed unto all.

Therefore, no matter how desirable God may consider it to make an exception in the case of His chief intelligences who are being trained for Godhood, nevertheless it cannot be done. Once we had fallen, God, the Father, was prohibited by virtue of His relation with all the other intelligences in the universe from ever taking us back on His own initiative.

This, then, was the problem of the Fall.

Lucifer sought to circumvent this difficulty by suggesting that if each of us was *forced* to live by celestial law while experiencing earth life, then there could be no objection by the other intelligences when we were readmitted to the celestial home of our Father. This plan, however, had two defects. First, it would involve coercion and subjugation of free agency—thereby violating the cornerstone of God's system of theo-democratic govern-

[25]D. & C. 1:31

ment. Secondly, it would have defeated the original purpose for which earth life was designed, i.e., to learn how to use our free agency in a "fallen" estate to overcome evil voluntarily.

So another plan had to be devised.

THE PLAN OF JEHOVAH

The plan presented by Jehovah or Jesus Christ was one which the Father, Himself, had previously worked out. This is borne out by Jehovah's statement when He offered the plan: *"Thy* will be done."[26] The plan, simply stated, was as follows:

Jehovah, a member of the First Presidency of heaven, would be born into the earth and live a perfect life— without sin. There could then be no objection to *His* returning to heaven when His life's mission was completed. While in the earth He would suffer violence at the hands of His brethren whom He would endeavor to teach and help. Then after returning to heaven, He would say unto His Father: "I went down among Thy children. At their hands I suffered greatly. I have spent much energy and effort to perfect them. Now I will be robbed of my labor if they are not allowed to come up and be with me."

Or, to quote the Lord directly: "Father, behold the sufferings and death of him who did no sin, in whom thou wast well pleased; behold the blood of thy Son which was shed, the blood of him whom thou gavest that thyself might be glorified; Wherefore, Father, *spare these my brethren that believe on my name, that they may come unto me and have everlasting life."*[27]

It is through the shedding of His blood and the suffering He endured while trying to teach humanity that He can say: "For my sake, let them come up."

Because of the love and respect which the intelligences of the universe have for Jehovah, they do not object when the Father accepts us back into His presence

---

[26]Moses 4:2
[27]D. & C. 45:4-5

(not for our own sakes, "for all have sinned, and come short of the glory of God;"[28] but for the sake of Jesus Christ who says He will not be happy without us.) Thus, what the Father could not do directly and on His own initiative, He is able to accomplish indirectly through the mission and sacrifice of His Beloved Son.

WAS THE PHYSICAL SUFFERING OF JESUS CHRIST NECESSARY?

The basis for the claim of Jesus Christ that He had "purchased" us had to be a very real and bona fide consideration on the part of Jesus Christ. It could not be merely a token offering or subtle gesture. It had to be so deep and poignant as to persuade any group of intelligences who might otherwise object that the human family did mean *that much* to Jesus Christ. His suffering was His proof that He had to have us with Him in order to be happy. This is the basis for the statement that the Savior is a "Bridegroom" and the Church is like unto his "bride" which He takes with Him back into the presence of the Father. It is for "His" sake that the Church membership is admitted back into the celestial home and it is through Him that the Church is made one with Him to share in His heavenly glory.[29]

That this suffering was an irrevocable part of Christ's mission and was so understood from the very beginning is borne out by the statement that He is the "Lamb slain from the foundation of the world."[30]

When He was born of the virgin, Mary, the conscious memory of the great Jehovah was blotted out by mortality. As with all of us, He gained an appreciation of His mission and identity only as He increased in wisdom and understanding through experience and instructions from above. At thirty-three, He was still only partially appreciative of His former power and calling and through the half-light of mortal understanding He still wondered if, somehow, the Father

---

[28]Romans 3:23
[29]D. & C. 88:107
[30]Rev. 13:8

could not save Him from the excruciating torture of Golgotha. In Gethsemane He posed the question to His
Father in humble pleading; but when He gained the final
answer, Jesus rose to the full stature of His Messiahship
and said " . . . if this cup may not pass away from me,
except I drink it, thy will be done."[31]

Eighteen hours later, bleeding and naked on a Roman
cross, Jesus of Nazareth suffered the torturous role of
"passing beneath all things." Not far away was His
grief-stricken mother, and near her stood John, the beloved disciple. But on the cross Jesus had to endure the
terrible anguish of that moment alone. To consummate
the work completely the Father even withdrew His
light which is shed forth upon all men, and, in doing so,
caused the Savior to cry out: "Eloi, Eloi, lama sabach-
thani? which is, being interpreted, My God, my God,
why hast thou forsaken me?"[32] Immediately afterwards
He said, "It is finished!"[33] And then, "Father, into thy
hands I commend my spirit."[34]

At that moment Jesus became the Christ.

---

[31]Matt. 26:42
[32]Mark 15:34
[33]John 19:30
[34]Luke 23:46

Immorality in Heathen Worship

"Among the ancient nations of the East, with the exception of the Jews, prostitution appears to have been connected with religious worship, and to have been not merely tolerated but encouraged. . . . In Egypt, Phoenicia, Assyria, Chaldea, Canaan and Persia, the worship of Isis, Moloch, Baal, Astarte, Mylitta and other deities consisted of the most extravagant sensual orgies and the temples were merely centers of vice. In Babylon some degree of prostitution appeared to have been even compulsory and imposed upon all women in honor of the goddess Mylitta. In India the ancient connection between religion and prostitution still survives." (*Encyclopedia Britannica*, (1952 Edition) Volume 18, p. 596)

"A dramatic tableau which summarizes the chief traits of Canaanite worship appears in illustration 238. It shows a clay cult stand found outside of an Asherah shrine. . . . Note the nude goddess seated in lewd posture. She holds her two symbolic doves. See the two warring male deities with a dove at the feet of one. Notice the advancing serpent, symbol of fertility, and the lion of power slinking along the side of the shrine. Imagine such crude glorification of prostitution in the name of religion and you gain an idea of the Syrian and Anatolian cults met by the Israelites moving up from Egypt to possess the land." (*Encyclopedia of Bible Life* by Madeleine S. Miller and J. Lane Miller, Harper Brothers, New York, 1944, pp. 446-447)

Abraham's Knowledge
of the Heavenly Bodies
and Modern Astronomy

By Milton R. Hunter*

"It is our purpose in this topic to make a brief comparison of Father Abraham's vision of the heavenly bodies and comparable knowledge had by astronomers at the present time. When we consider that Abraham's vision was recorded nearly 4,000 years ago, the facts presented therein cause us to marvel. Although his account is brief and a little of the terminology differs somewhat from the terms used today, nevertheless many of the ideas presented in the Pearl of Great Price are sustained by the knowledge had by modern astronomers.

"The science of astronomy, like the majority of the other sciences, has made wonderful advancements during the past few hundred years. Probably no time in history have mortal beings penetrated so deeply into the vastness of the universe as have the scientists during our day. Aided by powerful telescopes, the astronomers have penetrated billions and billions of miles outward into the universe, and have tabulated and named numerous galaxies of heavenly bodies—approximately one hundred millions of them. Each of these galaxies is composed of from two to five hundred billions of stars. Thus these modern scientists have verified through their discoveries the words of the Lord to the ancient prophets as recorded in the Pearl of Great Price. For example, in that holy scripture the God of heaven and earth made the following declaration:

" 'Worlds without number have I created. . . . For behold, there are many worlds that have passed

*Reproduction by permission from *The Pearl of Great Price Commentary*, by Milton R. Hunter

away by the word of my power. And there are many that now stand, and innumerable are they unto man; but all things are numbered unto me, for they are mine and I know them.'[10]

"We shall now turn our attention to an examination of Father Abraham's marvelous vision. In the foregoing scripture (Abr. 3:2-4, 9), the ancient Patriarch describes a massive body of matter which the Lord called Kolob. God showed him in vision many stars which were 'very great, and that one of them was nearest unto the throne of God; and there were many great ones which were near unto it; and the Lord said unto me (Abraham): These are the governing ones; and the name of the great one is Kolob because it is near unto me, for I am the Lord thy God.' Then the Lord explained to the Father of the Faithful that He had set Kolob 'to govern all those which belong to the *same order* as that upon which thou standest.'

"Modern astronomy holds the viewpoint that larger bodies of matter govern smaller bodies of matter through the law known as gravitation. Certainly that concept is in harmony with the words of the Lord to Abraham. However, astronomers have not, in our age, discovered one separate and distinctive body of matter which serves as the center of our galaxy and which seems to govern all the stars in said galaxy. In other words, they have not located a star which could be definitely designated as being Kolob. Instead of one large star serving as the center of this galaxy, astronomers maintain that there are numerous large stars located rather close together and that they are all nearly equal in mass. That idea seems to fit well with Abraham's statement that there were 'many great ones which were near unto it (Kolob),' although astronomers have not designated one of these stars as being the governor of the others.

"In verse 4 the Lord described to Abraham the revolutions of Kolob. The word *revolutions* is used correctly, according to modern terminology, when the

---

[10]Moses 1:33a, 35b.

description is referring to seasons. Then Abraham records the fact that 'one revolution was a day unto the Lord, after His manner of reckoning, it being one thousand years according to the time appointed unto' this earth. The word *revolution* in that particular phrase, according to our terminology, should be interpreted as meaning *rotation*,[11] because it is the rotation of the earth upon its axis that determines day and night.

"The Lord pointed out to Abraham that Kolob was immense in size. The fact that it took one thousand years of our time for it to make one complete turn on its axis— in other words, for one day's time to elapse—also is indicative of its enormity. Modern astronomers have discovered many stars which are gigantic in size. These they call 'super-giant stars.' One of the largest of them is named Betelgeuse. It has a diameter of approximately four hundred sixty millions of miles. Another super-giant star, being also enormous in size, is named Antares. This immense body of matter is located in the Scorpia constellation. It has a diameter of approximately three hundred millions of miles. Another giant star, being a little larger than Antares, is named Myra, and another is called Arcturus. The latter one has a diameter of thirty-six millions of miles. Any of these massive bodies of matter could easily be accepted as being comparable in size to the great star Kolob which God showed to Father Abraham.

"In verse 5 the Lord describes the motions of the moon (which satellite He named Olea in verse 13), comparing its motion to the rotation of the earth in determining the reckoning of time. He told Abraham that the moon rotates more slowly on its axis than does the earth, and therefore a day on that satellite is much longer than a day on the earth. The discoveries of modern astronomers have attested this revealed fact. Although the moon is much smaller than the earth, being only 2,163 miles in diameter compared to 7,900 miles, yet it takes $27\frac{1}{3}$ days (sidereal time—pertaining to the stars) for it to rotate once on its axis; therefore, a day on the moon

---

[11]Rotation is about an axis within the body as it turns; revolution is the turning about an axis which is outside the body.

is as long a period of time as 27⅓ sidereal days upon the earth. It also takes 29½ synodic days (pertaining to the sun) for the moon to revolve once around the earth; and so the same side or face of the moon is turned towards the earth at all times.

"According to the teachings of astronomy, the revolutions of the moon are faster than those of the earth. Since the moon revolves around the earth and the earth revolves around the sun, in addition to the moon following its own orbit around the earth—which it completes once every 27⅓ days—it is also accompanying the earth in its orbit around the sun; therefore, the moon has two voluntary motions compared to the earth's one, which results in its moving more rapidly.

"The Lord pointed out to Abraham (verses 6 to 10) that to each heavenly body He gave a law which governed the motion of that particular body of matter. Also, since each body of matter has its own separate movements, its rate of motion differs from the rate of motion of other bodies of matter. In modern revelation the Lord told the Prophet Joseph Smith certain truths which sustain the facts given to Father Abraham. To quote:

" 'All kingdoms have a law given; and there are many kingdoms; for there is no space in the which there is no kingdom; and there is no kingdom in which there is no space, either a greater or a lesser kingdom. And unto every kingdom is given a law; and to every law there are certain bounds also and conditions. . . .

" 'And again, verily I say unto you, he (God) hath given a law unto all things, by which they move in their times and their seasons; And their courses are fixed, even the courses of the heavens and the earth, which comprehends the earth and all the planets. And they give light to each other in their times and in their seasons, in their minutes, in their hours, in their days, in their weeks, in their months, in their years—all these are one year with God, but not with men.

" 'The earth rolls upon her wings, and the sun
giveth his light by day, and the moon giveth her light
by night, and the stars also give their light, as they
roll upon their wings in their glory, in the midst of
the power of God.'[12]

"Again, it can be said that modern astronomy verifies
the facts revealed to Father Abraham and to Joseph
Smith regarding the laws which govern heavenly bodies.
The speed of each body of matter which exists throughout the entire universe has been determined by the law
which was established and set into operation for the control of that particular body of matter. After the Divine
Omnipotent God put the laws into operation, each body
of matter traveled at its own definite given speed year
after year and age after age.[13]

"It has already been pointed out that the earth rotates on its axis many times faster than does the moon.
The fact could be mentioned that Jupiter rotates on its
axis as much faster than the earth as the earth does faster
than the moon. For example, Jupiter has a diameter of
88,000 miles and its rotation period is 9 hours 50 minutes
and 30 seconds. This planet is hundreds of times as large
as the earth and yet it takes a third as much time for a
day to transpire on it as it does upon the earth. Saturn,
another of the planets in this solar system, has a diameter
of 72,000 miles and a rotation length of time of 10 hours
and 2 minutes. The sun has a diameter of approximately
865,000 miles and its rotation period, or length of day,
is 25.14 days measured by our time at the sun's equator
or 35 days near the poles. Thus the speed at which each
of the heavenly bodies is traveling differs from the speed
of each other. To further illustrate this point, we shall
direct our attention to the speed of revolutions of some of
these bodies of matter. For example, the earth is revolv-
ing at the rate of 18½ miles per second in its course
around the sun in contrast to Pluto's speed of 1½ miles
per second. Thus we see that to every kingdom God has

---

[12]D. & C. 88:36-38, 42-45.
[13]In perfect agreement with the Laws of Planetary Motion as enunciated
by Sir Isaac Newton.

given its own individual law which law regulates the speed at which that kingdom moves throughout space as long as that Divine Being wills that it should do so.

"In verse 12 Abraham describes the eternal and innumerable amount of heavenly bodies that exist throughout the universe. To quote: 'I saw those things which his (God's) hands had made, which were many; and they multiplied before mine eyes, and I could not see the end thereof.' (Abraham 3) That statement suggests that there is no end to matter nor to space. As far as Abraham was able through vision to penetrate the immensity of space, he beheld body after body of matter, or in other words, star after star. The fact that matter and space have no limit is also confirmed by modern astronomers.

"There was a time a few hundred years ago when all the stars that were known were those that could be seen with the naked eye. Then came the invention of the telescope. By the use of that instrument numerous heavenly bodies were discovered which had not been known to man heretofore. Later stronger telescopes were invented and many new galaxies of stars came within view and these were studied by the astronomers. Following this, time and time again telescopes have been improved and numerous new galaxies have been discovered. At the present time there are a hundred millions of them known to man. Each of them is composed of two to five hundred billions of stars. Certainly the astronomers are of the firm conviction that if they could continue to invent more powerful telescopes that galaxy after galaxy of stars beyond the bounds of what are known today would be brought under observation. In other words, as Father Abraham saw in his vision, so are modern astronomers seeing and knowing today—that there is no end to the vast multitude of heavenly bodies, as there is no end to time nor to space."

Index

Egyptians not permitted to have Priesthood, 291

First rulers were righteous men with Patriarchal form of government, 291

First Pharaoh blessed by Noah, 291

Subsequent Pharaohs claimed they had Priesthood, 292

Egyptians become idolatrous people, 292

Abraham commanded to leave Egypt, 295

Modern scholars admit history of Egypt "unknown," 291

Egyptians passed on knowledge received from Abraham to Greeks, 294-295

Abraham given land from Egypt to Euphrates, 305

Egyptus, Daughter of Ham
Named after mother, 291
Meaning of name, 291
Discovers Egypt, 291
Her son, Pharaoh, became first ruler of Egypt, 291
Because of lineage, her sons could not hold Priesthood, 291-292
Her son, Pharaoh, a righteous ruler, 291

Egyptus, Wife of Ham
Wife of Ham, 228, 291
Meaning of name, 228, 291

Eislen, Frederick Carl
Gives modern evaluation of Genesis, 15-16

Eliezer of Damascus
Abraham's steward, 303
May have been the servant who was sent to Padan-aram to get a wife for Isaac, 303, 336-342

Elkenah
Name of heathen god, 262
Altar of Elkenah destroyed by power of God, 269
Priest of Elkenah smitten by the power of God, 269

Enoch, City of
See "City of Enoch"

Enoch, Land of
Enoch's mission to, 163

Enoch, Order of
See "Order of Enoch"

Enoch, Son of Cain
Cain's heir, 120
City named after him, 120

Enoch, The Patriarch
Born when Jared was 162, 155
Raised in land of Cainan, 155
Taught Gospel by Jared, 155

Suffered an impediment of speech, 155

Receives first revelation, 155-157

Enoch sees spirit world, 156

Enoch called "a Seer," 157, 160

The ministry of Enoch, 159-193

Enoch healed miraculously, 159-160

Ordained at age 25, 159

Questioned by Mahijah, 160

Reaction of listeners to Enoch's sermons, 161

Enoch preaches Jesus Christ, 162

Enoch predicts race war, 162-163

Baptizes in name of Father and Son, 163

Completes his mission, 164

Enoch rescues Saints from attack, 165-167

Given power to command elements, 156-166

People of Enoch prosper, 167-169

Building of City of Enoch, 170-172

Age 65 when city begun, 172

Age 65 when Methusaleh born, 172

Age 65 when he received Patriarchal Blessing, 172

Sees history of world, 183-188

Sees wickedness in days of Noah, 184

Knew name of Noah, 185

Saw Great Flood, 185

Saw life of Christ, 186-187

Saw the last days, 187

Saw the Millennium, 188

Made clerk of Adam's last conference, 188-189

Knew of other inhabited planets, 184

Promised his seed would be among all nations, 186

To return to earth with his city, 188

Enoch and city translated, 191-193

In his translated condition Enoch is a ministering angel to many planets, 311

Enoch appeared to Jude, 311

Enos
Born when Seth 105, 133
Enos probably not eldest son of Seth, 133
Enos ordained when 134, 134
Revelations to Enos recorded in Book of Remembrance, 135
Spoke and wrote a pure language, 135

Directed to lead Saints of God to new land, 135-136